# A LIFE
# IN THE DAY

# A LIFE
# IN THE DAY

## MEMORIES OF SIXTIES LONDON,
## LOTS OF WRITING, THE BEATLES
## AND MY BELOVED WIFE

## HUNTER DAVIES

**SIMON &
SCHUSTER**

London · New York · Sydney · Toronto · New Delhi

A CBS COMPANY

First published in Great Britain by Simon & Schuster UK Ltd, 2017
A CBS COMPANY

All photographs are Hunter's family snaps except for: p.1 bottom (*Sunday Times*); p.2 top
(*Mirrorpix*), middle left and bottom (*Sunday Times*); p.3 top left (Anthea Sieveking), middle
(*Sunday Times*); p.4 top left (Anthea Sieveking), bottom left and right (Frank Herrmann);
p.5 middle (Tyne Tees Television); p.7 middle left (Yui Mok/PA Archive/PA Images),
middle right (Rex/Shutterstock).

1 3 5 7 9 10 8 6 4 2

Simon & Schuster UK Ltd
1st Floor
222 Gray's Inn Road
London WC1X 8HB

www.simonandschuster.co.uk
www.simonandschuster.com.au
www.simonandschuster.co.in

Simon & Schuster Australia, Sydney
Simon & Schuster India, New Delhi

The author and publishers have made all reasonable efforts to contact copyright-
holders for permission, and apologise for any omissions or errors in the form
of credits given. Corrections may be made to future printings.

A CIP catalogue record for this book
is available from the British Library

Hardback ISBN: 978-1-4711-6129-2
eBook ISBN: 978-1-4711-6130-8

Typeset in the UK by M Rules
Printed and bound by CPI Group (UK) Ltd, Croydon, CR0 4YY

MIX
Paper from
responsible sources
FSC® C020471

Simon & Schuster UK Ltd are committed to sourcing paper that is made
from wood grown in sustainable forests and support the Forest Stewardship Council,
the leading international forest certification organisation. Our books
displaying the FSC logo are printed on FSC certified paper.

For Margaret,
obviously, so lost without her

# CONTENTS

# 1

# HAPPY DAYS

You don't often feel blessed at the time, only when you look back, but every day, every moment of the year 1960, I was actively aware and grateful for all the wonderful things that seemed to be happening to me.

Margaret of course was the number one happening. I could hardly believe she had agreed to marry me, which we did on 11 June 1960 at Oxford register office. The fact that I failed my driving test the day before, so our best man had to drive with us on the first stage of our honeymoon, was not a bad omen, did not seem like a worrying way to start a marriage, for I never believe in bad omens, preferring to smile and whistle, always look on the bright side, all is for the best, which is what I do, even though I know of course it is mostly total rubbish. As anyone who gets to the age of eighty well knows. Or even eight years old.

I did the actual driving. Mike Thornhill sat beside me. Margaret cowered in the back. There was an L plate on the car, front and back. That could also be seen as symbolic. We were aged twenty-four and twenty-two, still learning about most things in life, but it didn't feel like that.

Margaret was always middle aged and, also, more surprisingly, middle class, in that she had tastes and confidence, social skills and attitudes, which belied the background and family she had come from, the rough council estate with her dad going off in his boiler suit each day to the Metal Box factory. I don't really know where she had come from, how she got formed, but I could see it from the moment I first met her, back in 1956, when she was still at school, aged seventeen, and I was nineteen.

I was two years older, but only on paper. I had no idea what my tastes were, what I thought, what my opinions were, being ever so young for my age. That's what people told me. I looked young and acted young, which does not sound too bad, or juvenile and childishly enthusiastic, which is not so good but probably more accurate.

In 1960, at the time of our wedding, I was still being taken for young, which I was beginning to think was not all that much of an advantage. The opposite, if anything. I could tell when I started going to interview people for the *Sunday Times* they would often be slightly taken aback: could this callow youth really be on that paper, can we take him seriously?

Harold Wilson suffered from a similar problem. He became an MP in the Labour landslide of 1945 and Attlee made him President of the Board of Trade while still only thirty-one, making him the youngest Cabinet member in the twentieth century. I later asked him if it had been hard to be taken seriously – and he said that was the reason he grew a moustache.

I have worn a moustache most of my adult life, but I didn't start one till much later, and then the reasons were laziness rather than trying to look mature. I always had such a strong dark growth and would often need to shave twice a day if I was going out in the evening. I reckoned having a moustache would give me less face to shave. Oh, I was so virile in those days. Should I therefore have grown a moustache at twenty-two, not thirty-two, in order in 1960 to look the part of whatever part I was playing? Do I regret it? Stupid question. Wouldn't it be great if, as we went through life, growing or not growing a moustache, or having a fringe, dyeing our hair, was up there with the Big Things we now think we should not have done.

Mike did not actually come on the honeymoon. He dropped us off at our new London flat, then next day Margaret and I flew off to Sardinia. It was the first time Margaret had flown in a plane but I had flown to Cyprus as a war reporter the previous year, when working on the *Manchester Evening Chronicle*. An experience I boasted about for years, saying I had been a war reporter, oh yes, even though I had only been there two weeks on an Army PR facility visit.

It was John Bassett who suggested Sardinia. He was a friend of Margaret's from Oxford, who went on later to help bring the four Beyond the Fringe members together, all of whom had been at Oxford or Cambridge – Alan Bennett, Jonathan Miller, Peter Cook and Dudley Moore. I think John's mother had some connection with Sardinia. We liked the idea of going to an island, not a mainland place, and told ourselves we would always have our holidays on islands, from now on.

We went on one of the earliest package holidays – run by Horizon Holidays, the pioneer of post-war packaged hols. The notion of all-in tours had been created by Thomas Cook in 1841, when he organised a trip for temperance supporters between Leicester and Loughborough. He went on to organise packaged trips all over Europe and Egypt. But in those days they always went by train or boat.

Horizon, in 1950, was the first British company to run their package trips by plane, flying from Gatwick on charter planes to places like Corsica and Sardinia. In just a few years, one million Brits were going on packaged hols every year, mostly to Spain, their hotels, meals, flights, transport, all part of the package. It created a social revolution for ordinary Brits who otherwise would not have attempted going to any of those funny foreign places, not on a plane, not on their own.

I had interviewed the founder of Horizon just a few weeks earlier, Vladimir Raitz, a White Russian, who had come to London as a boy, studying at the LSE and working first as a journalist, before starting Horizon.

His office was in one of those streets behind Oxford Street, in Newman Street, traditionally a rag trade area. When I pass that way today, I still think about going to see him, but then I do that all the time, every day, everywhere in London. I am continually remembering going to certain houses, offices, streets to interview people, now going back almost sixty years ago.

I contacted Mr Raitz, after we had decided on Sardinia, reminded him of our meeting, and that I had written an Atticus piece about him, and managed to get out of him a 10 per cent discount on the holiday. I never revealed this to Margaret. She would have been appalled at my cheek and meanness. Getting a discount on one's honeymoon, how unromantic, how penny pinching. All true.

We stayed at a little hotel in Alghero where the head waiter,

Constanzo, took a shine to us, amused by us being a honeymoon couple. Every meal, even breakfast, when we asked what was on the menu, he said *freedmeexedfeesh*. That was the extent of his English. He was very ugly and bald and seemed very old, probably about forty, but he had the most stunning, luscious-looking teenage girlfriend. He had a little Fiat and used to take us out with her on his day off. Strange how you can remember, decades later, hotel waiters, yet it's unlikely they can ever remember you, once you have gone.

Towards the end of the holiday, I discovered a large spot on my bottom, which turned into a boil, which turned into a source of awful agony, Ivy. In the end I got the hotel to call an emergency doctor. She came to our bedroom, threw me on the bed, pushed and pummelled the boil. She was a large woman, with large muscles, and had clearly missed out at medical school when they taught the principles of charm and bedside manners.

I closed my eyes, trying not to show she was hurting – and heard a crash on the floor. Margaret had fainted. I could stand it, being a man, being brave, but she couldn't stand me having to stand it. When she came to, the doctor said, 'Un peu de courage, Madame,' in French. She did not speak English and we did not speak Italian, but I had boasted I spoke French. I did get an O-level in French, after a resit when I went to the grammar school.

The second really nice thing that had happened to us in 1960 happened straight after our honeymoon – our flat. I was nearly as proud of living there, and its address, as I was of marrying Margaret. How can you compare a house to a human? You can't, but they can each uplift your spirit, give you a warm glow when you see them, make you feel good and excited when you enter into them.

The address was 9 Heath Villas, Vale of Health, Hampstead, NW3. The postcodes were quite short in those days – and NW3, as I had already discovered from my few months in London, was one of the most desirable postcodes of them all. NW2, which was where my first flat had been, before we got married, had no cachet, no resonance. NW4, I never knew where that was. NW5 was on the other side of the Heath, the wrong side of the Heath, the Kentish Town side. No one I knew or came across in 1960 ever turned out to live in NW5, or at least admitted to it.

The flat also had a most desirable phone number – HAMpstead 3847. You just dialled the first three letters, then the number. When you gave it out, people always knew where you lived. In NW2, in Shoot Up Hill, my number was GLAdstone 4788 which nobody could ever locate. I never found out where the Gladstone bit came from, though later heard it was a park, but we never went there. Even living in NW2, we always headed to Hampstead and Hampstead Heath on Sunday afternoons, just to ogle the lovely houses, the lovely, affluent, sophisticated people.

The Vale of Health is easy to miss, a little enclave tucked away off the East Heath Road. It is a dead end, with just one road into it, totally surrounded by the Heath. The title was said to have come from the fact that it was the only place in London that escaped some plague or other, being so cut off. Lots of famous people had lived there, and there were plaques to prove it, such as D. H. Lawrence and Leigh Hunt. Opposite our flat was a plaque to a Bengali writer I had never heard of, Rabindranath Tagore, who turned out to have won the Nobel Prize for Literature in 1913.

I used to love coming home from work each evening on the Northern line from King's Cross, getting off at Hampstead Tube, then walking through the little Georgian squares and lanes towards the Heath. I varied my route each time, as there were so many ways, all delightful. East Heath Road was usually busy, with a long line of cars crawling up going north, but once over that road, it was like entering a rural oasis, so artistic, quaint, quiet and altogether wonderful.

We had found it through some friend of Theo's, Margaret's best friend at Oxford, who warned us that the landlord lived on the premises and was rather eccentric. We were told he would want to interview us first, check us out, before agreeing. Margaret was still at Oxford at the time, in her last few weeks, so she came through for the day and we were grilled by Mr Elton – Leonard Sedgwick Elton. Grilled is the wrong word, because he was incredibly shy and hesitant, did not look you in the face, muttered and mumbled. He was a bachelor, a retired civil servant of some sort. I did ask him if he was related to Elton the historian – Sir Geoffrey Elton, expert on the Tudors – whose dreary books I had ploughed through at Durham, and he muttered something about being a distant cousin. (Ben Elton, the comedian and writer, is his nephew.)

He was obsessed by three things. He wanted peace and quiet, tenants who would go to bed at ten o'clock, make no noise afterwards, and not even pull the lavatory chain. He worried that as we were so young, compared with the outgoing tenants, who were an older couple – must have been in their thirties – that we might be noisy. We assured him we always went to bed at ten, in fact one minute to ten, every night, even New Year's Eve.

He worried whether we could pay the rent. I assured him I had a staff job but Margaret did not, still being a student. And thirdly, he was terrified that once having moved in, we might have children, a thought which petrified him. And us.

We both immediately fell in love with the flat. Back at Oxford, Margaret wrote him a creepy letter about the wonders of his flat, saying that even if he did not see his way to us being his new tenants, she would never forget his flat. That seemed to do the trick. He offered us a three-month trial, at a rent of six guineas a week.

It was in fact the most inconvenient, ill-arranged house. It had not been arranged or converted at all, not in the normal sense, with no privacy, no facilities and no separation of living quarters. It was a four-storey, flat-fronted Victorian house, untouched, unaltered. Mr Elton lived alone on the top floor. We never heard him move around or even breathe. Each evening he made himself the same meal – sardines on toast – and drank a small bottle of red wine, the third of a bottle size, which you hardly see today.

We lived below him in a large through-room overlooking the centre of the Vale, with two large picture windows at the front and a kitchen at the back of the room, with a window over the pond.

We shared the WC and bathroom, which was on the landing, with Mr Elton. If by chance we met him on the stairs, or he heard us approaching, he vanished, disappeared. And if a full frontal meeting was unavoidable, he looked the other way, pretended he had not seen us.

We communicated by notes which we left for each other on the hall shelf behind the front door. This suited Margaret perfectly. She always adored writing notes, preferring them to telephone conversations.

Our bedroom was on the floor below, the ground floor as you came in, at the back of the house. Next to it, at the front, was the sitting room of Mrs Woodcock, an elderly lady we did not meet for some time. She had the whole of the basement, plus this one room upstairs, right next to ours. The whole arrangement was mad. It only worked if everyone was incredibly quiet and respected each other's privacy. Which we did. We might have been in our early twenties, but our lifestyle was more like folks in their sixties.

Mrs Woodcock was very refined, very snobbish, clipped and autocratic. She enjoyed ordering us around, commanding us to come to sherry, or to take her rubbish out.

She took to Margaret instantly, was fascinated by her, loved to hear her views on literature, all of them of course delivered forcefully, and on the theatre, on Hampstead and on Oxford, which Margaret had never liked, but was amusing in her criticisms. I don't think Mrs Woodcock had much interest in me, which I didn't mind. I was happy enough to sip her dry sherry and let Margaret do all the sparkling and entertaining.

Margaret then got into the habit of having sherry twice a week with Mrs Woodcock, just the two of them. They would sit upright in her button-back chairs by the fireplace and discuss serious, artistic and political matters. She was usually summoned at 5.30, before I had got home from work. Which suited me fine. I was not interested in uplifting, clever chat. Never being much good at it.

It was one of the ways in which Margaret always appeared to me some sort of cuckoo in the nest, being able to connect and interest and impress and understand the middle class and middle-aged people, as if she was one of them, despite her background. She just did it naturally. Even as a little girl at home in her council house, she had middle-class values and tastes, forever criticising Arthur her father for the way he ate, the horrible fatty breakfasts he scoffed, the way he spoke, how he came home from work in his boiler suit and washed himself at the kitchen sink. She would tell him it was revolting. And leave the room, even during a meal. Poor Arthur. Where had she got it from? She was not a snob, or pretending to be something she was not. It was just how she was – and she never drew back from expressing her opinions, whether asked or not, which of course someone like Mrs Woodcock so enjoyed hearing.

We both picked up one habit from Mrs Woodcock, drinking dry sherry, which of course we had never drunk in our Carlisle council houses, though I had been allowed a sherry allowance at Durham, when I had been Senior Man. Dry sherry was the smartest drink in smart social circles in the fifties and sixties. From then on, we always had a bottle in the flat, for special visitors.

We never had wine in the flat, not like today, when I have crates of it all over the shop for emergencies, such as getting to 5.30 without having so far had a drink.

If we were having friends for supper, we might have bought a bottle of wine specially, but regular wine drinking – i.e.

drinking it with every meal, and before and after every meal – did not exist in the circles we moved in.

Strange how drinking habits have changed. The history of the sort of wine we all drink, in all classes, has also changed over the decades, with dry white wine now being the most popular. Sweet or even medium white wine has disappeared, and as for Babycham, women drank that when out feeling quite sophisticated, not having acquired the taste for wine of any sort. Now look at them. Drinking as much as men these days. And swearing. As for dry sherry, I don't think I have had a glass of sherry, dry or otherwise, or kept a bottle in the house, since, let me think, about 1975.

Our flat was unfurnished, so we spent most of that first year looking for the sort of polished Sheraton-style dark wood bureaus and button-back chairs which Mrs Woodcock had in her flat, considering them the height of good taste. We made lists and on Saturdays trawled the second-hand shops in Hampstead – even the High Street had one or two second-hand furniture shops in those days, but most of the local ones were in Islington or Camden Town. I remember shopping at Ron Weldon's – the first husband of Fay Weldon. He used old ancient wood to re-create new but old-looking pine kitchen tables.

We didn't have beer in the flat, and I generally did not go to pubs, except for social occasions after work, but there was a large and ancient Victorian pub at the end of the Vale of Health which we often went to on a Sunday, after our long morning walk round the Heath. The barman was a rather moany, miserable Scotsman, who was always trying to chuck people out, long before the official closing. 'Have ye no hames to go tae? Your roasts will all be burning in the oven.'

Around the pub was a small, permanent encampment of caravans and boarded-up fairground stalls. It was strange to find them there in such a select, expensive location. This was the nucleus of the famous Hampstead Heath annual fair. Several fairground families, who had been there for decades, lived on the site all the year round. Once a year, at Easter, the encampment exploded, spreading right over the Heath. The posher Vale of Health residents would then always move out to their country cottages.

One of the fairground men, one of the residents, we always knew as Mr Shouter. Several times a day he would walk past our house shouting. It was alarming at first, worried that we had caused some offence, till we realised he was perfectly nice and harmless – just had some involuntary tic which caused him to go around shouting.

The only drawback to our Vale of Health idyllic, sylvan flat came after about a year – when I started to have asthma. I suffered from it all my childhood, but assumed it had gone for good. We put its return down to the fact that our bedroom window overlooked the Vale of Health pond. In the evenings, there was almost always a mist hovering and hanging over the pond, which soaked and seeped into our bedroom, and then sneaked its way into my lungs. That was my theory. It might or not have been the true cause, but it did not really matter as asthma is a psychosomatic illness. Once you begin to imagine you have it, you have it. So much for it being healthy, living in the Vale of Health.

It got so bad we decided I should go to a doctor. We had

not yet got round to registering with a local GP, but then you don't, in your early twenties, never thinking you will ever need a doctor, an accountant, a lawyer, an agent – nor a personal trainer, a yoga teacher, a masseur, or a brand manager. The last four are modern references. Still not got 'em.

We got the name of a GP from the Post Office board in the High Street, someone we were told was called Micky Day. I had presumed at first it must be a man. Her real first name was Josie, but for some reason she had always been known as Micky. It was a bit confusing, as her husband, also a doctor, was called Michael.

They lived in Thurlow Road – and she had her surgery in her house. The first time we went to see her, to register, we went into a front room where a young woman was sitting reading the *Manchester Guardian* with her feet up. I said we had come to see the doctor. She folded the *Guardian*, disappeared, and then put her head round the door and said come in, I will see you now.

She came from Macclesfield and had a broad northern accent, which was reassuring. It turned out to be her first week and I think we were probably her first patients. We remained with her ever since. In fact, fifty-seven years later, I am still with her, or at least with her practice. She has retired but the Hampstead surgery she created continues in Park End, beside the Heath. Today, I am always asking the young doctors in the practice, most of whom look about thirteen, if I am their longest-living patient. They just stare at me, not understanding what I am on about.

I did once call Micky in the middle of the night, when we were living in the Vale of Health. I had a bad attack of asthma, convinced I was going to choke to death. She came and gave me an injection. Which knocked me out.

I later decided that it was not the mist on the pond which had done it this time but earlier that evening, stuffing my face at a free press night meal in the West End, I had eaten crab for the first time. I was convinced it was the crab what done it. So I have never eaten crab again.

Dry sherry did not really agree with me either, causing a burning sensation in my tummy after five or six glasses, but that was not the reason I gave it up. Fashions and styles moved on.

On the morning of 4 February 1962, another fashion, another style, came into being. It was a Sunday and early that morning, lying in bed, we were awakened by the sound of Mrs Woodcock outside our bedroom, clattering about it, muttering loudly, which was not like her. We could hear her opening the front door, then banging down the dustbin lid, having dumped something into it, and then she returned to her sitting room, still muttering and complaining.

The very first edition of the *Sunday Times Magazine* had arrived. It was the beginning of a small but significant revolution in British weekend newspapers, but not as far as Mrs Woodcock was concerned. She immediately declared it to be a cheap, nasty, vulgar American abomination and she certainly did not want it in her flat a moment longer than necessary.

In talking to her the next day, still moaning on, furious at the impertinence of such a thing being delivered to her home, unasked, I discovered she had worn rubber gloves, so as not to be contaminated by this awful, disgusting publication.

# 2

# PAPER PLEASURES

There was part of me which rather delighted in Mrs Woodcock's reaction to the first appearance of the Colour Magazine.
I knew by then how vital the launch of the Colour Mag was
and how much had been invested in it. Their staff already
seemed to lord it over the so-called steam section, working
away in black and white and cheap newsprint, whereas their
product was glossy, colourful, glitzy, ever so trendy and fashionable. Just like the Colour Mag staff, or so we thought they
thought about themselves.

I had been on the *Sunday Times* just over a year by then,
having moved from the *Sunday Graphic*, a paper which no one
has heard of now. Not many at the time seemed aware of it
either. It was a popular, tabloid, national paper, one of several
in the Thomson stable – formerly Kemsley newspapers, which
I had joined in 1958 as a graduate trainee.

We were in the same building, 200 Gray's Inn Road, as
the *Sunday Times*, but we were below the salt, other ranks,
not exactly viewed with contempt but ignorance, as if we did
not exist, were not part of the same brotherhood, the same
profession.

The *Sunday Times* staff were rumoured to work in oak-panelled offices, like an Oxford college, not that I ever ventured into their quarters, or knew anybody who worked on the paper.

I used to imagine how wonderful it must be to work there. If you rang to say you were from the *Sunday Times*, they probably stood to attention, hanging on your every word. On the *Sunday Graphic*, when you rang up, you just got a grunt, and they never rang you back.

But of course on any paper, in any occupation, it is your colleagues who make it, not the bosses, not the outside image of your firm. I remember thinking at the time I was on the *Sunday Graphic* that it was unfair to stigmatise workers by the institutions they work for. On the whole, owners are remote and usually bastards. You have to remember that owners change, sell out, get caught out, but the workers carry on.

Coming to London as a total outsider, it took me a while to pick up the pecking order of institutions. The Savoy and the Dorchester were the two best hotels, no question. People wanted to stay there or work there, for having worked at the Savoy you could always boast you had trained there.

I had begun to interview quite a lot of authors, a breed I had never met before, and I picked up that a publishing house everyone admired was William Collins. It was felt if you worked there, you could go on to anywhere else.

In daily newspapers, the *Daily Express* was considered a brand leader, the one with the money and power, ideas and invention, well-designed, clever columnists, top-class reporters, both at home and abroad. The *Daily Mail* in the 1960s was a pale imitation, not quite as much of a rag as the *Daily*

*Sketch* – which the *Mail* eventually took over in 1971 – but generally viewed as a poorer paper, less professional than the *Express*.

In Sunday papers, the *Sunday Times* had for long been seen as the number one. It was not as dominant, or as fat and self-important as it later became, and was helped by the lack of competition in the so-called quality, broadsheet sector. In 1960 when I joined, the only real opposition was the *Observer*. The *Sunday Telegraph* was not founded till 1961.

During the summer and autumn of 1960 we were all aware that the *Sunday Graphic*, where I was still working, was going to close. Roy Thomson had made no major changes when he had taken over the group the previous year, but was now starting to shed the loss makers.

It was a miserable time on the paper. The older reporters, such as Dorothy Harrison, whom I sat beside in the news-room, were convinced they would never get another job. I never knew her age, probably mid-fifties, but she seemed totally ancient. When I was moaning on, saying what about me, I have just got married, I need a job to pay the rent, she always said the same thing: 'Oh you'll be fine ...' Which I always thought was an empty platitude, to cheer me up.

A few weeks before the *Sunday Graphic* finally folded, in December 1960, three of the staff were whisked across to join the *Sunday Times* – Robert Robinson who did films and show business for the *Graphic*, Peter Wilsher who was a brain box with a first in Mathematics from Cambridge, so I was told, and the sports editor. One day, all three suddenly got up, cleared their desks and departed the sinking ship.

I was so jealous, convinced that was it, the three chosen

ones had gone. I was clearly not going to the *Sunday Times*. I was probably going to be offered a job back in the provinces, in Manchester or Sheffield or Newcastle, on one of the group's local papers, or offered redundancy. I had only been working as a journalist for two years, so I wasn't going to be offered much money.

Then one morning I was called for an interview with the *Sunday Times* editor. I knew nothing about him, and had never even heard his name mentioned. He was called Harry Hodson, ex-Balliol and a Fellow of All Souls, and he was one of the dopiest, vaguest, least journalistic journalists I have ever come across. He was more like an absent-minded don than a Fleet Street editor. He had no interest in me, did not appear to have read the *Sunday Graphic*, was probably not even aware of its existence. He floundered around, abstracted, and then chanced to ask if I was interested in archaeology. I had studied Roman Britain for a year at Durham, and been totally bored, but I knew enough about the history of Hadrian's Wall to chunter on as if I knew what I was talking about.

On 23 December 1960, the week the *Graphic* finally closed, I got a note from him, saying I would be joining the *Sunday Times* on a salary of £1,350 a year. He welcomed me to the team. 'And I hope that you will work happily with us for a long time to come.'

In the event, it was he who didn't last long. In a few months, he was gone, off to become Provost of Ditchley. When I mention his name now to people working on the *Sunday Times* today, they have no idea who Harry Hodson was, yet he edited the paper from 1950 to 1961.

He was replaced by Denis Hamilton, Lt Colonel Hamilton, who was in his way an equally strange choice as an editor – in that he never wrote stuff, hardly read proofs, did not appear to be interested or involved in day-to-day journalism. He was more the leader figure, thinking and planning long term.

Being called to his office, for good or bad reasons, was a nightmare. He didn't speak, just sat there, austere and officer class, so in the end you blurted out any old stuff, comments and chat, stories which you should probably have kept to yourself.

Almost everyone on the *Sunday Times* when I joined seemed to me to have been to a public school and/or Oxbridge, which created a bit of a chip on my shoulder for some time, mostly imagined. Denis Hamilton, despite his upper-class demeanour, his clipped moustache, perfect suits, polished shoes, came from a humble background in the Northeast and had never been to university. Before the war, he had been a sub on the local Thomson paper in Middlesbrough. When the war came, he zoomed through the ranks, commanding a battalion of the Durham Light Infantry at a very young age, ending as a colonel and aide to General Montgomery.

After the war, he went back to journalism, but this time becoming editorial assistant to Lord Kemsley. When Thomson took over, he recognised Hamilton's efficiency, making things happen, organising the troops.

One of Hamilton's earliest coups was in 1958 helping the *Sunday Times* purchase Monty's memoirs. It ran for weeks and did so well, putting on a huge increase in circulation. Hamilton then bought further wartime diaries when he became editor. It began a long period of the Sunday papers competing to pay massive monies to serialise books. God, it made me scream, when I heard all the money being spent and the acres of space being devoted to these dreary old generals. I had lived through the war, as a child, and vaguely knew their names, and obviously was thankful we had won, but come on, surely we have had more than enough of wartime reminiscences, how about hearing from the new generation for a change? Such as, well, me for instance.

Looking back at editions of the *Sunday Times* in 1961 and 1962, when I was working there full time, not getting my name in the paper but thrilled to be there, I am surprised how flimsy the paper was, so few pages, so few sections. Just two in fact – the main paper and the Review pages.

There was of course no Colour Magazine, not till 1962, and that proved to be Hamilton's major contribution to the British media. Thomson had got the idea from the USA and Canada, where coloured supplements had long been common, but it was Hamilton who pushed it through, made it work, after a dodgy start. Mrs Woodcock was not alone in being appalled.

I sat in the newsroom, doing very little for a couple of weeks at the end of December 1960, till in the New Year I was eventually told what my job was going to be. I was to be the boy on the Atticus column, working with Robert Robinson, who had been with me on the *Sunday Graphic*. I didn't really know Bob on the *Graphic*. He was ten years older, wiser, smarter, rather cutting and cynical and world weary, but very cultured and literary, always quoting Dr Johnson.

Atticus was the paper's diary or gossip column, though not as we know such animals today. We had different forms of celebrity in those days, so we did stories about who would be the next Master of Balliol, or Archbishop of Canterbury, our Ambassador in Washington. As if I cared. But I had to ring round our so-called contacts and get names of people possibly in the running and do little bios.

The Atticus column had a long and distinguished history. Previous editors of it had been John Buchan, Sacheverell Sitwell and Ian Fleming. Sitwell was reputed to have got a lifetime's supply of Mateus Rosé after he had been the first person to mention the name Mateus Rosé in a British news-paper. Someone clearly to look up to.

Ian Fleming was still around when I joined the paper, supposedly foreign manager, but he didn't seem to do much, swanning off on Friday after lunch to play golf in Kent, which I thought was shocking. On a Sunday paper, Fridays and Saturdays are the two most frantic days.

We had our own Atticus office, me and Bob, a wood-panelled office – so the rumour was true. Our secretary, a debby-type girl, was best friends with Gillian, secretary to William Rees-Mogg, who was the paper's city editor. The two secretaries would sit and gossip in our office when Bob was out and I was supposedly working. I would listen to their chat about dear William, and discovered that he did not even seem to be aware that Gillian, his secretary, existed, and yet, so I picked up, she was secretly in love with him. Eventually she decided it might be best to give in her notice. I told William how lovely Gillian was, how much he would miss her if she resigned, and hinted that he had missed his chance.

The upshot was that he proposed, they got married and lived happily ever after and produced a large family including the Tory MP, Jacob Rees-Mogg.

That's my memory of the sequence of events back in 1961 – and I'm sticking to it. I have recently reminisced with Lady Rees-Mogg, formerly Gillian Morris, and she smiles and sighs and agrees, yes, that was roughly what happened. William died in 2012.

Everyone, apart from humble reporters, had a secretary and their own office. It was part of one's status, to have a good-size office and a smart, well-bred secretary. She answered the phone, booked lunch for you, typed your letters – bashing away at the office sit-up-and-beg manual type writer. Often not very well, for *Sunday Times* secretaries were prized for their breeding as much as their typing. The more brazen members of the staff had their secretary doing their bills, their personal affairs, buying presents for their wives or girlfriends. All gone. Almost all secretaries went out when computers came in.

Bob did try to shake up the contents of the Atticus column, make it a bit less stodgy and old-fashioned. He was a polished and amusing writer – but he was not a good interviewer, either on the phone or in the flesh. Probably too fond of his own opinions to be bothered listening to others. It meant I did most of the interviewing each week, a lot of which Bob would rewrite in his style.

I once went to an art gallery in Mayfair for the opening of an exhibition of drawings by L. S. Lowry. I had assumed he was long dead, so was surprised to find this funny, untidy old man sitting in a corner, smiling to himself at all the preening, phony Mayfair arty types bustling about. I sat down with him and got on well with him, so well that I arranged to go and see him at his house in Lancashire later in the week, and do a proper interview.

I had of course heard of Laurence Stephen Lowry (1887–1976), knew about his matchstick men drawings, his paintings of industrial Lancashire, knew that in his working life he had been a rent collector, which was funny, how he had turned down various honours, which seemed admirable, but was said to be something of a recluse, unmarried, living on his own. Most people in the sixties who had come down from the North had heard of him, felt affectionate towards his drawings and felt affectionate towards him, but the mainstream art world of London, or art lovers in London, if they had heard of him, saw him as a niche artist, a primitive even, not mainstream or important. I was so excited to have talked him into an interview, in his own home, which I don't think many journalists had ever managed.

When I got back to the office, I told Bob, half thinking he might never have heard of Lowry. He said well done – but I will do the interview, if you don't mind.

I was furious. I felt I had bonded with Lowry as a northerner, whereas Bob was from suburban London. I had shown journalistic nous in getting Lowry's address out of him and arranging a date.

I was upset when Bob came back from meeting him and wrote only a paragraph or so about him in the column. I had planned to rush to the features department and sell them the idea of a major interview, with a lot of space and illustrations, as I later managed with John Masefield.

I was even more furious when Bob let slip in the office that he had bought a Lowry painting – direct from the artist, not through a gallery or agent. I could of course not have afforded such a thing at the time, though I am sure Bob got a bargain. Today of course, Lowry paintings sell for millions, he is widely acclaimed and revered and has The Lowry art centre in Salford named after him.

Bob had gone to a local suburban grammar school, which he always said was the best grammar school in the land, with the finest headmaster, and then on to Oxford. I think he had always imagined he would go on to be a literary figure, a writer of some sort, but for years he had found himself interviewing second-rate film stars for the *Sunday Graphic*. At least on the *Sunday Times*, he had climbed a notch or two in status, as I had.

Bob introduced one new feature in Atticus which was our man Mayhew, who went out and met ordinary people, such as a dustman, a postman, a milkman. It was me who went out, stopped people in the street, and wrote down exactly what they said.

Bob got the name Mayhew from Henry Mayhew, whom I had never heard of till then, who was a nineteenth-century social historian and journalist (one of the founders of *Punch* in 1841) who produced a well-known book called *London Labour and the London Poor*, filled with first-hand, unadorned interviews and life stories. I was most impressed when I read it, and went on to discover his other journalism, thinking I could do that, I like interviewing ordinary people.

I produced hundreds, sometimes thousands of words for my Mayhew interviews with ordinary London people, asking them questions about their lives, till they got fed up. I was always on the lookout for an unusual turn of phrase, a cliché used wrongly, a malapropism, a quirky observation on life. I handed them over to Bob who boiled them down. He never took liberties, or added clever remarks, just reproduced it straight, linking all the best quotes together.

There was no name on the Atticus column – neither Bob's name nor of course mine either, as the mere assistant. That was the column's style. In fact the style of the whole paper. That's the other thing that struck me, looking back at those sixties copies of the paper – there were so very few by-lines.

About the only place the name of the journalist regularly appeared was on the review pages where Cyril Connolly on books, Dilys Powell on films and Harold Hobson on the theatre were the big stars. They were supposedly the reason people read the *Sunday Times*, which I could never believe, as I mostly considered them boring, pompous, humourless. Over on the *Observer*, our deadly rival Kenneth Tynan was so much more readable and amusing and of course cruel. The *Sunday Times* did not do cruel.

Even though my name did not appear, if I did a half-decent or vaguely amusing interview, almost everyone I knew or met next day had read it. They would not know it was me, unless I told them, but they had noticed the story. This was because there were only two Sunday papers, the *Times* and the *Observer*. Everyone I knew read both of them, as they were still quite thin with few sections, so didn't take up your whole day.

When Jimmy Porter in *Look Back in Anger* talks about collecting the Sunday papers – those were the two he meant.

As far as the arty or the intelligentsia were concerned, there were no others.

I went with Margaret to see *Look Back in Anger*, which was still running at the Royal Court, on free tickets. One of the perks of being a diarist on a national paper, then and now, is being on the list for press tickets for the new London shows.

I thought the play was terrific, loved the dialogue and the rants, and never worried at the time about the lack of a proper plot. It did seem so fresh and different from all those ancient Noël Coward and Terence Rattigan plays I had seen in Carlisle with my mother or performed by amateur reps in Manchester. We also went to see Joan Littlewood's *Oh, What a Lovely War!* at the Theatre Royal Stratford East and that again seemed a revolution, so spontaneous and mad, but wonderful. I was also astounded by *The Ginger Man* by J. P. Donleavy. In all these cases it was the lack of traditional framework and plot that struck me. I remember thinking you don't have to write so-called well-made, polished, crafted plays any more – they can be all over the shop, if they have the energy and humour. I wondered if I could have a go one day. I had begun to think I had a good ear for dialogue, even if the only dialogue I had ever written down was 500 words from a dustman talking to Mayhew.

The first time I got my name in the paper, on a piece I had written, was in May 1963 when I interviewed John Masefield, the Poet Laureate. It had taken ages to arrange, with letters and notes going back months, before I finally persuaded him to let me visit him in his pretty cottage in Berkshire. Masefield was born in 1878, so was eighty-five when I saw him in 1963.

He reminisced about meeting Thomas Hardy and Ramsay MacDonald, who had made him Poet Laureate in 1930, names which came naturally to his lips but to me seemed fictional, or existed only in school textbooks.

He had a cat called McGinty. 'A cat,' so he told me, 'of no distinction but much pretension.' He described how, before he got that cat, he used to fill his mouth with raisins, go out into his garden and let birds eat out of his mouth. Once he had acquired a cat, no birds would come near him in the garden.

If I had been into my stride as an interviewer, more experienced, rather than being slightly in awe and nervous about doing my first proper interview for the paper, as opposed to the Atticus column, I would immediately have pounced on this story. I am sure I could have talked him into having his photo taken, with his mouth open, feeding the birds, with the cat kept well away. He did seem an agreeable old chap, if a bit doddery. It would have made a great picture. It did go through my head, but seemed too cheeky and pushy to ask him to do it.

Bob Robinson edited Atticus for just two years, with me as his assistant, then was moved sideways, to write a personal column. I don't know whether he was pushed or not. Nobody ever seemed to get the sack in those days, not from the *Sunday Times*. The paper was so rich, so overstaffed, that if for some reason someone was relieved of his position or his column, he just carried on, on full pay, writing odd features, but nobody much caring whether he produced copy or not.

The national dailies were much the same. I often went to El Vino's in Fleet Street with Bob, who liked me to accompany him, as his sort of sidekick or batman, and I got to know a few of the main feature writers on the *Mail* and the *Express*. They seemed to do very little except play silly games in the office, then go to El Vino's and drink the rest of the day away. The *Daily Mirror* feature writers, ridiculously under-employed, would have oysters and champagne at their local pub each day at noon. The expenses were enormous, the abuses appalling.

There was always a lot of infighting and complaining about the print unions in Fleet Street, with the journalists and management accusing the unions of ruining our fine, noble industry, using Mickey Mouse practices, such as fiddling work sheets and wages for people who did not exist, then threatening to go on strike at the last moment, just before the presses started rolling, knowing management would have to give in to their demands. Both sides were in fact taking the mickey, abusing the privileges they had acquired over the generations for themselves.

Bob was always good to me, treating me when we went to these expensive Fleet Street watering holes, as I was still on a fairly low salary, unlike him. One day he also invited me – and Margaret – to his house for a meal.

He lived in a handsome Georgian house in Cheyne Row which he and his actress wife Josee had rented at first, I think from a relation of Richard Ingrams', and then they had somehow managed to buy it, at a very good price. Journalists, even reasonably paid ones, did not normally live in quite such period splendour.

One of the other guests at this dinner was Robin Day, the television broadcaster. For some reason he took an active dislike to me, turning and picking on me, calling me Bob's boy, Bob's lackey, mocking my northern accent and provincial university. I did not realise this was his style, to attack people for no reason, just to amuse himself. I was shocked into sullen silence, wondering what I had done to offend him.

Margaret of course had immediately got his measure, and when he talked to her, she let him get away with nothing, fighting back, giving as good as she got.

After the dinner, Margaret sent a thank-you letter in her best handwriting. In it, she must have made some semi-jocular remarks about the evening, which upset Josee. In reply she wrote: 'I expect my guests to write back prettily, whether they have enjoyed my hospitality or not, and if not, not to accept any more invitations.' We never got any more.


So who was going to take over from Bob, once he had been relieved of Atticus? I did not honestly and truthfully expect to get the job, though I felt well capable of it, after two years as the assistant. I knew how to do the boring bits, such as organising photographs, supervising the design and layout.

One of my jobs, as the assistant, was to go up on the stone on a Friday afternoon and stand there while the compositors made up the pages. If there was a line too long, or a headline did not fit, I would make a quick decision – and tell the printer what to do. Journalists could not of course touch the actual metal. The printers would be all out.

I realised that at twenty-six I was still a bit young to be in charge of such a well-known, long-established column, which had had so many famous editors. And of course Robin Day had got me on the raw. I was convinced I would always be discriminated against as a northerner from a provincial university.

Denis Hamilton, as editor of the paper, always had his ear to the ground, knowing who the rising stars were. It was he who really created the Insight column, hiring three journalists in 1963 whom none of us on the paper had heard of – Clive Irving, assisted by Jeremy Wallington and Ron Hall – to start a brand-new section which led to a totally different investigative team.

To be the new head of Atticus he appointed someone called Nicholas Tomalin, someone I had vaguely heard of, as he was currently the star writer on a trendy magazine called *About Town*. He was five years older than me, had gone to a public school and Cambridge, where he had been president of the Union and editor of *Granta*.

When I met him for the first time, I was struck by how handsome and well-dressed he was, in the latest American preppy-style clothes with button down collar shirts, which none of us were yet wearing. And he was sophisticated, amusing, clearly well connected, seemed to be best friends with all his Cambridge contemporaries who had gone on to do exciting things.

Oh God, I thought, I have had it now. Not only will he not like me, or get on with me, or want me, but he will insist on hiring his own assistant, which is the nature of most such sudden changes when an outsider comes in, be it journalism, politics, business, football management. It would prove what I had feared, that my background would be held against me.

# 3

# MARGARET'S FIRST NOVEL FAILS

When Margaret had been a little girl she had wanted to be a missionary. She was for a time very religious, thanks mainly to her mother. Then as a young teenager she wanted to be an MP, putting the world to rights. Both of those ambitions had long faded. Instead, almost the moment we were back from our honeymoon in 1960 and established ourselves in the Vale of Health, she started writing a novel.

Before going up to Oxford, she had gone for three months as an au pair in Bordeaux. Her Oxford tutor-to-be had said she should improve her French, if she wanted to read History. She was told that the French family she was fixed to stay with was middle class, educated, with the husband a teacher, but it turned out they were dirt poor, living in an attic. The father had been a teacher but because he was a communist, he had lost his job and just sat at home smoking. His wife took in laundry to feed their many children, all of whom Margaret had to look after. They did have well-off relations, so they often had weekends in style in a grand and pretty country house.

The contrast between the two lives, getting sucked into two

layers of French culture, had a profound effect on Margaret. But then almost anything, anywhere, after a lifetime on a Carlisle council estate in the 1950s, would have been a bit of a social and cultural shock.

She wrote to me every week from Bordeaux, long, graphic, amusing, colourful letters, which I still have, unless the rats have got into the garage and eaten them.

As a break from trying to furnish and equip our new flat, cooking for her dear husband when he came home from his awfully tiring day at work down the pit, I mean Gray's Inn Road, Margaret started writing a novel. She didn't tell me about it at first. She did it on the kitchen table while the flat was empty. It was called *Green Dust for Dreams*, which I immediately said was a poncey title. Did we say poncey in 1960? Pretentious, I probably said, which I said about anything smacking of purple prose, one of my hatreds in life.

It took her about three months of solid writing, working every day, all handwritten in ink. Someone then told her that no agent or publisher would accept any manuscript in longhand. So she painfully typed it all out, using two fingers on my new portable manual typewriter which I had recently bought for myself. I am at rubbish at typing, still am, but having done it for so long, since I was editor of *Palatinate*, the student paper, I am at least quick if slipshod, making endless mistakes and literals. Margaret, with her two fingers, never having used a typewriter before, took forever. It was agony for her. She also did it in single spacing, another mistake, in order to save paper.

Eventually she got it completed, parcelled it up and sent it off to an agent, Michael Sissons. I can't remember where we got his name from. Someone had said that he was young, just starting off, and might be looking for new authors.

He sent a letter back, fairly quickly. He thought it did not quite work as a novel, and could probably not be published as it was, but he invited her to come and see him at his office and talk about it.

Margaret immediately tore up his letter and binned the novel. I never even had a chance to read it all, but I can remember the physical look of it, about 300 close-packed pages with a purple ribbon tied round it. The type was so cramped it must have made it even harder to enjoy reading it.

So that was it, she was no longer going to be a novelist. The world clearly did not want her. I said come on pet, it's only one opinion, try somewhere else, but she was adamant. She was giving up trying to be a novelist.

Years later I did meet Michael Sissons, who soon became a very successful literary agent. He did have a memory of Margaret sending him a manuscript – and always wondered why she never replied. At the time, he thought he had sent her one of his more encouraging letters. Normally, he tried never to let young or new novelists anywhere near his office. After that, he made his replies to unsolicited manuscripts a bit more positive, if he did happen to think a new writer showed talent. But it was too late for Margaret. She had given up.

Instead, she decided to look for a job and became a teacher, at Barnsbury School for Girls in Islington, a girls' secondary modern, not far from Pentonville prison. She was technically only a supply teacher, but she stayed for almost two years. In those days, you did not need a DipEd – which I had, and never used. It was sufficient to be any sort of graduate to be allowed in front of a class.

Each morning she walked across the Heath, working her way down to Hampstead Heath railway station, and got on the Overground train to Barnsbury. It was a pleasant journey, as these things go, and at the school she made friends with two other young teachers, Di Regler and Mary Driscoll, drinking with them in a local pub at lunchtime. She kept in touch with both of them long after she had stopped teaching, but both of them, alas, died young from cancer. I often used to wonder, stupidly, if there had been something nasty in that pub. Or in that school.

Margaret was an excellent teacher, brilliant on discipline – nobody took any liberties – enthusiastic and energetic. Years later, women in the street would come up to her and recall her inspiring English lessons. Two of her old pupils ended up in *EastEnders* when it started on TV. She also had to teach current affairs, so on the train to Barnsbury she would buy the *Daily Mirror*, a much more socialist, educative paper in those days, which had a pull-out section on an important topic of the day, such as Vietnam, explaining what it was all about. Margaret would mug it all up, then repeat it to her pupils, as if she knew what she was talking about. Her knowledge of books, novels and plays was enormous. From about the age of sixteen, encouraged by her teachers at school, hoping she would try Oxbridge entrance, she had devoured everything suggested to her, averaging a book a day. But stuff like politics, economics or science, she had little interest in.

With Margaret working, it meant we had two salaries, not huge, but average for our age in London. I was now on £1,600 at the *Sunday Times*. We got an increase every Christmas, when Denis Hamilton would write to us and say well done, your salary will be going up by £100. You were not supposed to reveal it to your colleagues, which I suspected was a management conspiracy to keep us in our place.

After about a year in the flat, and us both now working, we had ticked off most of the major items on our lists, such as double bed, curtains, fridge, a cooker, and then, ever so posh, a Sheraton-style bureau.

My old 1947 Riley motor car, bought at the time we got married for £100, had caused endless problems, failing to start, the rain letting in through the roof. I blamed Mike Thornhill, our so-called best man, for making me buy it.

I then bought a brand-new car – a Morris Mini Minor. It had not long been launched, the first ones appearing at the end of 1959, so was still a novelty on the road. When I went back to Carlisle with it, and took my mother or Margaret's parents for a ride to Silloth, people in the villages on the way came out to look at it. I felt quite important. Someone clearly from London, at the cutting edge, or whatever cliché we used in those days.

I did once interview the inventor of the Mini, Alec Issigonis. He came from a Greek background but was a British citizen, educated at Battersea Poly, where he failed his maths exams three times, but managed to get a job as a motor engineer. What I remember about him was his pockmarked face. I wondered if he had had terrible spots as a teenager, as I had.

His Mini was a little miracle. The wheels were only ten inches high which made them look like toys. It had front-wheel drive and loads of other amazing innovations I did not understand, never having any real interest in cars. I suppose the most surprising thing was the enormous amount of space. You could not believe, looking from the outside, it was so spacious inside. Everything was pared to the bone, such as having a sort of pull wire instead of a door handle, which usually broke after too many tugs. You slid the windows open by hand.

I had one of the early models, so I discovered from the garage, which explained why it was hard to start on damp mornings, an initial teething problem not yet solved. I had to open the bonnet and dry everything in sight, then try to start it again.

But the Mini went on to become the most popular British car of all time, selling over 5 million. It's still highly prized and popular today in its modern equivalent. When I eventually started going abroad in the middle and late sixties, on hols or jobs, I always felt quite proud when seeing a Mini in the street, pleased that it had become so popular and fashionable, just as much as it had proved a huge success at home. It was probably a residue feeling from the fifties, when we felt a bit inferior to the Europeans, such as the French and the Italians, who seemed so much better and more artistic on design and fashion when it came to cars and clothes.

My Mini cost me £500, dirt cheap now, but seemed quite a lot at the time, a third of my year's salary. I got a car loan, interest free, through the *Sunday Times*, who were very generous at the time with helping staff. The colour of my Mini was blue. Or was it green? Or it could have been grey? The first time I happened to refer to its colour we had the most awful argument. Margaret shouted at me for being so stupid, so unobservant. Which happened quite a lot. Oh, the usual stuff: forgetting things when I did the shopping, asking the same thing three times, unable to remember birthdays and telephone numbers.

'Remind me again . . .' I would say.

'Certainly not,' she would reply. 'I have told you umpteen times. Just think.'

'Oh, come on, tell me, I'm in a hurry, I'll be your best friend . . .'

Not knowing the colour of my own car, which did seem rather dopey, turned out not to be my fault. It was after then that I discovered I was colour blind.

We were getting on by then extremely well with Mr Elton, our landlord in the Vale of Health. He approved of our puritan lifestyle, our regular hours, no singing, dancing, noisy guests, no playing loud music or getting drunk.

There was though one unfortunate domestic incident. Margaret foolishly agreed that a friend from Oxford could come and stay with us for a few days – who then asked if she could bring her boyfriend. I agreed as well. I had taken so much hospitality myself over the years, sleeping on people's sofas and floors when I first came to London, and when visiting Margaret at Oxford. It seemed only fair now that we were in the fortunate position of having our own lovely flat to help others.

We came home one day, both of us exhausted from work, to find the boyfriend trying to strangle the girl, blood everywhere. They had had some sort of fight. They apologised, were all remorseful, but it proved so hard to get rid of them.

Mr Elton, as a treat after our first year, invited us out for an evening. We went first to Overtons, a famous fish restaurant, and then to the Victoria Palace to watch the Crazy Gang. It was a music hall show, the sort I had been sent to review in Manchester at the Hulme Hippodrome, with jugglers, comedians, singers, ventriloquists. Mr Elton particularly loved a girl who did bird noises, nodding his head, saying how hard it was, bird noises were very difficult to do.

'But she does them awfully well, every night.'

You what? How did he know?

It then transpired that two days earlier, he had gone on his own to Overtons, tried the exact same menu he had ordered for us, and then to see the Crazy Gang. He had wanted to check everything out, to his satisfaction, that it would be suitable for us. We felt like a couple of maiden aunts being sheltered from the realities of West End life.

When I got my Mini, I started driving to work each day, as parking was easy in the side streets off Gray's Inn Road. I had always hated the Tube, feeling claustrophobic, telling myself that one of my ambitions in life would be never to go on the Tube again.

Over that Christmas period of 1962, the car disappeared. Minis were so easy to steal. You slid open a window, yanked the wire door handle, and you were in.

It had been stolen from the side street behind the office where I had left it, filled with Christmas presents for the family. We were going to be driving up North the following week for Christmas. The car was found, just in time, before we left for Carlisle, but the presents had gone. It had been discovered abandoned near Windsor barracks. It was presumed some squaddie had nicked it, wanting a quick way home. Unless it was Prince Charles, after too many cherry brandies, tee hee.

This was one of the funnier stories of 1963 – Prince Charles, then aged fourteen, on a school trip, had been spotted in the bar of a Stornoway hotel knocking back the cherry brandies. We all felt a bit sorry for poor old Charles when he was sent to Gordonstoun, his father's old school, for which he appeared totally unsuited; he would have been happier at Eton, which is where, allegedly, the Queen Mother wanted him to go.

In October 2016, this rumour turned out to be true, when some of the Queen Mother's unpublished letters became public. Writing in 1961 to her daughter, whom she addressed as 'My Darling Lillibet', she said she feared that Charles would feel 'cut off and lonely' at Gordonstoun.

The cherry brandy incident in fact made Charles appear less soppy and drippy than we had all imagined, with his awful floppy hair and strangulated voice – and presumably Prince Philip thought much the same. But Charles had been caught doing what normal fourteen-year-old boys, and girls these days, do at that age. So we all warmed to him.

I took the Mini one day when I went to interview Aldous Huxley, over on a rare visit from California. He was staying somewhere in Kensington and, after the interview, he said he had to go to his publisher in Bloomsbury. He was incredibly tall, going blind and a bit doddery. I said I would give him a lift; it would be on my way to Gray's Inn Road. He came out and saw my car – and was horrified. This was the period in which all Americans had monster cars. I had to coax him to get into it.

As we were driving down Piccadilly, we found ourselves between two giant London double-deckers. Huxley was nervously looking out of the window – but all he could see were the wheels of the buses towering over us.

'Let me out of here!' he yelled, convinced we were going to be squashed to death. He tried to pull open the door, fiddling with the mechanism, and the stupid piece of wire. Fortunately he could not find or understand the door-opening system, so he was forced to stay seated. Very soon, at the next lights, I was able to zoom away from the two scary double-decker monsters he was convinced were going to kill us.

Coming home in my Mini, to the Vale of Health, in the winters of 1960 and 1961, was a nightmare. When the London smog descended it covered everything in its horrible, thick, yellow, mucous-y vapour. It made you choke, unable to breathe. It reduced visibility so much you could hardly see your hands in front of you. No wonder so many thousands had died every winter in London, and had done so for centuries, back to 1200, which is when records of London fog first begin. London's position, on a river near an estuary, and all the overcrowding, had always made it vulnerable. The Industrial Revolution made it worse, and the image of the fog in London, permanently in a pea souper, was known throughout Europe.

Perhaps the worst winter ever was in 1952, when all those post-war cars added to the pollution. I was still living at home in Carlisle, on our lovely rural, sylvan council estate where there was no smog as we had no cars, and we felt very smug. I remember seeing the photographs of the London streets and we all thought poor things, having to live down there, in the Smoke. They don't know who their neigbours are and now they can't even see them. Poor petals.

Between 4 and 8 December 1952, it was estimated that 100,000 Londoners were made ill and 12,000 died prematurely. Ten years later, when I had become a Londoner, older locals were still moaning on about the Great Smog of 1952.

Looking back, the total eradication of the smog, after the various Clean Air Acts, is one of the many miracles of my lifetime. Just shows what governments and authorities can do, once they put their minds to it.

The arrival of Nick Tomalin as my boss on Atticus resulted in slightly more interesting people appearing in the column, most of them interviewed by me.

Nick turned out not to be the superior, supercilious ogre I had feared. In agreeing to take on the job as editor of Atticus, he had secured from the management an unusual concession. New people, when they are wanted, in football or business, can usually dictate their own terms in their honeymoon period. For the first time ever, since Atticus first appeared in the paper, decades earlier, the column suddenly had a by-line.

The title Atticus still appeared at the top, the name of the column, but at the end there was suddenly plopped in the name of the person responsible for it – in this case Nick Tomalin. So sensible, really. Not just to indulge the vanity of the journalist concerned – and by and large the journalistic vanity is enormous, the sight of his or her own by-line can send any journalist into raptures – but it meant when people wrote or rang with a story or a suggestion, they knew whom to address.

I was immediately worried this would demote me even further in the eyes of my colleagues and contacts, such as they were. People would now assume Nick had written everything. Under Bob Robinson, when it was all anonymous, I could always boast I had written the best bits, even when I hadn't.

Nick sensed my agitation and fears and very graciously offered to put my name in somewhere, every week, inside the column, in small print. So if I had interviewed Aldous Huxley that week, in the middle of the interview there would suddenly appear the words 'as Mr Huxley said to Hunter Davies'. The print was tiny, and the sudden appearance of an internal by-line clumsy and confusing, but I was well pleased.

It soon began to happen that some weeks I had written the whole column, all the interviews, all the bits and pieces, the funny bits – yet Nick's name would still be at the end, in bold letters. My name would appear just once in one interview, as if that was all I had done, in titchy eight-point Bodoni bold italics, floating about in one of the grey bits in the middle of the column.

Nick was always tremendously grateful when this happened, when I had manned the fort, done everything, as he had been unavoidably detained elsewhere, sometimes for the whole week. At first he gave off hints that he was working on some future project for CD, as Hamilton the editor was usually known in the office. (Brian Glanville, on the sports pages, deliberately always pronounced this as Seedy, which

I thought was unfair. I always admired Mr Hamilton, or Sir Charles Denis Hamilton as he became in 1976.)

I began to realise that Nick always seemed to be ringing up midweek from Brighton, to say he had been detained. It slowly dawned on me he was having an affair. Until then, I had never known personally anyone having an affair. Having lived a sheltered life, and still very puritan in my general outlook, I was rather shocked. He was five years older, and always seemed much more a man of the modern, fashionable world than I did.

I then picked up that it was a young female student, daughter of a then famous father, whose name I can't really reveal even now as perhaps her subsequent husband still doesn't know. I always assumed that Claire Tomalin, Nick's brilliant, attractive, wonderful but long-suffering wife, suspected as much.

So while Nick was spending all week shagging this stunning-looking young woman, for her photograph had appeared in the papers, I was stuck in Gray's Inn Road not just writing all the column but organising pictures, layout, doing the subbing, headlines, dealing with the lawyers, then working on the stone to get the page to bed.

The main frustration was that nobody knew. Apart from Nick himself. I could not boast around the office, as that would be tantamount to shopping Nick. Going behind your boss's back to sneak on him is rarely a good move. I just hoped other people would eventually find out, that it would leak out around the office.

On the other hand, I enjoyed being in charge of myself. I had a free hand to pick the interviews I fancied, use the bits I liked best. Journalists always complain when the stupid subs or an idiot editor cuts out what you think are your best lines. I managed, now and again, to introduce into the column one or two of the people I really wanted to interview, such as footballers and pop stars, though the managing editor, Pat Murphy, who supervised the column and passed the proofs, still wanted boring stuff about politics or the Athenaeum or the Garrick.

We normally got a page to ourselves, for the Atticus column, and I tried to have three interviews, running to about 500–750 words each, with little fillers in between, jokes, anecdotes, and observations. Not all the interviews were done face to face, some took place on the phone.

I liked ending each week with my main interview and photograph already lined up for the following week. If I managed that, it felt great coming in on a Tuesday morning, knowing I need not panic about having a whole blank page to fill.

So it suited Nick, during the height of any of his affairs, that I was doing so much, and he so little. We got on very well, never a cross word. He was incredibly sociable and I was often invited to his house for drinks after work.

I would go with him sometimes when he went to pick up his children from school in his VW camper van. He jumped out of the driving seat one day and shouted to me to take over, telling me just drive it back to his home in Gloucester Crescent. Two of his kids were in the vehicle at the time, who both started crying. I was petrified, never having driven such a large ungainly vehicle before. I couldn't change the gears, or turn the steering wheel. He hadn't asked me if I could drive or was insured, he just went off on a whim, having spotted someone in the street he wanted to talk to. Probably famous, or fashionable, or female.

On his daily rounds, meeting people or talking to them on the phone, he was always inviting people he had just met, and hardly knew, such as, say, Peter Hall. He would gaily tell them to come to supper that evening. Often they said yes, if just out of politeness. He would get home and tell Claire, oh by the way, X Y and Z are coming for supper tonight. Claire would rush around making more food, setting more places. Then of course they often did not turn up. I would be suddenly invited, to make up the numbers, fill the gaps.

He came home to our place once and I gave him a glass of dry sherry in the garden. He then took Margaret aside and said that unless the two of us – me and Margaret – were more sociable, had dinner parties, went to parties, moved around town, made contacts, invited well-known people to our home, I would never succeed as a journalist, not the sort who might eventually edit the Atticus column.

Margaret told him to get lost. If that's what I had to do to succeed, then she didn't want me to be that sort of journalist. Anyway, it was all nonsense and pointless, that sort of hectic social life. There was no need to do any of that to get on. She personally had far better things to do with her time and her life than become a social butterfly.

# 4

# Buying a House

One of the things we were doing was saving like mad, working our way through our 'To Do' list. Nick was miles ahead of me in most things, such as his family. He and Claire had five children, one of whom had died aged one month, and then a fifth child, a son, Tom, was born with spina bifida. I never knew how Claire coped with it all, and with Nick, plus running a huge house in what was already a fashionable, attractive area in Camden Town.

But after two years, our own modest list had begun to be whittled down. In fact only two major items on the list remained, one of them a fantasy, which I had made Margaret write down. That was to start a family.

I forced her one Christmas Eve to make a list of names for the children we might have some day, possibly, maybe. I still have that list, for I put it in a Bible, my Lord Wharton Bible, the one I had won aged thirteen at Warwick Road Presbyterian Church in Carlisle for reciting reams of psalms, all of which I had forgotten. My names for a girl included Morag, as it was my favourite girl's name and sounded so Scottish. Margaret said she hated it, which was typical. She never quite liked things, or didn't care, or didn't know, or was not bothered. So we compromised by only listing names which the other did not actively hate. Top of the girls' names was Caitlin, followed by Kirsten, Joanna, Amanda, and Lucy. Boys' names included Mark, Gavin, Simon, Nicholas, Callum, Piers, Adam, Justin, Saul, and Dominic.

You think you are being unusual, individual and different, when you are looking for a name for your child, but looking back, we were picking on names which thousands of other young marrieds at that time in that place were also alighting on. Though we did not know it. They just seemed to be absorbed into your head by osmosis. So in the end, depending on the name you choose, for the rest of their lives, a person's first name can so often give away the year they were born, where, and into what social class. So much for free will.

But top of the list, toppermost of the pops, the Number One Goal, which was beginning to appear at long last realisable, was to buy a house.

I suppose the most remarkable thing about our house saga is that from scratch, having no capital, with parents who had no money and had never owned their own houses, was that we worked out that if we saved up out of our wages, without any help whatsoever, we could get on the property ladder, buying an actual, real house, not a flat – in just over two years. Two years! That dates us far more than the Christian names of our children. In fact it now sounds like a story from the Dark Ages.

There has hardly been a week in the last fifty-five years since we bought our London house in which I have not managed to drag in how much we paid for it. I do it to annoy, to piss off the neighbours, boast, make people jealous, show how clever we were, which of course we were not. It was just how it was, at that time, in that place, at that stage we were at.

Today a young London couple, on average London wages, would have to save for forty years to acquire an average London property, which in 2016 was around £550,000. Probably over £600k by the time you get to the end of this sentence. And for that of course, you would be unlikely to acquire a whole house but have to be content to scrabble for a flat in a crummy area.

The London property world has gone mad, everyone knows it, everyone says it, and it means that the average young couple of the present and next generation is unlikely ever to be property owners. They will have to rent all their lives, or move out of London. London will become a ghetto for the rich.

When I start my spiel, boasting to the neighbours, I end it by saying that of course we did not think it was easy back in 1962, oh no, it seemed a hell of a struggle, there were loads of obstacles and problems, don't think it was a doddle, oh no, which of course they don't want to hear. They just roll their eyes and mutter lucky bastards.

Towards the end of 1962, after two years of saving hard, we had amassed the sum of £1,500 in a building society account. This was to be our deposit. Our first desire was to stay in Hampstead. Obviously. Lovely place, lovely houses, ideally somewhere near the Heath. Dream on.

We looked at Flask Walk, in the middle of the village, just off the High Street, where the houses appeared to be artisan terrace houses, nothing special, small front gardens, no side passages, all a bit cramped. Then we found out they started at around £7,500. Christ Church Hill was nearer £10,000 while houses in Downshire Hill, the street we really, really ogled most of all, were going for nearer £15,000.

It soon became clear that our target would have to be £5,000 houses, max. The rule of thumb at the time was that, to get a mortgage, you needed a deposit of one-third. We might increase marginally our £1,500 deposit by the time we found somewhere, but it was clear we had to aim for houses no more than £5,000.

We looked at a map of the Heath, decided the so-called wrong side, the Kentish Town side, would be the best bet, as it would still be near the Heath. If and when we ever made any money, we vowed to come back to Hampstead, our spiritual home, so we imagined, so we told ourselves.

Moving to the Kentish Town side would be a bit like slumming. We did not know anybody, had never been there. Even walking the whole circuit of the Heath, which we always did at the weekend, right round the boundaries, right up to Golders Green, which could last three hours, the Kentish Town side always seemed a bit scruffy, the people not as, how to put this, refined as on the Hampstead side.

We had referred to it till then as the Kentish Town side, but KT is technically further south, which just appeared to be one busy, scruffy, noisy High Road before you get to Camden Town. We soon discovered that the area we fancied, simply because it seemed achievable, was called Parliament Hill Fields. That's what it still says on the C2 bus which has its terminus at Parliament Hill. Local people, in the local streets, who had been there for some time, always talked at the time about going on the Heath as 'going over the Fields'. It made it sound rural and agrarian, as if they were all farm workers.

We got a list from a local estate, Jennings and Samson in Fortess Road, a scruffy, duplicated, badly typed sheet with no photos, no full addresses and certainly no flowery prose. There were whole houses available in Tufnell Park and in Camden for about £5,500 – all vacant, i.e. with no tenants. In 1962 almost every house in our area had been divided into flats with one or two sitting tenants who had been there forever and were protected by law.

The one that caught our eye was very near the Heath, in Parliament Hill Fields. 'Ideally suited for the discriminating buyer who is desirous of carrying out repairs and re-decoration to his own requirements.' Notice the use of the word 'he' which they would never use today – and I should think not.

It was three storeys high, flat-fronted, with a neat little iron balcony on the first floor outside the main drawing room, which was the handsomest room in the house with double windows. The house looked as if it was in a terrace but was in fact semi-detached, which meant we had a side passage to the left of the front door, which was a great help when the builders started.

There was a sitting tenant whom the agent explained was an old lady, currently in America living with her daughter, who had the top floor and paid 32/6 a week rent. The agent said she would probably never come back, which of course I did not believe, being cynical about all estate agents, even in those days, when I had met so few.

The asking price was £5,250. I offered £5,000 and it was immediately accepted, a clear sign, which I did not translate at that time, that the old woman would come back and that the condition of the house was probably even worse than they had suggested.

I found a lawyer, John Carey, of Moon Beever and Kinsey – purely because he lived in the street where we were buying the house and someone gave me his name. I paid the 10 per cent deposit of £500 in December 1962.

When I went to my building society, the one we had been saving with for two years, on the understanding that they would provide us with a mortgage in due course, they said oh sorry, we are no longer giving mortgages on pre-1900 houses. Our house was 1860s. They had never told us that, bastards. So I was left with having paid a £500 deposit – but was now unable to get a mortgage.

I went to the *Sunday Times* personnel department and they recommended another company, the Norwich Union, whom they used, saying they would act as my reference. They organised a survey of the house and agreed yes, they would give us a twenty-year mortgage. Twenty years! Would we live that long? Would the world live that long?

We moved in in late January 1963 without having yet seen the garden. It had been covered in snow when we looked at the house in December, so we had no idea what it contained.

Spring was a constant delight. It was such a surprise as pears and apple trees emerged, plants and bushes shot up, flowers appeared which we had never imagined were there. Even more amazing, an Anderson air raid shelter was revealed at the bottom of the garden, up against the back wall.

Anderson shelters were the wartime shelters half dug into the ground, with corrugated iron on top over which soil and turf was usually laid, which was why we had not identified it, thinking it was a mound at the bottom of the garden. The shelters that were erected inside your house, and which we had in Carlisle during the war, were known as Morrison shelters. They were like a steel coffin, under your kitchen table. Hell to get into, hell to sleep in and liable to knock you out flat if you happened to get up quickly without ducking your head.

Frank Herrmann, a young photographer on the *Sunday Times*, one of my closest friends on the paper, with whom I often contrived to work, was around the same time paying £7,500 to buy his first house not far away in Highgate. I could not work out how he could afford so much more than me – till I discovered he had family help. I thought this was cheating. I was a bit jealous of course, but then rationalised it, feeling pleased that we had bought ours all on our own, from scratch. Even if it was not in such a desirable area as Highgate.

At that time, Frank and I buying houses in what is roughly inner London, was fairly unusual. Not in buying a house, at our age, but the norm among my contemporaries, when they tried to get their first steps on the housing ladder and think about a family, was to move out to the suburbs. Another of my friends on the paper, Mike Hamlyn, an Oxford graduate, had, like us, a flat in Hampstead when he first got married, but when it came to a buying a house, they moved out to Beckenham. We went there for a meal once. It seemed to take forever and I got totally lost. When I got there, I still felt lost. It was one vast, featureless suburbia.

Most subs on most papers, as they had been in Manchester, lived out in the suburbs, wanting a semi-rural life, nicer houses, bigger gardens. We so-called writers, like me and ahead of me Nick Tomalin, rather looked down on subs for having no imagination – and being frightfully provincial. We wanted to be in inner London, among real people, from all classes, even if the area had its scruffy, scary, low-life element, though naturally we would be looking for a bijou Georgian gem, a Regency square or a spacious Victorian terrace.

I never for one moment contemplated the idea of commuting from the suburbs. I felt instinctively an inner Londoner. There was no real reason for this, I don't know where I got it from, nor Margaret, as we had lived almost all our lives in the North and London was still much of a mystery to us. We just loved being in the heart of the capital. Charing Cross, the traditional centre of London, was just four miles away. In the suburbs, we would have got a whole, empty house for £5,000 and had green fields within walking distance, yet we had 800 open acres of the Heath on our doorstep. It was well worth having the inconvenience of a sitting tenant. Whom we were still hoping would never actually appear.

We found a local builder, J. P. Brown, who lived nearby in Fortess Road. He was a stage Irishman, and all his workers were stage Irish. He was full of blarney and delighted in ignoring all safety rules, climbing on broken roofs, walking over sky lights, always cheerful.

I went round one day to his house to find out why he had not turned up. In the basement I could see benches, little more than large shelves, where two Irish workmen were asleep. At one time, Kentish Town and Camden Town had large Irish populations, most of them in the building trade. Now the Irish have gone, replaced by Poles. Probably still sleeping on the same shelves.

JP ripped the house apart, put in central heating and tore

out fireplaces – which in a few years we bitterly regretted. We had never had central heating in our own homes in Carlisle and assumed you always had to get rid of fireplaces to install CH, as we began to call it.

Mrs Hall, the sitting tenant, did eventually return. She turned out to be Irish as well, though she denied it, for some reason. She had a strong Irish accent and all her friends who came to visit her were Irish women, several of them retired nurses, always addressed as Nursey. Mrs Hall was about seventy, lean, grim-looking, a bit like Old Mother Riley but without the laughs.

She suddenly appeared in our kitchen one evening, while we were eating, asking me to come up at once and mend her leaking tap. Margaret got up, showed her the kitchen door, and told her never to do that again. She was always coming down to complain about something, or stopping us on the stairs while we were going up and down, our stairs of course, to moan on.

Mrs Hall had the whole of the top floor to herself, three rooms and a kitchen on the landing, but she shared our lavatory which was on the middle floor. Every time she used it, she insisted on spraying it with the most revoltingly scented spray. Her only entrance was through our house, sharing the front door, which was endlessly annoying, giving us no privacy in our own house. She would stagger her way past our bedroom door every evening, heaving and sighing, dear God this, dear God that, or sometimes Sister of Mercy.

Margaret became pregnant in the autumn of 1963, at the end of our first year in our house. We had waited to have a house of our own, and a garden, which we never had in the Vale of Health, before starting a family.

One day I got a letter from the Royal Free Hospital, addressed to me, as the father to be, asking if I would like to attend a fathers' class. This was the first such class they had organised. I wondered what they could teach me, as surely I had already done my bit, but then I thought, brilliant, that must be 1,000 words. A cry which has crept out of my lips ever since, whenever anything remotely interesting, however personal, or trivial, ever happens to me.

I rushed along to the first fathers' class to find a young BBC reporter, Wilfred De'Ath, was already there, his tape recorder at the ready, also hoping to get a feature out of it.

I didn't actually witness the birth. Despite it being the early sixties, a time of endless novelties and innovations, or so we thought, the fathers' classes did not lead to fathers being present at the birth.

In fact I wasn't even in the hospital when Margaret gave birth on 6 March 1964. I had been sitting in the hospital with her all night, holding her hand and other manly contributions, but nothing appeared to be happening. By the morning, I was fed up and hungry so I decided to go into Hampstead Heath Street to buy a pie. When I got back, Caitlin had been born, weighing 8 lbs 3½ ounces, with incredibly thick black shiny hair – which is what I used to have, er, many decades ago.

Caitlin had been top of our list for girls' names. We had got into our head it was Welsh, and would go well with Davies, thinking of Caitlin Thomas, wife of Dylan Thomas, not realising that she was Irish.

I was never forgiven for missing Caitlin's birth, especially for such a prosaic and unromantic reason as buying a pork pie.

But I was there two years later for the birth of our second child, Jake, born in 1966 on 24 May, the day before Margaret's twenty-eighth birthday. So that was a nice present for herself.

We decided to have a home birth this time. By now we had most of the downstairs alterations completed, to our part of the house. A little outside room downstairs in the back addition, which had been a coal hole when we moved in, had been converted into our spare bedroom.

The midwife was delayed, and so was the doctor. Jake came out so quickly he got the cord stuck round his neck. He could well have strangled himself, coming out so quickly, but I managed to untangle him. Thus my fathers' day classes had not been wasted. The midwife and doctor both eventually came and said jolly well done.

After Margaret, and the baby, had been cleaned up, I asked the midwife to give me the placenta. She asked why I wanted it, but I did not reveal the reason. Just said I was going to bury it in the garden, saving her the bother of disposing of it. She said it had to be destroyed or buried properly, to make sure no rats got at it. Government rules.

I had read somewhere about a woman in America who had eaten her own placenta – fried it with onions and pronounced it tasty, a bit like liver.

Naturally my thoughts were on a thousand words. I did get a piece out of it for the Women's pages of the *Sunday Times*. I cooked it in the frying pan, and I did eat a bit of it, but not much. Liver is one of the very few foods I have never cared for.

So now, with two young children, it meant that Mrs Hall had more space proportionally in our house than we had. The four of us – two adults, a baby and a toddler – shared two floors, while she on her own had one whole floor to herself. We explained the situation, as if she didn't know it already, but she would not move. She was protected by law. We did not have the financial resources to offer her a suitable bribe, I mean inducement. So that was it.

When I boast endlessly today about how little I paid for our house, what a bargain, doesn't it make you sick, clever old us, I do tend to forget about all those years in which I was driven mad by Mrs Hall. I did begin to think at the time that perhaps we hadn't got such a bargain after all. Unless somehow, from somewhere, we ever got the money to buy her out, we could end up with this old grumpy woman being part of our household for ever and ever.

The very primitive, cheapo estate agent's handout details of our house in 1962 – just think what a glossy brochure they would produce today. It is the one at the top, in Parliament Hill Fields. I got them down to £5,000.

# 5

# WRITING LIVES

One reason we did not have such an active social life as Nick Tomalin was not just because we were saving money but that after about a year in the Vale of Health, after a hard day at work for each of us, we had started writing. All our spare time, and every weekend, we were writing away. Margaret at the kitchen table with her fountain pen and me in the living room, on my portable typewriter, sitting at the repro Sheraton bureau.

Margaret started first. She had got over what she considered had been the disaster of her first attempt at a novel, and had decided to try again, writing a different sort of novel, a lighter, more amusing story based on the sort of people she knew, not what she had imagined had been the life and feelings of the French family she had lived with in Bordeaux.

She was so disciplined, so organised, doing a thousand words almost every day after work. I was so impressed I decided I would have a go as well, at so-called creative writing, as opposed to journalism. Not that I would have used the term creative writing, being wary of all pretentions. Anyway, isn't all writing creative? The page is blank, till you create some words on it.

I decided against fiction, believing I did not have the right sort of imagination. So I started a TV script, a series about a school, called *Silver Street.*

There were lots of police dramas at the time on TV, such as *Z Cars*, which had begun in 1962 and was incredibly popular, and *Dixon of Dock Green*, which began in 1955, still limping on, and being mocked for being old-fashioned. Not that I knew much about TV. In the Vale of Health we never had a TV set, nor later in our Boscastle Road house for many years. It wasn't snobbery, which was prevalent at the time, with the aspiring middle classes looking down on everything on TV, boasting how they never watched the box. It was just that it didn't fit in with our lives. But I had picked up that there was nothing much about schools on TV and thought a staff room was a naturally dramatic setting.

So there we sat in our Vale of Health flat, in 1961 and 1962, night after night, bashing away. No one had asked us. No one was waiting for us to finish. No one except each other knew what we were doing. Or cared.

I have no memory of either of us, when we first met and were courting, telling the other that really, pet, what I want to do in life is write. The subject was never mentioned. Margaret read avidly, but that was after she had done her school or college work. At Durham, I did write a fairly pretentious story once which was published in *New Durham*, a literary magazine, but I did not put my name to it. I think I thought it was too soppy – and anyway I saw myself as a humorous writer.

I am sure it was Margaret's example which spurred me on – but when I asked for her help or opinion, which I did all the time, she always refused. I would say please read this bit of dialogue, it's really good, or this scene, you'll love it. She would never read anything I had written, not till it was all finished, then she would give her honest and brutal reaction.

I had the same problem when I began to move on from simply doing 500-word interviews for Atticus. I felt I had mastered that length, could bash them out without too much worry, but when I came to do longer interviews, such as John Masefield, the Poet Laureate, which was more like 3,000, I used to panic. I was never sure where to begin, how to shape it, what to leave out. It was like running a mile race when all you have ever trained for is the 100 yards.

Then there is the other problem, which is the one all beginners have, then and now – who do you send it to? As an outsider, you imagine there is a magic circle which somehow you have to enter, or need help to enter. When you do become a published writer, the most common letter you get is from people wanting advice. Even people who have distinguished themselves in their own field, such as judges and surgeons, still imagine that someone who has had a few books published can help them get their book published. Popular and successful writers, such as George Bernard Shaw and J. B. Priestley, in the end resorted to duplicated replies, refusing to read other people's manuscripts.

When I finished my TV script, I sent it to the BBC. Seemed the obvious thing to do. Just popped it in the post to BBC, London W1 or whatever. I failed to get the name of anyone, or the title of a suitable department. It came back after three months with a duplicated rejection.

I then started on a stage play. Again, I find it hard to believe

I did this. Today, I have no interest in the theatre and probably have not been to a play for over fifty years, but plays were in the air, we had seen lots in the sixties, there seemed to be so many exciting new playwrights.

I based it on an incident and characters we knew, a bloke who had two families. In each case the mothers of his children went out to work, while he did nothing at all, all day long, except take out his various children and play, often in the same playground.

I sent it off to the literary agency Curtis Brown. By this time I had learned that you needed to contact an agent first and I had been told they were the biggest in town. To my amazement, their theatre man wrote back agreeing to handle it. A few weeks later, he had sold it to a West End theatre director, Allan Davis.

I then started working with him in his Mayfair flat, as he showed me how to shape the scenes, shape the plot. He talked airily of opening in Brighton, before the West End, and which stars he would get, and how Hugh Beaumont, known as Binkie, a famous producer with whom he had worked, would put the money up.

On 18 January 1962, Beaumont wrote personally to Allan – turning down my play, *The Herring Gulls*. I still have a copy of the letter. In it he did say a few nice things – some very amusing dialogue, potential talent – but that a lot of the play was incoherent and I needed more experience. He signed it Yours Binkie, so I knew his nickname was not a newspaper myth.

But encouraged by my first attempt, I started another play, based on my father dying. Allan Davis turned it down as did the theatre man at Curtis Brown, John Barber, who had been so encouraging with my first play. In fact he wrote me a most awful letter, saying how disappointed he was. After all the time and energy he had spent with me on my first play, he said I had learned nothing, had been wilful, not working hard enough on the characters and the narrative.

I was totally devastated by this reply. Yet again I have kept the letter. I still have it filed in Volume One of My Life, a row of folders in which I have kept all the scraps and documents from my early life. At the top of the letter, in pencil, Margaret has written 'Oozeefinkeeis? How very unnecessarily unpleasantly put.'

So that was it. My life as a playwright had come to a dead end.

Margaret's attempt at another novel, however, was immediately accepted. It was called *Dames' Delight* and was about her time at Oxford, not the usual dreamy spires stuff, but how a northern working-class girl goes there and finds it all nonsense. She too sent it to Curtis Brown where the boss, Graham Watson, sold it to Jonathan Cape.

However, excitement at having a first novel published by such a distinguished publishing house was ruined when she ran into libel trouble. The mother of one of her friends recognised herself in a proof copy sent to her and complained. Tom Maschler, the boss of Cape, called Margaret into his office and said it was all her fault. She was almost in tears. She was only twenty-five, with no experience of publishing or libel. It seemed so unfair that she got blamed. I always felt her editor should have checked and changed certain things before it got to the proof stage. She had to pay for reprinting costs and legal fees which came to more than the £250 advance she had received for the book.

After various changes were made, all of which I considered piddling, *Dames' Delight* eventually came out in February 1964. It sold well, got good reviews, but you can't buy this book in any shop today as it has never been reprinted. Not because of the trouble associated with it – but because almost immediately Margaret decided she hated it. She had got published, at last, but felt she had got off on the wrong foot. It was not really the sort of novel she liked or wanted to write. In later years, when publishers regularly asked to reprint it, she always said no.

I have just looked at a copy, one I hid in my room before she destroyed them all, and I see her heroine, the girl who goes to Oxford from the North on a scholarship, was called Morag Graham. I had completely forgotten that. If asked her heroine's name, I would not have been able to answer.

Graham is of course a very common surname in Carlisle and the Borders while Morag was my first choice of a girl's name, which she had rubbished at the time, refusing to consider it.

I think I was more excited by Margaret being published than she was herself. It had all seemed so easy and pleasurable, till it all went wrong and ended in tears. But all the same, I was greatly encouraged that she had done it, so I decided I would have a go at a novel. If Margaret could do it, perhaps I could? I knew her, had known her for ages, since she had been a schoolgirl. Had I not seen her sitting in the kitchen, her pen poised? I knew she had no connections to any magic circle;

she had used no contacts to get published. 'Ah kent his faither,' which is what my mother used to say when people did well, or more likely, got above themselves. Meaning she knew their background.

Margaret had used her student days for her novel, so I decided I would base my novel on my own teenage life, looking for the girl of my dreams. In my mind, I have exaggerated over the years about how long we had gone out, saying we went to school together, which was not totally true. I had known of Margaret, and spoken to her from an early age, but it wasn't till I was nineteen and she seventeen, and still at school, that we really got together. And by that time, er, I had had quite a few girlfriends, all in the best possible taste of course – i.e. nothing happened.

I knew I could not handle a proper plot, or do anything imaginative, but I had just read *Catcher in the Rye* and was impressed how Salinger did not really have a plot, not much happened, it was all in the character of the hero, Holden Caulfield.

So I wrote my teenage novel in the first person, mainly for laughs, but with suitable doses of teenage sexual frustration and sentimentality and soppiness, moving on quickly whenever I got bored.

I sent it to Curtis Brown again but instead of Graham Watson, who had handled Margaret's novel, and turned out to be the boss man, I got a new young agent, Richard Simon. He wrote back saying it could not be published as it was, but if I was prepared to do some work, it might have a chance.

He suggested that instead of just having the same girl in the book from the beginning, whom I idolised from afar, I should have lots of girlfriends, one after the other, keep it fast and furious. Which, in reality, was very much what happened. Till I eventually do meet up with the girl of my dreams.

When Margaret had had that rather low-key response from Michael Sissons, she immediately gave up. Richard's initial response to my first attempt had been similar, but I was immediately encouraged by his suggestions and at once set to work. For several weeks I slogged away at building up the minor girlfriends, under his direction. When I had finished to his satisfaction, Richard sold it to Charles Pick of Heinemann.

Mr Pick, who seemed a bit pompous and stiff for someone who presumably liked my racy teenage saga, took me out to lunch in Mayfair, near their office in Queen Street, and told me how excited they were and about all their great plans for the book lunch.

They had devised an amusing gimmick for the book cover – which was to have a pair of three-dimensional plastic lips stuck on the cover. Quite a technological and printing achievement for 1965. The lips would appear to kiss you, as you walked round the bookshop. Everyone loved it – until people started inspecting the actual book. When customers pulled the book off the shelf to buy it, the plastic lips came off. They would then demand a proper copy. Hundreds of copies were sent back. By the time of the paperback version, the lips were abandoned. But the reviews were good and there was soon talk of several film companies being interested.

Meanwhile Margaret had started on her second novel, determined this time not to send it to Cape. It was a novel called *Georgy Girl* and was totally fictional, not like her first novel. Several of the women in it were vaguely inspired by some of the good friends she had made while teaching at Barnsbury School, at least the concept of female chums. She even managed to persuade her new publisher, Secker and Warburg, to let one of her friends, the art teacher, Mary Driscoll, to design the cover for the book. Publishers are always being asked by authors to employ their friends or relatives to design a cover – and they always say no.

*Georgy Girl* turned out to be the most amazing success – and Tom Maschler, so we were told later, was furious, suspecting that Margaret knew she had a better book in her and had deliberately kept it from him.

Before publication, film offers were coming in, though the people who bought it, getting in first, were a small company, who then did a deal with a bigger company, so it seemed to take ages before there was any real progress.

If 1960 was a big year for us, getting married and me joining the *Sunday Times*, 1965 was running it close. *Georgy Girl* was published, Margaret's second novel, and so was my first novel, *Here We Go Round the Mulberry Bush*.

We had our own house and family by now. A shame about Mrs Hall, but she did go off for long spells to stay with her daughter in the USA. And now, with the prospect of some monies to come, we might eventually be able to buy her out.

It always seems to me, looking back, that what we now describe as the sixties did not come in till 1965. That was when I was really aware that changes in attitudes, culture, styles, and clothes were really happening, at least in London. And I was there. I have a photograph of me with sideboards, granny sun specs and the grandfather buttoned T-shirt vest to prove it. But then so did many thousands of others.

In the world at large in 1965, which I didn't really worry about all that much, there was martial law in Rhodesia, with more problems to come. At home, the Labour Government under Wilson was about to instruct local authorities to introduce comprehensive education, which was something I thought an excellent idea. In football, which I was interested in, Sir Stanley Matthews, the first footballer to be knighted while still playing, had his last game in the First Division, aged fifty. The Kray Brothers were arrested, Ronnie Biggs, the Great Train Robber, escaped from Wandsworth prison and then there were the Moors Murders. So loads of fodder for the popular papers in 1965.

Kenneth Tynan said fuck on live TV, which had them all in a tizzy, but I couldn't see what the fuss was about. Not that I swore. Never did, nor did Margaret. In fact it is only in the last few years that I've taken up swearing – and it's really good fun. Everyone now does it, from Downing Street to Buckingham Palace. I say fuckinhell all the time, appalling, I know.

One of the major events of 1965 was the death Sir Winston Churchill. I was among the scores of reporters sent to cover his funeral procession on 30 January 1965. The funeral was a Saturday, so perfect timing for all the Sunday papers. Everyone on the *Sunday Times* was out that day, office staff, photographers, management, people who had not written a word for years found themselves positioned somewhere on the route.

Churchill had died six days earlier, on the Monday. His coffin was displayed in Westminster Hall and 321,360 people filed passed it in three days. He was given a state funeral, the first for a politician in the twentieth century. Only politicians in the distant past, like the Duke of Wellington and Gladstone, had been honoured with a state funeral.

I remember being quite thrilled and excited in 1945 as a child at primary school when Attlee had surprisingly kicked out Churchill and become Prime Minister, joining in with the runny-nosed kids chanting in our street: 'Vote Vote Vote for Mr Attlee, kick old Churchill up the bum.' But of course we revered Churchill all the same, and knew he had won the war for us. And he did come back once again as PM, as a very old man, in 1951.

By the time of his death in 1965, aged ninety, he was hugely admired all over the world, especially in the USA, so his funeral was a massive event. There were 120 different countries represented at the funeral service, the cortege took ages parading round central London, including a river trip, before eventually heading out of the capital to his burial place near Blenheim Palace. The BBC had forty camera crews providing the coverage which was watched by a worldwide audience.

It was an appalling day, wet and dull, miserable and cold, so uncomfortable for all the hundreds of thousands who had turned out to watch, but I had an enormous piece of luck. I managed to bag a really cushy location – sitting in the Savoy Hotel. I talked the newsdesk into letting me cover it from the Savoy press office, which I knew was at the back of the hotel and looked out over the river. Perfect position to observe the river procession. I often popped into the Savoy on stories, while interviewing famous people who were staying there. In those days, the Savoy and most of the big hotels had gaggles of young debby-type press girls who would issue to their chosen and friendly hacks a weekly list of well-known people who were staying in the hotel. I knew all the lovely press girls who kindly plied me with drinks and sandwiches. Most of my colleagues on the paper were stuck either in massive crowds in the streets, unable to see anything, or marooned on an overcrowded boat on the river, cowering in the cold and rain.

I wrote a poignant piece which made the front page – in which I, alas, admitted to shedding a few tears. I don't think it was just due to the huge emotional occasion, as it was for everyone who had lived through the Second World War. I think it was also the fault of the Savoy gels, continually filling up my glass.

I was worth treating, so they thought. For by 1965 I had at long last been put in charge of the Atticus column. A small event in journalism, but a big event in my life.

# 6

## ATTICUS

Until it happened, I was convinced it never would. I had already started once again to look around for other papers, other jobs. At the *Sunday Graphic*, when we all knew it was closing, I was sure I would not be moved to the *Sunday Times*, and had applied for a job on the *Sunday Express*. I had a friend working there as news editor, John Robson, who had told me how good it was. I got an interview with John Junor, one of the best known editors of the time. He offered me a job on the *Sunday Express* at £28 a week. I seriously thought about it, but a few weeks later, the call came from the *Sunday Times*.

By 1964 I was getting itchy feet again, convinced I was not making progress. Although Nick Tomalin had put my name in the column, I was doing most of the work and felt unappreciated.

I had talked one day to Jack Lambert, who was the assistant literary editor to Leonard Russell. Jack seemed to do most of the work while Leonard – married to Dilys Powell – seemed to be at home most of the day, supposedly reading proofs or manuscripts. Jack explained that I had to try to establish myself outside of the office – for that was when they would take notice of you inside the office. He had got himself a minor niche on the radio as a theatre critic, which didn't seem much of an achievement to me. Having a book published, which I hoped to do soon, that would surely make them take notice on the paper.

Nick Tomalin was taken off Atticus in the summer of 1964. It happened gradually and I never quite worked out the details. He started going off, officially this time, on various foreign stories, leaving me to run Atticus that week. I used some of his stories in Atticus, giving him a by-line in the middle of the column, but printing my name in bold at the end. But then the weeks went on – and he never came back to Atticus. It slowly transpired that he had become a roving foreign correspondent. After a few months, it was confirmed. I was the new Atticus. Sounds very piddling now, all these decades later, but at the time I could not sleep, driving Margaret mad, trying to work it out, read the signs, worried that I was just holding the fort while some exciting, better connected, better known person was being lined up to come in and take over.

Having been officially appointed, I was then allowed to hire my own boy assistant, just as I had been the boy assistant to Bob Robinson and then Nick.

We were already having occasional help from a young free-lance Nick had found, just down from Oxford, Tim Heald. He was incredibly quick and confident for one so young and inexperienced. Before ringing someone, I would still sit for ages reading all their cuttings, writing out notes, preparing myself for fear they might be difficult and put the phone down. Tim would just pick up the phone and bash away, ever so smooth and convincing. He was even quicker than me at bashing out copy.

He looked amazingly young and fresh-faced, with a lovely linen suit and a rose in his button-hole, floppy fair hair, very public schoolboyish. He had gone to Sherborne and Balliol, just the sort of background I would normally have been prejudiced against, someone who seemed to have had it easy in life, the looks, the charm, the exclusive education, with contacts and confidence, able to land a job on the *Sunday Times* straight from Oxford, while I had had to sweat it out for two years in Manchester and then on the *Sunday Graphic*.

That did not actually worry me. I just thought lucky Tim. What concerned me was whether he could do the job or not – and he clearly could. We got on well, though I did get annoyed when he insisted on calling me Edward. Somehow he had found out it was my real first name and it amused him to address me as Edward or write me notes and letters addressed to Edward.

It did of course amuse me, with my background, to be hiring someone from his background, something I never thought I would be in a position to do. That year, 1964, when I became Atticus, was the end of my silly obsession and persecution complex, feeling that people were prejudiced against me and always would be. It had all been in my head of course, seems so ridiculous now. Ever since, if anything, they have been prejudiced in favour of me, partly because of my background, which of course is equally unfair.

It was not just me, in my own little world with my own little phobias. It was also happening out there. Suddenly, the world seemed to have reversed its old class prejudices and someone like me, with my interests, was now being given all the advantages, benefits of the doubt, space and encouragement.

So much has been written about the sixties, mainly by people who were never there, and the image has grown up that it was all drugs, sleeping around, wild living. Not where I was, not in the circles I moved in. Ordinary people did none of those things. It only happened, if it happened at all, among a handful of pop stars or in Soho clubs. It was only in the seventies that the drug culture began to trickle down to ordinary young people doing ordinary jobs, in ordinary parts of the country.

The big noticeable change in the sixties was one of attitude and deference, rather than drugs and sex. And I would say it began around 1964–65. The fact that I was being allowed to interview, even encouraged, to write about people from the so-called traditional lower social classes, as long as they had done something, achieved something, was a reflection of what was happening generally in society.

In Britain, there had been strict class and professional hier-archies for so long, right up to and throughout the fifties, the sort of deference that the war had failed to eradicate, that in fact had made worse because the military mind had taken over, making people not questioning but accepting the status quo.

In so many careers and professions, you had to come from the right background, or at least appear to have the right background and accent, hence people assumed the right accent, believing it was the way to get on. You can see and hear all this in those old pre-war and post-war films with even humble secretaries and receptionists having unbelievably posh accents.

Even in the so-called creative professions, where you might assume it was talent that mattered most, people had to look and talk the part. Not just actors and actresses but photographers. I could not believe it when I interviewed Cecil Beaton just how posh he was, yet all he did was take snaps of women in frocks.

Along with no longer having to have the right accent it became acceptable, and even fashionable, not to have had any proper training or education. You could take photos, cut hair, make clothes, make music, write novels, without having had to put in the years and pretend you were grander, more experienced, better educated than you were.

Fashion designers just out of art school, or even those who had never been there were starting their own lines and had people rushing to buy their products.

Art designers, on newspapers and magazines and in publishing, had traditionally been rather upper crust, or so they appeared. Many of them of course were just pretending, putting on airs, assuming graces. At the *Sunday Times* in the sixties a very grand, immaculately besuited art designer and typographer called Robert Harling used to wander in, as if straight from his club, at the end of the week and supervise the overall design of the paper. I could not see what he added, but I could see he was awfully smooth and sophisticated. He was a friend of Ian Fleming's and had been a distinguished naval officer in the war.

And then I met Alan Aldridge, someone of my age, who

became a friend and neighbour and work colleague. He had the impressive title of Art Director of Penguin Books, traditionally an important position. Yet he had never been to art school and always talked about drawing as if it had an *r* not a *w* in the middle.

He was one of the new breed of young people who got promoted to important jobs in the fashion and art and design world at a young age and became flavours of the month, got written about in the quality papers, people wanted to meet them and talk to them.

I had always been fascinated by such people, along with gritty northern novelists, Merseyside pop groups and footballers. These were the people I wanted to meet, talk to, and write about. I had never wanted to interview bishops or ambassadors or cabinet ministers who had been the staple diet of columns like Atticus, and similar ones in the *Telegraph* and *Times* and other so-called Establishment papers, forever, or so it seemed to me.

Gritty novelists .had been around for some time, and jumped-up fashion designers, but the Establishment had largely ignored such people. They were not deemed worthy of our attention. Now suddenly they were fashionable.

And so, once in charge of Atticus, I was able to rush around seeing people I wanted to see, for my own interest and amusement, knowing I would get space in the *Sunday Times*, of all papers, to indulge them, and myself, and probably annoy quite a few readers.

In 1965 I went up to Manchester and interviewed a nineteen-year-old youth from Belfast called George Best who had just got into the Manchester United first team. He assured me he didn't drink or smoke, though on a rare occasion he might have a lager. He was in digs with another boy and got very bored in the evenings as most players in the team were married, such as Bobby Charlton and Denis Law. He had been in awe of them from afar but now he found they were just ordinary blokes.

His basic wage was £50 a week but that week he had earned £175, as he had three games, one of them an international for Northern Ireland. 'What I'd like to be is a millionaire. If it means not playing football again from this minute on? Well perhaps I don't want to be a millionaire after all.

'I would like to have a flat of my own. But the boss, Mr Busby, thinks there might be temptations. Perhaps when I'm twenty-two. I've got no complaints, I like my landlady.'

David Hockney seemed the sort of bright, chirpy northern lad made good, still with a strong Yorkshire accent. In 1966 he was twenty-seven and had just won a Gold Medal at the Royal College of Art. I went to interview him at an enormous but rather rundown flat in Bayswater.

While staying recently in the USA, he and a friend were watching an advert on TV which said 'Blondes have more fun'. So at two o'clock in the morning, slightly drunk, they both went out, bought some hair dye and became blonde. David had decided to remain blonde from then on, despite having naturally dark hair.

In his lavatory I noticed a cut-out photograph from a newspaper of Denis Law, scoring a goal. I asked if he was a football fan. He said no, he just liked Denis Law's thighs.

The subs cut that remark out of the story, to save any gossip or legal problems. In 1966, homosexual activity could still be an offence. It was not till July 1967 that the Sexual Offences Act decriminalised homosexual acts in private between two men, as long as both were over the age of twenty-one.

As a teenager I had always been a fan of the *Goon Show*, as most of us were, so I indulged myself by going to interview Spike Milligan in 1964. Spike recounted, using funny voices, that when Peter Sellers had got married to Britt Ekland, Spike had sent Peter a telegram saying: 'You rotten swine, Bluebottle. You promised to marry me. Send me back my ring – Eccles.'

Today, it would take too long to explain the names, and the funny voices, though I am sure Prince Charles would still laugh.

Spike also remembered, in the days when they were hard-up and struggling after the war, how Peter Sellers had come to his flat door one night. 'He was standing there stark naked with a tray of matches. In a Jim voice, he said, "Can I interest you in a thriving timber and sulphur business?"'

One of the modern young writers I interviewed in 1964 was James Baldwin, over from the USA. He was gay, but again this was never talked about. I walked round Bloomsbury Square with him. 'I suppose I am exotic. A dancing doll. A Negro who is a writer.' I complimented him on the Beatles-style suit he was wearing. He said he had bought it in Germany and had not heard of the Beatles at the time. 'Perhaps it does look like theirs. But I could never follow their hair style.'

*

I was always keen to do young writers and playwrights, fancying myself as one of course, and went to see Dennis Potter in 1966. He had come down from Oxford and become an angry TV playwright, causing lots of controversy with scenes about sex, violence, politics and the royal family. I was worried about doing him as I had met him when he was at Oxford, acting with Margaret in a university production of *The Caucasian Chalk Circle*.

I always felt he didn't like me – as I suspected he fancied Margaret. I was probably jealous of him. I did a fairly cheeky, mocking interview with him in 1966, which I was beginning to do, though telling myself I was just trying to amuse the reader. I described how he was working on a play called *Message for Posterity*, which was about a senile Tory Prime Minister, a bit like Churchill, which the BBC was worried about broadcasting. The play sounded a bit pretentious and self-important to me, but of course did not quite say so.

I finished the piece with just one sentence. 'You can't keep these lads down, can you ...?'

Nothing he could object to, but he was not best pleased at being teased.

In 1965 I interviewed Auberon Waugh, the son of Evelyn Waugh, who was seething after some bad reviews for a novel. He had listed all the names of his enemies in a black book. 'I am incredibly vindictive. I have none of the humble acceptance of the civilised man.'

As I left, he asked me to give a plug for his new book, but not in his words, put it in my words. Naturally I quoted him verbatim, as follows: 'Can't you slip in somewhere that my

new book is brilliant? Oh, and if you have room, say further-
more it is selling *very* well . . .'

He never forgave me for that. Years later he regularly got
his own back in his *Private Eye* column with nasty remarks
about me.

I went to a see a new young playwright called Tom Stoppard
in 1967, one of the first interviews he had given. At the age
of twenty-nine, he had just had his play *Rosencrantz and
Guildenstern Are Dead* put on at the National Theatre. He too,
like George Best, said his ambition was to be rich. 'Naturally
I won't be corrupted. I will sit in my Rolls-Royce, uncor-
rupted, and tell my chauffeur, uncorruptedly, where to go.'

I discovered he had not been to university and since leaving
school at seventeen had worked as a local journalist, spending
eight years on papers in Bristol. For a while, his ambition in
life, so he said, so he maintained, had been to be me. I didn't
quote him saying that, as that would have been far too self-
indulgent, even for me. But I believed him, of course. Which
young provincial journalist in the mid 1960s would not have
fancied having the space and freedom and fun of running the
Atticus column in the *Sunday Times*?

# 7

# FILM FUN

I find it hard now to believe that both our novels got turned into films, appearing almost at the same time. They did not happen suddenly, all decided in a day. Talks and meetings, discussions and plans, went on for ages, appearing not to be going anywhere. Films creep forward incrementally, so there is not really a moment when they can say yes, it will be made. Only when I look back does it seem to have happened quickly, smoothly, inevitably, perhaps even miraculously, but at the time, the films seemed something of a distraction, not real, not our proper concern, keeping us from other things, involving us in meetings which we did not really want to go to and were glad when they were over, half hoping it would all collapse so we could get on with our real work.

The producer who bought the rights to *Georgy Girl* was always going on about cinema noir and wanting long intellectual discussions, driving Margaret mad. It did sound to me like total pretentious time-wasting. Film producers have to be obsessive, to believe in the project day and night, whereas the writer is more like a hired hand, wanting to get on to the next thing.

Margaret had been pregnant with Jake when it all began, so she had enough to think about, plus the house was still being knocked into shape. It was a while before a director was on board, Silvio Narizzano, and then finally a leading Hollywood company, Columbia, agreed to make it.

Margaret was asked to do the film script, which she agreed to, thinking it can't be hard, she knows the story. She did several versions but at the very end, Peter Nichols the playwright was brought in to do work on the final screenplay, which was quite a relief. They were given joint credit for the screenplay, with Margaret's name first. These things matter in films.

We got to know Peter Nichols and his wife, as they lived not far away. He was very funny, cynical and caustic, moaning about the new young playwrights like Tom Stoppard who seemed to be getting all the critical praise and best jobs. But Peter did go on to write some very successful plays, such as *A Day in the Death of Joe Egg*, first produced in 1967, which was based on his experience of having a handicapped child, and then later the extremely funny army play *Privates on Parade*.

Vanessa Redgrave was going to star in *Georgy Girl* at first but it clashed with some other job so her younger sister Lynn got the part, her first break, and made an enormous success of it. Charlotte Rampling was also relatively new and she played Meredith who in the film has a baby. Charlotte had never had a baby and didn't appear to know what one looked like, or how to hold one, so the producer insisted she came to our house for tea to meet Margaret and hold baby Caitlin. Charlotte did not seem at all comfortable, rather austere and cool.

James Mason had been a big star for decades and was utterly charming, and so was Alan Bates. James Mason had been Margaret's mother's favourite film star, so once we had met him, we had to tell her every detail. We both got invited on to the set at Shepperton to watch them filming, meet the cast and crew, but we only went once. It seemed such a faff, getting there, then standing around when nothing much was happening, except the same thing over and over again.

Margaret did not go to the world premiere of *Georgy Girl* in the West End in July 1966. I am not even sure she got invited. Once a film is at that stage, they have lost interest in the original creator. Not that she was bothered. Or would have gone anyway. She did not see a future for herself in writing scripts and was just glad not to be involved any more.

The film was a huge success, won a prize at Berlin and Cannes, and was particularly successful in the USA. It had cost only $400,000 to make but in a year had earned $7 million. The theme tune played by the Seekers was in all the charts. I read somewhere at the time that Jim Dale, who wrote the vocals – i.e. wrote the words for the song, not the music – earned £20,000 from the song, whereas Margaret, who had created the whole project, the novel and the original script, earned just £3,000. Which seemed unfair, but the film world has a different set of priorities to the book world. The writers get involved at a very early stage in a film, when there is little money, little hope it will ever get made. But when the paperback of the novel was later published, once the film was out, and the stars were on the cover, it did of course sell loads. Not that Margaret was at all interested.

I got a lot more up front for the film version of *Here We*

*Go Round the Mulberry Bush* – around £20,000 altogether. Unlike *Georgy Girl*, it was acquired from the very beginning by a big Hollywood company, United Artists. The director was Clive Donner who had directed *What's New Pussycat?* and he had done a successful film version of Harold Pinter's *The Birthday Party*.

I too was hired to do the first screenplay, which I jumped at, not realising how much time it would entail, having to fit it in with my work as Atticus. Luckily I had Tim Heald helping out by then. He probably felt the same about me as I had about Nick Tomalin, leaving him in the office to do all the boring stuff while I swanned off to attend script meetings.

I had to go once a week or so to Clive's flat off Marylebone High Street. It was like a tutorial, arriving with my essay. Clive would read what I had written, go over it, discuss it, make suggestions, and then I would have to go away and do it again. Very often he would want me to write a brand-new scene, not in the book, which he had just thought of. I would struggle with it all week in the evenings after work, and then duly bring it back to Clive. He would say fine, that is interesting. Oh no, we are not going to use it, I just wanted to see what you would do with it, so thanks. Which would leave me spitting. I have always hated unused copy.

A young, handsome, Ivy League American called Larry Kramer began to appear at these film script meetings. I could not at first work out who he was, what his role was. I thought perhaps he was Clive's boyfriend, yet on the other hand, Clive did appear to have a girlfriend, Penelope Mortimer, the first wife of John Mortimer, who herself was a very good novelist.

Clive eventually explained that Larry was simply an assistant producer, called in by the American film-makers in Hollywood, to keep an eye on the script, make sure it did not become too English and therefore hard for Americans to understand. The only thing I remember Larry querying was the word knickers, as in 'oh knickers', a very mild English expletive, or one boy asking another boy: 'Did you get into her knickers?'

Larry was charming and friendly and came to our house several times and always brought wonderful presents for our children. One day he brought some high-class wooden toys from Galt, which I knew were expensive, very educational and sustainable, greatly desired by caring, concerned middle-class parents in the sixties.

I had a slight disagreement with him at the end when the final screenplay had been completed. I discovered that his name was going down as co-writer. I protested, knowing I had written almost every word, under Clive's direction. I appealed to the Screen Writers Guild, which I quickly joined. I had to produce all the various versions I had done of the scripts myself – and they agreed with me, that I was the screen writer.

Larry then came to me almost in tears. He explained that his future was in films, this was his big break, he desperately needed as many screen credits as possible, whereas to me it did not matter, and my future was going to be writing books and journalism. In the end, I did get solus credit for the screenplay, but underneath it said: 'Additional dialogue by Larry Kramer'. I was not totally happy with that wording, but accepted it and it pleased Larry. (Later, back in the USA, Larry went on to be a notable playwright and gay rights activist.)

I had hoped my film would be shot in Carlisle, where it had been set in the novel. I looked forward to impressing my old neighbours on our council estate, especially the ones on my paper round who had never given me tips at Christmas. But it was felt there were already too many gritty North of England films, such as *Saturday Night and Sunday Morning* and *A Taste of Honey*. Instead it was decided the whole location of the film would be moved to a New Town. It was an interesting idea, and I could understand the reasoning. There had not been a film so far with such a setting, yet more and more New Towns were being planned.

The New Town chosen was Stevenage, just less than thirty miles from London. That meant costs were kept down. If the location had been any further away, they would have had to pay all the actors and crew overnight rates.

Margaret's film was full of stars whereas mine had nobody of note. It was of course a teenage film, so most of the actors and actresses were young, apart from Denholm Elliott, in a minor role. Instead they tried hard to make a feature of introducing an unknown Barry Evans, as the hero, and Judy Geeson as a star in the making. I thought Barry looked attractive enough, but he did not convince me in the part. He came to our house one day, we had a walk on the Heath, and he told me his ambition in life was to have a herd of white horses. Oh help, as my other used to say. I much preferred the actor who played a lesser, wideboy-type character, Spike, who was Christopher Timothy, later well known for playing the vet in the long-running TV series, *All Creatures Great and Small*.

I didn't think much of Judy Geeson either, who was

supposed to be so alluring, panted after by everyone. I didn't think she could act. But what did I know about acting. Nor was I pleased with my own screenplay. Despite all those meetings and rewrites, when it came to them acting the lines it all seemed so corny and banal. I had always felt the novel itself was funny, and touching, but that seemed to have been lost on the way to the screen. The dialogue was clunky and obvious. I can't blame anybody but myself.

But the music was brilliant – with Traffic and Steve Winwood and the Spencer Davis Group – who produced excellent tunes and background music all the way through. There was also an original element, thought up by Clive. In the novel, I had moments of fantasies, like many teenagers, imagining how things might turn out. Clive cleverly introduced moments of animation into the film, when Jamie, our hero, is having his reveries, created by the brilliant animator Richard Williams. It was unusual for the period to have animated scenes in a feature film. They did not quite work or fit, but they were imaginatively done.

Margaret's film *Georgy Girl* was in black and white. *Here We Go Round the Mulberry Bush*, which came out in January 1967, just six months after her film, was in full, glorious, state-of-the-art colour, and featured all those clichés of the sixties such as miniskirts, kipper ties, psychedelic shirts.

My novel, when it had been first published in 1965, had been seen as quite racy at the time. For many years, I used to meet people who had been in the sixth form and had read it on the back seat of school buses, under a plain cover. Can't believe now there was anything rude in it, or sexy, but then I haven't read it since I wrote it. Couldn't face it. I still have not reread any of my books. Now and again I have had to look up a page or paragraph, when some reader has pointed out some glaring stupidity, but I have never sat down and read the whole thing again. I always find it a slog reading proofs, of anything, articles or books. I am always more pleased when I can move on to writing something new.

I did go on location to a river somewhere near Stevenage one day when they were filming a nude scene. Barry and Judy had to strip stark naked and go for a swim. Barry kept on getting an erection, till eventually they had to tie down his manhood with Sellotape. It might have been the freezing cold water that caused it, or of course the sight of the luscious naked Judy. Probably the former, for it turned out later that Barry was gay. That particular scene, with them naked, was cut out of the versions shown in the UK or USA, but was shown in Sweden. In the sixties we believed that all Swedes were stripping off naked and doing naughty things all the time. Hence the popularity of Swedish au pairs.

My film got rather snotty reviews, the critics feeling that it was vulgar and commercial. Margaret's *Georgy Girl* got excellent reviews. It was in black and white and seen as an art film, while mine was in lurid colour with pop music and trendy clothes, which I tried to maintain was the reason the critics did not like it. Snobbism really, so I argued, but without much conviction.

All these decades later, each of them gets occasionally shown late at night on TV. There now seems to be more affection for *Mulberry Bush*, seeing it as a piece of amusing nostalgia, a good example of an awful sixties teenage film. In fact a year or two ago there was a retrospective evening at the National Film Theatre on the South Bank. They showed the film and I answered questions about it. Not that I could remember much about it.

The premiere of *Mulberry Bush* was a swish affair at the London Pavilion in Piccadilly Circus in January 1968. Lots of celebs of the time came, such as Paul McCartney and his fiancée Jane Asher. I did make sure I got invited, unlike Margaret to her film, as she did not care. I also got invited to the party afterwards which was at Tramps, the night club. Nobody talked to me or Margaret and we left early.

Very recently, I met Alan Johnson, the Labour MP, former Home Secretary, and he told me that he had christened his son Jamie, the name of my hero in *Mulberry Bush*, having just watched the film. No, he hadn't thought much of it either, but he had loved the music.

The writing and making of the film had been spread over two years, since the novel had first appeared in 1965, by which time I had finished two more books, both published in 1966.

The first was a non-fiction book for Heinemann called *The Other Half*. I wonder now why I did not do another novel, to follow up the success of *Mulberry Bush*. Perhaps I was too well aware of my limitations as a novelist, compared with Margaret.

*The Other Half* was semi-sociological, consisting of interviews with the New Poor and the New Rich. I defined the New Poor as people who had to have a long and proper education and training, who contributed greatly to society, but were earning comparatively little money. My examples included school teachers, nurses and social workers. The New Rich had little or no education but were making small fortunes, such as a barrow boy working in a street market, or a hairdresser in a fashionable West End salon, such as Vidal Sasson. I did not make any heavy moral judgements or draw conclusions. Just presented their lives, as they were living it now, in 1966, alternating the chapters, the New Poor then the New Rich, deliberately of course highlighting the contrasts in their work and values.

The other book, *The New London Spy*, was one I edited for a new, young, thrusting, amusing Old Etonian publisher called Anthony Blond. It was a guide book to underground or hidden London that most people did not know about, written by people in the know, or so we proclaimed. I had to find the writers, explain it all and brief them, then edit their work. Anthony Blond assumed that as Atticus I would have contacts everywhere.

One of the sections was about London vicars and London churches, which was quite scathing. I got John Betjeman to write it. He must have been hard up at the time to agree to it. I had interviewed him, for Atticus, which helped me approach him.

I went to see him in his lodgings, a very small and crowded flat in the East End. When I mentioned I was from Carlisle, he insisted on pressing upon me a two-volume antiquarian book from 1814 called *Border Antiquities*. I protested it was too valuable but he insisted, saying he had too many books and wanted an excuse to clear his shelves. I asked him to sign it. He wrote 'Tae Hunter Frae John MacBetjeman', a dedication which probably won't make much sense, if anyone ever comes across it in the future.

Once the film was out, I did get approached about a couple of other film scripts, but I turned them down. I did not want to go through all those meetings and tutorials again. I had enough work with my full-time journalism job, plus my books. Looking back, I can't believe that I managed to fit so much in during the sixties. Constantly cutting corners, that is probably the answer.

But I did agree to do a TV play. I was approached by Tony Garnett from the BBC who was a producer of the *Wednesday Play*, the most prestigious slot in original British TV drama. He was a cult figure in TV at the time, having produced two social classics, *Up the Junction* in 1965 and *Cathy Come Home* in 1966, which was directed by Ken Loach. Tony said he had liked the dialogue in *Mulberry Bush*, which was a surprise to me, and asked if I had an idea for a TV play.

I couldn't think of anything at first, and then remembered my stage play, which had so nearly got performed a few years earlier, about the young man with two wives and two families. I rejigged it, changed the title from *Where the Dragonflies Play*, which was awful, and made it simply *The Playground*. It got made, got shown, got decent reviews, and had a good director and some decent actors – all of whose names I have now forgotten. It was one of those early BBC *Wednesday Play* dramas which was performed live, played at the time you were watching it. Most records of them were destroyed. If some viewer did have an early video machine, and managed to copy it, they probably wiped it off soon afterwards. I never managed to get a copy. So my TV career came to a dead end.

But my non-fiction book *The Other Half* got very favourable, encouraging notices. Despite not very good sales, the publisher asked if I had any other similar ideas. Imagine such a thing happening today. You are smartly dumped by almost all publishers if you don't immediately make them money on your last book.

You would also find it hard today to persuade any half-decent publisher to publish a book of interviews. They would be more than likely to dismiss it as purely journalism, not worthy of a hardback. Unless of course you were a big name, such as a newsreader or a reality TV star.

Charles Pick, the boss at Heinemann, and I devised a book to be called *The Class of '66*. In it I would interview a selection of people at British universities – students as well as lecturers, Oxbridge as well as Redbrick.

Charles's own son Martin had just started at the new University of East Anglia, so I decided to do him. I also did a girl student at Sussex University, Buzz Goodbody, and went to Manchester and interviewed a young girl called Anna Ford who had become the first female president of their Students Union.

Halfway through working on the book, when I had done six interviews, a better, more exciting, book project came up. I immediately decided to stop interviewing any more university people. Not forever. Just for a year or so, as I still thought it was a good idea. In my mind, I planned to return to it, when this other, new project was completed, perhaps changing the title to *The Class of '68*.

# 8

# THE BEATLES

What had come up was the Beatles. In September 1966 I went to see Paul McCartney for an Atticus interview. 'Eleanor Rigby' had just come out and it seemed to me the words, not just the tune, were wonderful, possibly the best poetry we would hear in 1966, not that I am an expert on poetry.

I had earlier interviewed the Beatles, or at least tried to, in 1964 on the set of *A Hard Day's Night* at a theatre in Charlotte Street. The girls in the audience screamed all the way through, so I couldn't hear a word, but I managed to get myself on stage after they had finished playing and had a few words with John. He was making some complicated joke about a sign which said 'Sound On' by repeating the words 'Sounds On, Sounds On', which was a sixties phrase meaning something was good, something was possible.

My little piece never appeared. Either I failed to explain the joke, Nick Tomalin didn't think it was amusing or the hierarchy had no interest in reading about the Beatles. Even in 1964 there was a feeling we knew everything we wanted to know about the Beatles.

By 1966, this was still a general feeling, that everything to do with Beatlemania was known, had been done, there was boredom in many quarters – outside of course the fans – which very often happens in Britain, when an initial and intense manic stage is over. But by going to ask Paul about the lyrics of one song, how he had written them – if indeed they were all his work – instead of asking them yet again about their hair or why they said 'Yeh Yeh' not 'Yes Yes', it seemed to me to be a chance to break some new ground.

I can't say I remember, back in October 1962, 'Love Me Do' coming out, being too preoccupied with other excitements, such as looking for a house. 'Twist and Shout' seemed to be too shouty. But I could see how totally different they were from all the bubblegum mid-Atlantic pop groups we had been brought up on during the fifties. They did have a voice of their own and most importantly, every album was always an enormous development, moving on, trying new things, new sounds and instruments, unlike the normal pop groups. I rushed out for each new album, amazed they had done it again, wearing out the tracks by constant playing till I had memorised every note, every pause between the tracks so I knew what was coming next, even when there was silence.

This still must happen. Impressionable youth still fall in love with music which seems to be aimed at them, which takes them over, which they play constantly. Or does it? You always try to ascribe unique qualities to things you love, believing that it must be special, just because it speaks to you.

I don't think the mass popularity, and mass acceptance, and mass love for the Beatles, from all sorts of people, all over the world, has quite been equalled. They were indeed a phenomenon. Today there is so much diverse music, coming from so many sources, listened to in so many different ways, that the overall impact of one song or one group is not quite the same and does not last as long.

I went to see Paul at his house in Cavendish Avenue, St John's Wood, which he had not long moved into. He still has it today, being at heart a conservative sort of feller. He appeared to live alone, apart from a housekeeper, no sign of his girlfriend Jane Asher, whom we had all read about in the papers. He seemed mature and confident for a young man of only twenty-four, not someone you might take liberties with. After three years of worldwide fame, he had clearly become used to the limelight, but he did not appear arrogant or big-headed. There was something of the teacher about him, liking to explain things and make things clear.

The house was quite untidy, clearly lived in, which I felt was partly deliberate, to show he was not the sort of young millionaire obsessed by designer glitz and expensive glitter. It was vaguely arty, indicating he was artistic, appreciated the modern art world. There were pieces of modern sculpture around and on the mantelpiece in the main living room I noticed a Magritte – not the sort of painting you would normally associate with a lad from a Liverpool council estate. The garden was overgrown, again a statement that he was above the normal suburban mania for neat lawns and flowers. The other three Beatles had already moved out into the London suburbs, with lush gardens and rolling lawns, while Paul was in the heart of London in an old period house.

'People think we are not conceited – but we are,' he said,

when I complimented him on the house, and admired his possessions.

I remarked on the number of girls permanently outside his house, waiting for a glimpse. He said he did not despise them. 'I don't think they are humiliating themselves. I queued up at the Liverpool Empire for Wee Willy Harris's autograph. I wanted to do it. I don't think I was being stupid.'

I then got him to explain where the words of 'Eleanor Rigby' had come from, which was the point of the interview. He enjoyed taking me through his whole thought process, how the name which first came into his head was a woman called 'Daisy Hawkins, picking up rice in a church where a wedding had been'. He had no idea where that line had come from. In Bristol, where he had been visiting Jane who was acting there, he was walking round and saw the name Rigby on a shop, and thought that would be a better name. 'You got that? Quick pan to Bristol.' This was quite a witty, self-aware comment to make, very sixth form-ish.

I wrote the interview in short sentences, rather staccato, working in all his best, smartest remarks. I referred to Mr McCartney and Mr Lennon, not Paul and John, without being satirical or mocking. That was being polite in print in the *Sunday Times*, back in 1966.

I got a note after it appeared from Ken Tynan, the star of our rival paper, the *Observer*. He agreed with me that the words of 'Eleanor Rigby' were indeed poetry, probably the best which would appear in all the sixties.

About three months later, in December 1966, I went to see Paul again, this time with a different hat on, as a screenplay writer. I went with Clive Donner in the hope that Paul might write the theme tune for the film we were working on. At the end of our chat, Paul said he would think about it, but he later said no.

But during the time I was with him, I suggested there should be a proper biography of the Beatles, a full-length hardback. I was surprised there had not been one, just a couple of fairly flimsy paperback books, one produced by the fan club and the other a slice of life on tour by an American journalist, Michael Braun.

Paul thought it was a good idea, but said Brian would have to agree to it. He would help me write a letter to Brian Epstein, their manager. There and then he sat me down and suggested points to mention, such as my *Sunday Times* position, which would impress Brian, that I had done three books and this would be a serious, big book.

My appointment with Brian was for 25 January 1967, but he cancelled at the last moment. I saw him the next day, at his house in Belgravia, 24 Chapel Street. A butler let me in and I sat around for a while, admiring his fine furniture and noticing two oil paintings by Lowry. Despite having met Lowry, briefly, I had at the time not really been aware he painted in colour, in oils, not just matchstick pencil drawings.

Brian appeared looking smooth and healthy, with rather chubby pink cheeks, immaculately dressed and coiffured, very much a successful London impresario, if perhaps of a slightly bygone age as opposed to what we liked to think were the fashionable sixties.

It's hard to believe now that he was only thirty-two, just two years older than me. Until relatively recently he had been working in a record shop in Liverpool. Now his habitat was Belgravia and Mayfair and the West End, a sophisticated man of the world, so at home in the best parts of London.

He seemed a bit distracted, as if his mind was elsewhere, but he got out some tapes of 'Penny Lane' and 'Strawberry Fields' and played them to me, watching my face with paternal pride. I was astounded by 'Strawberry Fields'. It was so discordant, avant-garde, experimental that I wondered what on earth the fans would make of it. It was clearly their biggest leap forward so far. If I got agreement for the book, I felt my belief would be correct – that the Beatles were still breaking boundaries, which not everyone was currently thinking.

I asked Brian what 'Strawberry Fields' meant, but he had no idea. He appeared to have little knowledge of the background to either song. He then quickly packed them away in a safe saying he couldn't be too careful. Some earlier tapes had been stolen and ended up on pirate radio.

We eventually got round to my project. He seemed to think it was a good idea, but would have to talk to all the Beatles, so we arranged another meeting.

At this next meeting, Charles Pick from Heinemann came with me. He had done my first two books and I already had a contract from him for *The Class of '66*. I had expected Richard Simon, my agent from Curtis Brown, to meet us there as well, but in walked a tall elderly gentleman who said he was Spencer Curtis Brown. He was the founder of the firm. I did not know he was still alive. Having heard about the meeting, he was keen to meet Epstein, a man of the moment, and get into his house.

I let Spencer discuss the details of the contract, which appeared to be going ahead, though nothing officially had been said. Brian then offered a clause in the contract none of us had suggested. He said he would give no access to the Beatles to any other writer for two years after my book came out. We were talking in early 1967. The book would come out in late 1968, if all went well. So we would be given till 1970 to have a clear run, with no rival author being able to have access to the Beatles.

It was a nice offer, but at the time, I did not really think of it as particularly important. The Beatles would surely be with us for decades to come, so they would obviously in the future allow other biographies.

Never for one moment, during the whole of the next two years while working on the book, did I envisage that I would end up as the only ever authorised biographer.

Charles was willing to transfer the contract for *The Class of '66* to the Beatles biography, paying the same advance, which was £3,000. Not a huge amount, in fact it turned out I got less as we agreed with Brian that a third of the Beatles biog would go to the Beatles. I would also have to do a bit of foreign travelling, which might be expensive. But I was very happy, thrilled at the prospect of talking to the Beatles, visiting all their homes, watching them at work. Not all the directors at Heinemann were as thrilled. 'We know everything we want to know about the Beatles,' said one, 'and anyway their bubble will burst, like all pop groups.' I said they were more than a pop group – this book could be a piece of social history. 'Who needs social history?'

\*

I started work on the book on 7 February 1967 – and that same day I got a call from a funny-sounding woman who said she was called Yoko Ono. She had been told I was the most eminent columnist in London and she wanted me to appear in a film she was doing about bare bottoms. I told her to piss off. I assumed it was some joker from the *Observer* winding me up. She convinced me it was serious, so I decided to go along and watch the film being shot. It might give me a funny story. But I said no, I would not appear in it. How kind. But my agent would not allow it.

She had put an advert in *The Stage* – the actors' news-paper – asking actors if they would like to be in a film, their appearance guaranteed, but there would be no money.

When I arrived at the address off Park Lane, they were queuing down the pavement. One by one they were let in, through an ordinary front door of an ordinary-looking house, told to drop their trousers and knickers. They then stood on a children's roundabout where a fixed camera focused on each bare bottom as it went round. Once round, they stepped off, put their pants back on, were ushered out of the door and back on the pavement again, all a bit bemused.

I wrote a fairly amused, mickey-taking piece about it, trying not to ridicule it too much, in case Yoko might object. She rang me afterwards and said thanks, it was great publicity, and the first time she had made it into a UK publication.

I did not meet her again in the flesh till one day in 1968 I walked into Abbey Road studios, working on the Beatles book, to listen to their latest efforts. There she was, entwined with John. Both of them appeared to be in a transcendental state. The other three Beatles were staring at them, clearly thinking, 'Who the fuck is this?'

Meanwhile, back in 1967, with the contract signed, I don't know how I imagined I was going to cope with doing a major biography and still running Atticus, though I had managed so far to balance books and journalism, a film script and a BBC play. Over the last five years, in fact during most of the last seven years since we were married, we had both been writing away in all of our spare time. Even when Margaret had two children, and gave up teaching, she was clearing the kitchen table every evening when they were in bed, getting out her pen and ink and sheets of blank paper.

I didn't really want to give up the *Sunday Times*. I had yearned for so long to be Atticus, and it still gave me such pleasure. I always thought, and still do, that I can't really turn anything down because very soon no one will be offering anything, so I have to grab everything while I can.

But with the Beatles book, I realised I would have to spend a lot of time in Liverpool, going to see their parents and friends, and to Hamburg of course, where their career had really begun, and probably to America.

I was still wondering what to do, to leave the paper or not, give up journalism, when Harry Evans arrived. He had gone to the same Durham college as me, but was eight years older, and I had first met him in Manchester. I had last heard of him in Darlington, where he was editor of the *Northern Echo*. Out of the blue, he rang me up, saying he was down in London for an interview on the *Sunday Times*. I was the only person he knew on the paper. Denis Hamilton was offering him the job of managing editor. I suppose Hamilton was impressed by the job Harry had done on the *Northern Echo* and also attracted by his northeastern connections.

On cross-examination, Harry had to admit that being offered the position of managing editor meant nothing. He had no remit, no staff and no department he would be in charge of. Being a space baron, controlling pages and journalists, is the only vital thing for any newspaper executive. I said it sounded a non-job. And anyway, he was a provincial editor; they would eat him alive in London at the *Sunday Times*. My advice was not to take the job.

But he did. He and his wife Enid rented a house near us on Highgate West Hill and then bought a house, also nearby, on the Holly Lodge estate.

Harry spent about six months moving around various departments, knocking them into shape. Unlike almost every other journalist I have ever met, Harry could do everything – write leaders, economic analysis, political columns, sports articles, crop photographs, lay out pages, sub edit, encourage and enthuse the troops. But of course as Managing Editor (Fuck All), which was roughly his title, according to the sceptics, i.e. me, you get taken for granted, get landed with all the rubbish jobs, have to sort out the awkward squad, don't appear to have achieved anything.

But then he had the most amazing stroke of luck. In 1967 Roy Thomson bought *The Times*. Denis Hamilton became editor-in-chief of both newspapers. William Rees-Mogg, who had been deputy to Hamilton on the *Sunday Times*, became editor of *The Times*. And Harry became editor of the *Sunday*

*Times*. So much for me telling him to go back to Darlington and be happy as a provincial journalist.

I was by then well into the Beatles biog, which of course I had told Harry about. As the new editor, he was very keen to acquire the serialisation rights for the paper. So we did a deal. I promised him he could have it for the paper. He would let me give up Atticus, but stay on the staff as chief features writer. It meant I had a roving brief, able to go abroad when I wanted, at the paper's expense, as long as I was doing some interviewing or features for them.

In August 1967 I went to New York to interview U Thant, Secretary General of the UN, and then up to Toronto to interview Marshall McLuhan. Both interviews made the front page of the Review section of the paper. So I had fulfilled my part of the new arrangement.

What I remember of U Thant was being allowed into his private flat in the UN building. When he was called away, I peeped into his bedroom. Around the room were loads of unopened boxes, presents to him from world leaders. One was from the Pope, which clearly he had never opened.

Marshall McLuhan was an internationally known academic and professor. His work on the media is even more relevant today than it was then, as it he was he who coined the phrase 'The Medium is the Message'.

He started boasting about the research he always did for all his books and lectures, so I asked if I could see it. He took me into a room in his house filled with cardboard boxes. In each of them he had shoved in newspaper cuttings, just torn out, unfiled, unmarked, unorganised. That was his research material.

While in New York, after I'd done U Thant, I spent most of my time working on the Beatles book. I went to the stadiums where they had played, meeting the organisers of their various concerts, such as Sid Bernstein, met record company executives, and also American Beatles fans who had been there, screaming when they first arrived, still talking about their Carnegie Hall performances or seeing them on *Ed Sullivan*. Their memories were all fresh, as their American debut had been only three years earlier.

I managed to organise a trip to Hamburg, going to visit a state-registered brothel, which had just become legal, and did a feature about it for the Colour Magazine. But mainly I was following the Beatles' tracks, visiting the clubs they had played at.

I secured an interview with Astrid Kirchherr, who had been engaged to Stu Sutcliffe, the Beatle who died of a brain tumour. She was sitting on a portfolio of what I still think are the best ever photographs of the Beatles – yet she was refusing to capitalise on them. Instead, she was working as a barmaid in what was partly a lesbian bar, dancing with customers when required.

I suppose the best fun, the most exciting part of doing the Beatles biog was sitting for months in Abbey Road, watching them perform. Along with of course visiting them at home, interviewing each of them on their own, one to one.

I was keen for them to meet Margaret, so she could see what I was spending all my time doing, rushing round the world. Margaret was not at all interested in their music, having no interest in music at all. And she did not really want to meet them. She suspected it would reveal the worst parts of my character – i.e. arse licking, hanging on their words, charming for England, being a total creep, hero-worshipping them. I always denied this. And was rather upset by her accusations.

In my mind, interviewing people for the previous ten years or so, I had always treated so-called stars as ordinary people. I liked to believe that had helped me get so much out of them. I always tried to put myself in their shoes, working out their worries and problems, their jealousies, as of course all apparently hugely successful people have chinks, deep down worried they are not getting the high-class acclaim or the mega sales figures of some of their rivals. You have to think hard to work it out, decide what might be bugging them. My other self-taught rule was never to ask a question which must have been asked a hundred times already. Answers to the obvious questions will be somewhere in the cuttings. Always try to ask something new, bring up a new topic.

But Margaret did meet them in the end. After a bit of arm twisting, she agreed I could invite them home to NW5 and she would make something for them. I had by now taken a lot of hospitality at their homes, having endless meals, especially at Paul's. Not to a dinner party with other guests, she put her foot down about that. That would be appalling, unbearable, and just showing off.

Paul, George, and Ringo, with their respective partners, came home for tea or supper. John cancelled, when he had said he was coming with Cynthia, but Margaret did talk to John for some time at the *Magical Mystery Tour* private party to which we were both invited. So she did meet them all, and their wives.

Oh, if only I had used a tape recorder during the almost two years I was hanging around with them. I never did have a tape recorder, even for journalistic interviews.

Back in 1963 I was sent to interview W. H. Auden, who was staying at Stephen Spender's house in St John's Wood. It was fixed up by Leonard Russell, the literary editor, who gave me an envelope to give to Auden. On the way there, I opened it, unable to resist it – to find £100 in notes. I quickly sealed it up again.

After some idle chat, Auden asked if I had anything for him, so I handed over the envelope. The minute I did so, he seemed to lose interest in the interview.

Meanwhile I was struggling with a tape recorder. I had borrowed it from someone in the office, an early Grundig, about the size of a Mini Minor. It was the first time I had used one and was so worried I wouldn't be able to work it.

It did, after a fashion, but the interview never made the paper. I got nothing of interest out of him. I blamed the tape recorder. And vowed never to use one again.

I always think tape recording doubles your work. You have to listen to it all over again, and most of what anyone says is boring, and will never be used. With a tape recorder, you can't capture all the extraneous things that happen, or the atmosphere. Which you can do when you are writing down notes. When they are being boring, you can write down what the room looks like, the wallpaper, what their wives or husbands or children said when they came into the room.

When they say this is off the record, and then tell you something juicy, you nod and put down your pen. Then later, when they say they love children and always help old people across the road, instead of writing that down you write down the juicy bit they came out with earlier.

If I had used a tape when doing the Beatles, I would not only have had historic material from them, talking about their own work, at the time it was happening, but I interviewed so many associated with them who are now long since dead – such as John's Aunt Mimi, Paul's father Jim, George's parents, Ringo's parents.

I even managed to track down Ringo's real father, who had split from Ringo's mother when Ringo was very small. He was working as a window cleaner in Crewe and had so far refused all interviews and publicity. He had never come forward when Ringo became famous, unlike John's father Alfred. John had refused to see Alf for several years but I tracked him down, washing dishes in a roadside pub, not far from where John was living. He was a great talker and very funny. I told John about him, and John decided he would meet him, but secretly. It would have been good to have had Alfred on tape, a spoken record of his memories of meeting and marrying John's mother, and then abandoning John when he was young. I do have it all in my countless notebooks, but it would have been good to have captured his actual voice.

Then of course there were their road managers, Neil Aspinall and Mal Evans, both now dead, and Derek Taylor, their PR and close friend, and also more recently George Martin. Brian Epstein died many years ago, back in August 1967, while I was with them. I spent quite some time with Brian Epstein, in London and at his country home in Sussex.

I got so much material from all these people, some of which in the end I could not use, as the book was getting too big. I didn't actually want to stop interviewing the Beatles themselves. Every week they were into something new, still developing, and I didn't want to miss the next interesting or potty thing they might be getting into. But the publishers were desperate for me to finish.

At the proof stage, there was a bit of moaning and messing around, not from the Beatles, but from some of their management figures. Then John's Aunt Mimi somehow got a copy of the manuscript, began moaning to John, so John asked me to deal with her. I went to see her and it turned out she wanted me to take out John's bad language. I refused to do so. Instead, I kept Mimi quiet by putting in an extra quote from her at the end of an early chapter, quoting her as saying that John as a boy was 'as happy as the day was long'.

The book came out in the UK in September 1968. By which time I was not there, having left the UK.

# 9

# ABROAD

I was always rather ashamed of going abroad, and would deny for years what all my reasons were. I probably lied to myself, trotting out loads of different reasons, hoping that one of them would convince me, that I wouldn't be considered as just another nasty, two-faced tax exile, the sort I had always criticised.

I don't know how I talked Margaret into it. Probably the same way I talked myself into it. Going abroad would be fun, an adventure, if we don't do it now, we never will, so let's go.

Health reasons, that was one of the things I told people. Which was true. I was knackered. For five weeks, in the early stage of the book, and while I was still writing the Atticus column, I had collapsed with jaundice. I lay in bed downstairs in the little back bedroom, where Jake was born. I moaned and groaned, turned yellow, lost pounds. Except strangely enough, I did not lose my taste for alcohol, which was what everyone said would happen when you have jaundice. I drank all the way through – and maintained that was why I recovered fairly quickly and started to put on weight again.

I was visited one day when I was still in bed by Michael Bateman, a local journalist friend I had made at Durham, who had told me about the graduate training schemes, one of which he had joined from Oxford. It was thanks to him I had applied to Kemsley. He was now in London, as a freelance journalist, and I was getting him work on the *Sunday Times*.

He arrived one day with a large bunch of something for me – which, when he took it from behind his back, was revealed to be a cabbage. I laughed so much I thought I was going to be sick. He was rather hurt. It was not a joke, or silly. It was a genuine, carefully thought-out present – some unusual form of cabbage with health-giving qualities for invalids. He had become a total foodie by then, not just cooking stuff, but investigating and researching all forms of food. I had never met a foodie before. Food is what you eat, at meal time, that's it. Michael was not just obsessed by everything to do with food, where it came from, how it was grown or made, but had a fantasy of making a journalistic career out of writing about it. Not recipes. People have done recipes for centuries. But food as a subject, like politics or sport.

Caitlin and Jake were just four and two by this time – which was another rationale for going abroad. They were not yet at primary school, so perfect time to expose them to different cultures, before they started full-time school. When we came back, they would have missed very little, because Margaret would teach them while we were abroad. That was the plan, as I outlined it to Margaret.

Another reason for going off for a year was realising a fantasy, one which so many people have, especially in writing and journalism. I had heard so many people on the *Sunday Times* and in Fleet Street generally chuntering on with the same sort of lines: 'Oh if only I could make a killing on a book, or even get a half-decent advance, I will be off, no question, catch me hanging around horrible old Gray's Inn Road or rainy London any more. I will be off writing in the sun, oh yes, no question . . .'

With both of us now being writers, we could in theory go off and live anywhere in the world. Even in those days, without computers and the internet, everyone knew that writers could go anywhere, and still work, still be employed, still send their stuff in.

We had in fact never had this fantasy of going off to the sun, not the way so many of our contemporaries had it. We had been so busy for the last eight years, enjoying so much what we were doing, and just wanted it to go on. But during the awful winter of 1967, it had come into our heads that when I finished the Beatles book, we were now among the few fortunate people who need not be here, so yes, we could be on a tropical beach. See what it was like.

Then there was the attraction of doing it – in order to have done it, to have got it over. Coming back, we would have had the experience, and still be young, with most of our life still ahead of us. Didn't that sound attractive? Why wait for years, putting it off, till we might be too old. Then wouldn't it be awful, if we didn't like it when we did try it, having waited so long.

So, let's do it now, get it over with.

Those were all the reasons I trotted out, to myself, to Margaret and to anyone who asked. All true, all real. But I have to admit in all honesty, gritting my teeth, that what really sparked it off, to go off for a year, at that particular time, at that particular stage in our lives, was the financial element.

It was my accountant, at least the one I had at the time and later left for other reasons, who first suggested it. Many British writers and actors had been doing it for some time, going to live abroad for tax reasons, such as Noël Coward. More recently Desmond Morris, after the success of one particular book, had gone off to live in Malta. In fact I did a whole Atticus column one week about all the tax exiles in Switzerland. No one really criticised them, only when they pretended they had not gone for any financial reasons. Most people accepted that they would probably have done the same, in their position.

We did not want to emigrate, leave the UK, as we liked it here. All our relations were here, we loved our house, the area. And I did not want to set up a company abroad, which some people had suggested. I did not want people I didn't know handling my money. Brian Epstein had done this: losing £1 million in some dodgy bank in the Bahamas. He was too ashamed to admit it to the Beatles. His image in their eyes, so he thought, was that of an awfully smart businessman.

Our accountant explained that you need not set up a company, nor go abroad for more than a year and a day. That would be enough. He had taken advice, gone to counsel. As long as you had a good reason to go abroad. Which I had, as the paper's roaming features writer.

The biggest argument, which was one I never admitted at the time, was tax. Looking back, it now seems unbelievable. Tax, at the top rate, was 98 per cent. I still can hardy credit that figure, but that was what you paid on unearned income over a certain level. It crippled anyone who happened to have a good run, making it all meaningless.

We were already on a good run, and paying the top rates, long before the Beatles money. Most of our books had had only modest advances, but over the last two years we had had this remarkable period in which we had a film each, which greatly increased our paperback sales.

The advance I personally got for the Beatles book, of £2,000 (as one third of the £3,000 went to the Beatles), had initially made little difference to our lives. Then suddenly, at final proof stage, before it was published, there had been an auction in the USA for the American rights, handled by Curtis Brown. All the main US publishers made offers and it went to McGraw-Hill for $150,000. I wanted to keep this quiet. It was so obscene, so mad, but it leaked out in the USA.

It meant that now for a short period we were likely to make more money than we would obviously ever make again in our whole lives. The accountant pointed out that it was therefore only prudent and sensible to protect what we had, in order to provide for the leaner years which were bound to be ahead. It seemed clear we could never possibly be as fortunate in the future.

We should of course, if we had been smart and really mercenary, gone abroad two years earlier when the good run had started. We had already paid a lot of tax, with more to be paid that tax year, but if we spent the next year abroad, legally and correctly and properly, going to live and work in another country, we would make tax savings on any monies that came in during that particular year. Though of course the exact amount was not quite certain.

We had not had a Year Abroad on our bucket list when we first married in 1960. That was topped by a bed, a bureau, a car and then a house and children. All of which we had done. This chance, to go abroad, had been unexpected. So why not? What an adventure!

We thought of California, but decided it was too far away. If our parents were ill, it would take a long time to rush back. Europe sounded more sensible. We thought of the South of France, but decided our French was not up to it, despite Margaret's spell as an au pair in Bordeaux. And I did fail my French O-level. Not my fault. That dopey teacher at the Creighton School for Boys. It wasn't till I was at the Grammar school that I successfully re-sat it. But I was still rubbish.

In the end we chose Gozo, the little sister island of Malta, for reasons I cannot quite remember and were not totally clear even at the time. They spoke English, which was one reason. The hospitals were supposed to be good, another attraction. Jake at that age was endlessly doing stupid things, falling and cutting himself, so we felt we must be near decent medical help.

A friend of a friend who worked at the BBC, hearing we were thinking of going abroad for a year, arrived and showed us a little Super 8 video of a house on a beach he had to rent in Gozo. It looked charming. We and the children could go straight into the sea every morning before breakfast. So we signed the rental agreement. And off we went, renting out our London house for a year to a New Zealand dentist.

I staggered onto the plane, helped by the attendants. I had recovered from the jaundice but had now caught pneumonia. All those books and projects in the last couple of years, while still doing the day job, had taken their toll and weakened my puny body. In 1968 I was only 10 stone and still getting lost in 32-inch waist trousers. Yet another good reason to go off to the sun. Obviously. (Today I am 12 stone and last week I bought new shorts with a 38-inch waist. Oh Lord.)

When we arrived in Gozo, it was to find that we couldn't get the house on the beach we had been promised. The present occupant would not leave. Our BBC friend offered us another one, which he also owned, saying it was just as nice. Except it turned out to be inland. It was miles from a beach and would mean we would have to drive there every time. I hate driving and Margaret refused to learn.

We never really took to Gozo, perhaps put off by that disappointment of not getting the house we had fantasised about. We did like Comino, an even smaller island nearby, which had a nice hotel and quiet beaches.

But Gozo's social life was interesting, when we eventually discovered it. There was an extensive expat gay community, British bachelors of a certain age, mostly very discreet, well bred, who had left their constrained lives in England, and their families, to be themselves in the sun. They were all excellent foodies and gave good parties. One or two of them, though, fled the island before they had paid all their lobster bills, which gave the Brits and gays a bad name.

While we were there, the Archbishop of Gozo decreed that men and women could not dance together in bars. I assume this was to restrict males and females getting too intimate in public. But he did not ban men dancing with men. Which of course was great news for all our bachelor friends.

We became friends with a young Englishman called Trevor Nunn who suddenly arrived next door to our house. He was on holiday with a girlfriend. After a few days, and a few drinks, he swore us to secrecy about the fact that he had just been appointed artistic director of the Royal Shakespeare Company at the incredibly young age of twenty-eight. It would not be announced till he returned to England.

Jonathan Aitken, later a Tory MP, came to stay with us. This was in order to write a piece for the London *Evening Standard* about us, two so-called Young Meteors, escaping to the sun. Our children were continually trying to get into the shower with Jonathan, in order to see him naked. It was an open-air shower, with no door, just a screen.

Over drinks one evening I tried to get him to confess that he had had an affair with Antonia Fraser. This had been talked about in London before we had left. Naturally, he refused to be drawn, being such a well-bred gentleman.

I stupidly confirmed to him, showing off, that the US advance for the Beatles book was officially $150,000. But I stressed that was the total USA sum, not what I would person-ally get. The Beatles got a third and there were lots of agents. In the piece, that was not made clear. In fact the headline said I would earn £150,000, which was a figure that haunted me for years.

In his article, he quoted Margaret as saying that 'at least the Beatles book has got Hunter over his inferiority complex'. Margaret had no memory of saying that to him, nor did I hear her say it, but it sounds like her. And it was partly true. While she was at Oxford, and in my early years on the *Sunday Times*, I had felt slightly paranoid, intellectually and socially.

Over the years, over the cocoa late at night, sometimes almost ten o'clock, when the subject of me had come up, not sure how, Margaret – who never talked about herself – often said that I had always been pushy, cocky, always with both elbows out, full of confidence, showing off. I was always hurt by that. It was not my memory of myself. Oh goodness, do we ever know the truth about ourselves? Or how we are perceived, what other people really think of us?

After six months in Gozo, we moved to Portugal. We had been moaning about Gozo on a beach one day to some Brits and they said try Portugal, you'll love it.

So we rented a converted sardine factory on the beach at Praia da Luz, near Lagos. There were no modern developments, no clubs or estates. We arrived in October 1968, the summer season was over, and so we had the beach to ourselves. We immediately fell in love with Portugal. The beaches were lovely, the food and wine wonderful, the culture seemed richer, deeper.

We made a very good friend of an elderly literary lady who lived next door, Alison Hooper. She appeared very haughty, clipped, blue stocking, buttoned-up but, as is often the case with such fearsome-looking women, she was full of hidden passions and hatred, keeping us endlessly amused with awful gossip about her enemies – and friends. She introduced us to all her friends, both expat and Portuguese. In Gozo, we had not got to know any of the local Maltese.

Mainly of course we mixed with the British expats, as we had in Gozo. This time there were a lot of colonial types who had fled from Africa. They considered Britain was the pits, hated Harold Wilson, the country had gone to the dogs, full of socialists, they would never go back. They had of course hardly ever lived in the UK. They were the sort of right-wing people we would have run a mile from in England, but thrown up against them in a foreign land, and keeping off politics, they were amusing and generous and sociable.

Alison was a Cambridge graduate, one of the first women, and had had a fairly racy life. During the war she had worked on *Lilliput* when it had been a literary magazine. She had had lots of lovers in her time, some quite well known, especially during the war.

I have talked to several women over the years who boasted about the good times they had during the war, getting drunk, sleeping around. It used to make me quite jealous, thinking that the young adults of the thirties and forties seemed to have had a freer, more liberated, more fun time than us in the fifties and sixties. Apart of course from the war.

Alison had a gentleman friend, the Brigadier, who came to visit her every few weeks, parking his camper van in her drive. She moaned every time he was due, saying what a bore, but we noticed that at night the lights would go off in his camper van and go on in Alison's bedroom. Could they be at it? Surely not. She must have been in her sixties and he seventy. Clearly impossible. So we thought, aged thirty.

We invited him for drinks one evening, along with Alison, and he arrived in yellow corduroys. It was the first time I had encountered this fashion among upper-class county and ex-military gents. They are otherwise conservatively attired, but have a passion for ill-fitting, luridly coloured corduroys in bright green, flaming red, startling yellow, screaming purple. It is an affectation which goes on to this day.

Alison had a dog called Homer – Homy Hooper – whom she shouted at all the time. I often think people have dogs to shout at them and not be shouted at back. She loved Margaret dearly, and me, but had no interest in our children, dismissing all young kids as ankle biters.

She had had one well-received book published, a semi-autobiographical novel under a pseudonym, and several short stories. She wrote something every day, but without being published again, complaining about the present day publishing establishment, how lucky we were to get published so easily.

When she popped in to see us, she always brought tasteful, artistic presents – hand-painted plates, bits of furniture, fruit and wine. Now that I too am old, I always make a point of bringing something whenever I am invited anywhere, especially by younger people, and I think back to Alison in the Algarve in 1968 and how kind and generous she was to us.

She had a beautiful large antique desk, roll-top with lots of little cubbyholes and secret drawers, which Margaret always admired. When Alison died, about ten years later, Margaret discovered, to her surprise, that she had been left Alison's desk. By this time we had no need in our house for further furniture and anyway could not face transporting it from Praia da Luz to London. So we arranged for it to be sold at an auction house in Lagos – and the proceeds to go to a local charity. A shame, really. I imagined Alison imagined Margaret writing on it for many decades to come.

*

In the middle of one night, Paul McCartney arrived with his new girlfriend, Linda, whom we had never met. When we left London he had been engaged to Jane Asher and we thought they made a very good couple. They had with them a girl called Heather, aged about eight, who was Linda's daughter by a previous relationship.

That evening in London, Paul had suddenly thought it would be a good idea to take his new girlfriend and her daughter to see us, as he knew we had young children, having been to our house. All service flights to Faro had gone, so he told Neil, their roadie, to hire a private jet. Which was why they arrived in the middle of the night.

We might well have not been in, or had even left Portugal, gone somewhere else. They had not rung, for we did not have a phone, nor had they written. Typical Paul. He would not have been fazed if we had not been there, seeing it as an adventure, take life as it comes, let it all hang out.

When he arrived, out of the blue, at two in the morning, he had no money and an irate taxi driver who had driven them 80 kilometres from Faro airport. Paul had landed at Faro with a £50 note, but had given it to someone to change for escudos. Then he noticed a taxi driver, waved him across, and jumped into his taxi, forgetting to pick up his currency.

They stayed for two weeks. At first we had assumed Linda was a groupie, a one-night stand, who appeared to be hanging on to him all the time, but as we got to know her, we realised she was a strong character, better for Paul than we had imagined.

When we got back to England, Linda kept in touch with Christmas cards, presents and invitations, but when she died, and Paul married Heather Mills, we lost touch with Paul and his family for a while.

Not long ago, Paul invited me to a party for old friends, which provided a chance to meet his new wife, Nancy. His older daughter Mary was there, with her own children. I had not seen her since she was a teenager.

I decided to tell Mary something I had always believed but not mentioned to her when she was little – that she had been conceived at our house in Portugal. The dates were clear. Exactly nine months, almost to the day, after they had stayed with us, Linda gave birth to their first child together, Mary.

Mary was charmed. She gave me a hug and said I must be er, what is it, step-godfather or something?

Margaret was not at Paul's party, of course, as she always refused to go to such events. When I told her afterwards what I had said to Mary, she said it was an awful thing to do, so embarrassing, she would never have done that, but typical of me, showing off.

We were glad to have had that year abroad. And did not regret it, then or afterwards. But we were never interested in or attracted to the idea of doing it again. Not for that length of time. After six weeks of the sun we were saying oh no, not another perfect day.

The people you end up being friends with abroad, however charming, are not the friends you would make or meet in real life at home. You can never properly, truly, deeply get to know people, either locals or expats, when you are only ever passing through their lives.

I missed so much reading the English papers every day,

and the magazines, and the radio. I did buy one of those so-called worldwide radios, supposedly capable of picking up London, but I could never get it tuned properly to the BBC. Or remember what half-hour in the day there was an interesting programme. There were some lessons learned from that year abroad. I am a little Ingerlander at heart. And a creature of routine.

On the other hand, every January after that year abroad, when it came to my birthday on 7 January, I moaned and groaned, saying oh if only we were still on a beach in the sun, now, do we always have to put up with these English winters?

# 10

# LONDON LIFE

We came back to London at the fag end of the sixties. While we were away, nothing much new seemed to have happened. People still looked and dressed the same.

We have a photo of us on the beach at Praia da Luz in 1968 with Paul and Linda and it is interesting now, all these decades later, when I look at it, to see that Margaret has a Vidal Sassoon-type hairstyle, which clearly she must have had done in that style a year earlier, before we left London. And she is also wearing a miniskirt.

She did go to Vidal Sassoon now and again, and so did I – because men went there as well. I was doing it for copy reasons, to find a West End barber I could interview for my *New Rich and New Poor* book. Trendy sixties snippers were said to be making a fortune.

Despite that photograph, we did not consider ourselves in the fashion swim in the sixties. I always felt dowdy when with the Beatles. But everyone who was alive and well in the sixties could not help reflecting in some way the times we were living in. Even if you only realised it later. My mother, in her pre-war snaps with my father, looks ever so chic in what appears now to be fashionable twenties clothes, but she was never remotely a fashion plate. You reflect your times, even if you are not aware of it at the time.

There is another snap of me walking up to Brookfield primary school with Caitlin and Jake. I am wearing very fashionable slightly flared white trousers, a sort of grandad T-shirt with buttons down the front and rimless sun specs, the sort John Lennon used to wear. I also have sideburns. That photo, so the family always says, makes me look a bit like George Best. Their implication is that I must have been trying to ape Besty. I always reply, oh no, George Best was trying to look like me. Well not me personally, but that was the style we all copied, chaps of my age, trying to look vaguely fashionable. George Best looked like lots of people, but of course his image is set in aspic, as being so typical of the sixties, whereas everyone else who was there has changed their styles and moved on. Or is dead.

The further we get away from that decade, it does strike me that there was a certain, identifiable sixties style, so different from the boring clothes and styles which went before, such as they were. There were no teenage styles when I was growing up in the early fifties. For a start, there were no teenagers.

On returning to London, I did go and visit Carnaby Street, which had seemed the world centre of young London fashion before I went away, but now was full of people up from the suburbs, walking up and down, gaping at the windows, and now and again buying stuff. They were all Brits, from the provinces. Not many foreigners, they all came later.

The sixties shop which most amazed me was Biba. Their

first store had opened in 1964, and had modest publicity, but a big new one had opened in Kensington High Street which we visited not long after we came back to London. I thought it was incredible. Every nook and cranny, every corner of the vast emporium, had been decorated and designed in the most amazing materials and drapes in all colours, a visual explosion of art deco and modern psychedelia. The shop itself was a work of art, before you even looked at the items on sale.

The staff were equally amazing. None of them seemed to be working, in the sense of actually trying to sell you anything. They stood or lay around, looking beautiful, considering themselves part of the overall design. Customers were being ignored, left to push and shove, allowed to try things on with no supervision. A lot of them walked out in the clothes, without paying. The losses must have been appalling.

I remember seeing Donovan there, the pop star. He stopped and spoke to Jake and Caitlin who were wearing floppy, purple Biba caps. He wanted to know where we had got them. I told him they came from Biba. While there, Margaret had bought herself a pair of knee-high purple canvas boots, which laced all the way up. Took ages to put on but they looked great, as she always had good legs. So I suppose it was not quite true that we were not in the fashion swim.

Habitat was also a revelation, but in a different way. That was more professional and organised. It too opened in 1964 on a small scale, gradually getting bigger premises. When the Tottenham Court Road one opened, we seemed to go there every Saturday. We started chucking out our dark, elderly furniture and Victorian button-back chairs and sewing tables we had been so proud of just a few years earlier. Instead we were filling the house with Scandinavian-style, hard-edged, unadorned, gleaming pine tables, chairs, day beds. Then we moved on to covering the kitchen and bathroom walls with pine boards which we then sealed with Ronseal. Which of course we regretted, about ten years later, when stripped pine became awfully old hat.

The more I think back to the sixties the more I am convinced it was a fascinating decade. Not just the changes in cultural and social attitudes, which helped me progress on the *Sunday Times*, but in the streets, the shops, the homes.

I do find it very hard to think of what were the styles of the seventies, apart from awful flapping trousers, platform heels and long hair. I can't even think of anything which symbolised eighties style, at least which affected me. As for the nineties, we are still in them, aren't we? Practically yesterday.

I know I do romanticise the sixties. But it did mean so much to me, when so many things in my life and Margaret's life happened and when our family and careers began. I know it was as much the fact of being aged in our twenties and early thirties, rather than it being the sixties. Most people look back to their twenties and thirties with fondness and nostalgia. I assume there are people now who go dewy eyed about the 1990s or 2000s. Do they refer to it as the 2000s? Who cares. I am still in the sixties.

In 1969, when we came to London, we each came home with a completed novel. We had taken it in turns every morning while abroad, two hours on, two hours off, to look after the children while the other one wrote.

I had dropped entirely the book about university students, originally *The Class of '66*, which then became *The Class of '67* and then *'68*, and then I gave up. It was all out of date. Students had changed so much in just three years. More so on the continent with various demonstrations and action groups, but even in the UK they had become more political and involved.

I had completed half the interviews, which I then never used. They are lying around the house somewhere. Anna Ford, who had been at Manchester University, later became a well-known TV presenter and newsreader. Buzz Goodbody, then at Sussex, joined the Royal Shakespeare Company, becoming one of their first and youngest female directors. She committed suicide in 1975. There is still an annual award for young directors in her name.

While abroad, I had decided to write another novel, *The Rise and Fall of Jake Sullivan*. My hero was a lout, a working-class yob, who has become a property millionaire. In my mind, he was a bit like John Lennon in his attitudes, and a bit like John Bloom, a washing machine magnate I had interviewed, and also a publisher friend called Gareth Powell. I had not used anything from their lives, just how I imagined they looked at the world.

To my hero, Jake Sullivan, fighting to make his property millions, it was all a laugh. He didn't mind if he did go bust, in fact going to prison for debt or bankruptcy would be part of the process. Failure was part of a being a success, so what did it matter. I interviewed quite a few people who had made money out of property, so I got to know how the system worked.

In the book, the hero Jake, now very rich and flash, meets an old friend from school who has gone to university, got a proper job, done the right things, but has no house or money, unlike Jake who was useless at school, but ducked and dived and amassed a massive property empire. Jake hires his friend – whom I based upon me – as his Surprise Assistant. All he has to do is organise surprises for him. Once I had thought of that wheeze, it was good fun to write. If the plot got stuck, and I got bored, then I could spring another surprise. Jake does end up in prison.

Naturally it was full of bad language, farting, wanking, grabbing people's balls in meetings, with Jake insulting and humiliating people and being foul-mouthed, just as he had been at school. Charles Pick at Heinemann was appalled. He wanted all the bad language out. Even the success of the Beatles biog could not make him change his mind.

I stuck to my guns, said he was a hero of our times, this is what the new breed of self-made tycoons are like. I suppose the success of the Beatles biog had given me the confidence not to worry about possibly not getting another publisher to accept it. I did have the security of some money in the bank – though I had decided not spend any of it for seven years. This was the period I was told that the Inland Revenue can always come back and demand more tax.

Richard Simon, my agent, had left Curtis Brown and set up on his own. When Heinemann finally said no, Richard agreed to try it on another publisher. This turned out to be an enormous stroke of luck. The book was taken on by Tony Godwin of Weidenfeld and Nicolson, with whom I worked so happily for the next ten years, producing seven books.

When I first went to see Tony, I was so impressed that he had read the novel twice and made notes, created graphs, charted the rise and flow of the narrative. I could not believe anyone would take my fiction so seriously. I always felt I was a fraud as a novelist, compared with Margaret. I was writing novels because, well, I can't now quite remember. It just seemed the thing to do. Everyone with any sort of writing ambition always thinks they would like to write a novel.

In fact I went on to have three novels published with Tony, till I realised I was better off, life was easier, sticking to non-fiction.

*Jake Sullivan* did well, got a lot of coverage, and the film rights were sold to Robert Stigwood, a pop music impresario who had a big success with the Bee Gees. I had met him by chance at Brian Epstein's country home, when they were doing various pop music deals together. He had now decided to go into films and this would be his first film venture.

I was to do the script and he hired a clever and bright young director, Tony Palmer, who had made his name in TV. We were given the use of an office in Mayfair, just vacated by a supergroup he was handling, called Cream.

Tony and I went off to scout locations, found possible places to shoot, spent a lot of time and money on the script and did auditions. The person we chose for the part of Jake was John Alderton. He turned up in character, wearing a flash suit, shouting his mouth off, and seemed perfect. So we signed him up.

But the film never got made. Robert Stigwood decided instead to put his money into a pop music film, *Saturday Night Fever*, which turned out to be a Hollywood blockbuster.

I still have the film script of *Jake Sullivan* lying around somewhere. Perhaps one day somebody will see it as a period project about the sixties, but I doubt it. So my brilliant career in films, as a screenplay writer, ended with one film made and one script lying gathering dust.

I can hardly remember now the four other novels which I went on later to do – three with Tony at Weidenfeld and one for Bloomsbury. I can't recall the names of the characters or the plots, if any. So you will be spared.

One of them, *A Very Loving Couple*, published in 1971, appeared a few years ago on a reading list from some new university. Which surprised me. One called *Body Charge*, which was about gay bashing on Hampstead Heath, plus football, has recently been republished in America. A Californian publisher who specialises in gay books from the past had somehow come across it and brought it out in a new edition.

I have just got down a dusty copy of *A Very Loving Couple* from my shelves, to check the date, and I noticed that the copyright belongs to the Multiple Sclerosis Society of Great Britain. I had forgotten that. It was the beginning of a period in which Margaret insisted we should start giving money away. I put it off at first, saying we might need our money some time, if one of us falls ill, needs years of care, but she said no, we should do it now, while we are both young and healthy. She argued that we were now earning enough for our needs, plus we had the money saved after our year abroad. (It came in total to about £50,000, which I left in various building society accounts for seven years.)

In the end I gave away about five books and Margaret did

the same. What happened was that once a book idea had been accepted by a publisher, and the contract drafted by the agent, we then put the contract in the name of the charity. They then received all the monies. In effect, we worked for a year for nothing. The charities we donated books to included Shelter, Marie Curie Cancer Care and several others.

People used to think it was some sort of fiddle, that Multiple Sclerosis was a company owned by us in the Bahamas, and that all we were doing was avoiding tax. We were, in a sense, avoiding tax – by avoiding any payment and working for nothing. John Fowles, whom I had interviewed for Atticus early in his career, and who was now at the height of his fame and fortune, wrote to us to ask about it. He said he wanted to donate a book to charity, and wanted to know what sort of wording should be used. I think Fowles heard about what we were doing through one of our publishers. They could not believe it at first. They did not lose, of course, nor did our agents, because they got their 10 per cent by still representing the book, even though it was now owned by a charity.

Tony Godwin eventually left Weidenfeld and moved to the USA, which was a loss for me. For about ten years he had commissioned almost every book idea I thought of. However dopey. We got on so well, he was so supportive, even with topics, such as football, in which he had no interest at all.

Tony lived for a while in a penthouse flat in Gloucester Crescent, Primrose Hill, after he had separated from his wife Fay Godwin, who became a well-known photographer. He invited me and Margaret one evening to a dinner party. He had cooked and prepared and served it all on his own, after a hard day at work. I was most impressed.

There were about six couples there, mostly authors published by him, and for some reason, towards the end of the meal, the chat got on to Antonia Fraser. She was not there, but she was one of Tony's authors. The conversation had turned to her biog of Mary Queen of Scots, which was selling very well. Margaret was not asked her opinion, but that of course did not hold her back. While admiring the research and the work Antonia had put it into, Margaret declared that she felt it was a shame Antonia was not a better writer.

Tony jumped up, absolutely furious. He said he would not allow any of his authors to be criticised in his house. Margaret should either retract what she had just said or leave his table.

We were all stunned, people looking at each other in amazement. We had never seen this side of Tony, though of course as his author, it was nice to realise he defended his authors, even behind their backs.

Margaret said if that was how Tony felt, then fine. She then got up and left the table. I did not quite realise at first what she had done, or where she had gone. Perhaps she had just gone to the lavatory, so for a few moments I quietly carried on eating, my head down, saying nothing. When I had finished the dish, which was the pudding, and she had still not reappeared, I got up and went downstairs to find her. I found her outside, further down the street, standing beside our car. She had no key and could not drive. She was patiently waiting, leaning against the car.

I made a face, glared at her, waiting for her to tell me what she was going to do. Was she coming back or not? Along the pavement suddenly arrived the panting Tony. He had run down the stairs after me, not wanting to lose a second guest before his dinner party had ended.

Tony said he was sorry, he had not meant to dismiss Margaret, and never thought for one moment she would leave. Margaret said she was sorry she had spoken out in that way.

Then Margaret pointed at the car, pointedly. She was indicating that she wanted it unlocked and driven home. I thanked Tony for a lovely meal. We both got into our car and left. I saw Tony lots of times after that for work reasons, but the incident was never mentioned again.

In 1972, our third child, Flora was born, a surprise package, after a gap of eight years. I can't remember planning to have another. It just seemed to happen. A blessing. We used to say she was a mistake which turned into a flower, hence her name. Though of course not in her hearing. No one likes to think they were not planned.

Margaret had been writing a biography of Bonny Prince Charlie, which is how she came to think of the name Flora. We both liked the name. It sounded nicely but not too madly Scottish.

I had to get another car, now we had three children. At the time I had an MGB GT, a little sports car, which only had a bucket seat at the back, room for just two children, whose heads were already getting flattened by crouching inside.

We had bought a country cottage in Oxfordshire, at Wardington, near Banbury. Another middle-class fantasy, like wanting to live abroad, is to rush off out of London after school on Friday to one's country cottage, tra la. Of course we were middle-class by now, and the country cottage sealed it, despite me still pretending I was northern and working-class, grew up on a council estate, don't you know, though perhaps I did not harp on about it quite as often as in the past when we first arrived in London.

At Wardington, I played for the local village football team on a Saturday, then moaned all Sunday that I was in agony, by which time it was Sunday evening, ready to come home again for school the next day. So not a lot of fun for Margaret.

When we knew that Margaret was pregnant, we were driving up to Wardington one Friday evening with the two of them, crammed into the MG.

'Something lovely is going to happen to our family,' I said, turning round to smile at them.

Caitlin and Jake, then aged eight and six, stopped pushing and shoving each other, and moaning about the lack of space, to contemplate what this nice thing might be.

'We're going to have a dog,' said Jake.

'We're going to have a cat?' said Caitlin.

We had always refused to have any pets. Bringing up children seemed hard enough without any extra burdens. Feeding, watering, healing, caring, worrying about children needs enough energy and love without the worry of blooming pets. The most we ever allowed them was a tortoise, which is still in our London garden, almost fifty years later. We never feed her, except for amusement reasons, to show visitors or children, such as giving her cucumber or strawberries. We don't water her either, or take her to the vet. In fact we do nothing for her. Perfect. Oh, if only children were like that. If we ever went away, we never gave her a second thought.

We bought her from the pet shop in Park Way, Camden Town. You can't buy them now. Tortoises are an endangered species. In London, you now get tortoise burglars who come over your wall in the dark and steal your tortoise, selling it on the black market or eBay.

When we bought her we were told to put her in the garage every winter in a straw box so rats wouldn't get at her during her hibernation. We did that for the first winter, and let her out in the garden again in the spring when she started stirring. Next year, as winter approached, we couldn't find her. She had disappeared. We feared the rats had got her.

In the spring I was giving the grass its first cut with a Flymo and realised I had gone over a bump in the lawn. It was the tortoise. The silly animal had buried herself right in the middle of the lawn. Before I could stop myself, I had shaved a bit off the top of her shell. The children were distraught, convinced I had finished her off. But she was fine. The shell grew back. And every year since she had put herself to sleep, on her own, but in a more sensible position, digging a hole against a wall.

I once made some money out of her. I was approached by the BBC children's department who asked if I had an original story which could be done on *Jackanory*, a popular children's series of the time, which ran from 1965 to 1996.

The tortoise had taken to coming into our back kitchen, hauling herself up and over the back step from the garden and into the kitchen-dining room where we had a laid an ever so nice and shiny new wooden parquet floor. She would skid across it, then reach the comfort of the carpet in the living room, very pleased with herself – except we had to ban her in the end. She kept leaving her little secret shits behind our best Habitat day bed.

I wrote a story about her, how she imagined that our kitchen was a skating rink. So she skates round and makes friends with the children of the house. It was read on *Jackanory* by a well-known actress of the time, but I can't remember her name.

With the birth of Flora and now three children, we moved up to a Volvo, one of those monster tank-like ones with extra seats at the very back. Awfully middle-class, but I never liked it. It never felt safe either. Driving up the M1 on a Friday after school it used to sway and shudder, yet the whole image of a Volvo was of utter reliability and safety. For someone who has always said he does not like cars, has no interest in them, I seem to have had quite a few in my long life. When not sleeping I still try to remember them, in order, and their colour.

With a third child, it was now even more important that we found a way to take over the whole house. Yet still Mrs Hall would not be moved. I offered her more and more money, and she always said no. We were beginning to think we would have to move to get more space, in order to provide a bedroom each for the children in due course.

I eventually discovered that the only condition on which she would move was if I bought a flat for her, somewhere she could live for the rest of her life, at the same rent.

The moment she mentioned this I agreed at once. I started immediately looking locally for something suitable, only to find there were further conditions she had not mentioned, one of which was the precise area. I had been to look at a very nice flat in a block at the top of Chetwynd Road, just two streets away. She dismissed that. She said it was Kentish Town. What a snob. She wanted to move in the other direction, and be in Highgate, or at least have an N6 postcode.

That of course would put the price up, but having started the process, and got her to agree to move, we had become excited by the thought of having our whole house to ourselves.

I kept looking. And eventually came across a new block, with eight flats, going up a few streets away in Swain's Lane, excellent position, at the bottom end of Highgate West Hill, near the Heath, with some nice, upmarket shops opposite.

I took Mrs Hall to see the block just before it was finally completed. She agreed she would move there, but demanded a flat on the first floor. I was surprised, at her age, assuming she would have preferred to be on the ground floor. She said the ground floor might attract burglars.

It had one bedroom, sitting room, security entry phone, her own front door to her flat, modern bathroom and kitchen and full central heating, none of which she had in her/our house. The price was £7,500 for a 99-year lease. I was furious at having to pay so much. It was 50 per cent more than we had to pay for our own house, just to get her out. And she didn't seem at all grateful.

I was the first purchaser of any of the flats in the block but the other seven quickly sold – almost all of them to Russians. The Russian trade delegation had a big residence nearby, over-looking the Highgate ponds on the Heath. They had featured in various newspaper stories and scenes in John le Carré-type stories about hidden letter boxes, rendezvous with spies behind trees. Allegedly, MI5 had managed to bribe a window cleaner, who was cleaning the windows in their residence, to fix a listening device to every window.

Many of the Russian families sent their children to Brookfield School, the local primary that Caitlin and Jake attended. The Russian children integrated well, but the parents never smiled and chatted, though I got to recognise a few in the playground. When you met any of the mothers coming towards you on the Heath, they would suddenly stop talking, as if they feared you might understand their Russian.

The Russian fathers played football on the Heath on a Sunday. We played a game against them once. By 'we' I mean Dartmouth Park United, a Sunday morning team I began with two other local dads which went on for many years.

Not long after Mrs Hall had finally moved in, I got a call from a posh-sounding man who wanted to ask me about her. I was a bit suspicious, but he seemed to know all the details, of the flat, that I owned it and that she was my tenant. He just wanted to know who she was. I asked who he was and he muttered something about some government depart-ment and gave me a genuine-sounding official number and address. I said all I could tell him was that Mrs Hall was a single woman, aged about seventy, born in Dublin. He hung up.

Not long afterwards I got a similar call from a Russian-sounding voice, asking the same sort of questions. They explained they were the owners of some of the other flats, which I knew was true. When I mentioned Mrs Hall was Irish and seventy, they too hung up.

The first was clearly MI5 or one of our security departments, the second was the Russian equivalent. Each was obviously suspicious that Mrs Hall had been planted. Or could be planted. She was for a long time the only non-Russian living in the building. I suspect their lack of interest in her, once I had given them a few details, was ageism.

Getting Mrs Hall into that flat was a triumph of persuasion and money. Getting her out of our house was wonderful. At long last we had our own house, all to ourselves.

## 11

# BACK TO JOURNALISM

I began to miss journalism. I didn't really enjoy being stuck at home all day long, every day, even though we now had the whole house to ourselves. I didn't need the money journalism might bring in, or the work, as I had enough books being commissioned. I just missed the fun of being a journalist.

I had been doing it full time for around ten years, from 1958 till 1968 when we went abroad for that year. Margaret never felt the need to do anything else other than sit and write books, or sit and read books. She never wanted to be with other people, far less sit in an office.

In the early years of being published, feeling so grateful to your publisher, most authors do what they suggest, so Margaret did do some bookshop signing sessions, appeared on TV and radio programmes, talked now and again at literary festivals – and was brilliant at it, being so fluent, intelligent, far better than me. She always had complete silence, people hanging on her words. It was the actress in her coming out. All public appearance is acting. But she did not enjoy it, in that she did not like herself liking it, did not approve of herself doing it, feeling it was catering to her worst instincts. She did not feel anyway that it was an author's duty to appear in public. She much preferred being at home, on her own.

I did not want to want to go out full time, as I loved being at home, but I also wanted to go out, now and again, be in contact with people. I fancied some sort of part-time journalism, keeping my hand in, if only now and again. I told myself if I had been a plumber or a carpenter, and had enjoyed it, I might still have wanted to go back and do a bit of plumbing now again, even if I did not need to.

I had come off the *Sunday Times* full-time staff, once we were back in London, and stayed full time at home for a couple of years working on books. Then, Harry Evans, the editor, suddenly offered me a part-time position, any time I wanted it. Nothing was written down, it was just a verbal arrangement that I would come back to the paper for around six months every year and do whatever he felt the paper needed. I would not be a threat to other people, scheming to get their jobs. They would know that in six months, whatever I was doing, I would be off, back home, working on a book.

This strange off and on routine ran for most of the 1970s, doing other things at the same time, such as books, but for longer or shorter periods I would put on my journalist cap and become a hack again, going to the office, working with other hacks.

It began when Harry asked me to become the women's editor of the *Sunday Times*. That was not the exact title. In fact it was all a bit hazy. Harry just blurted it out one day, on the run, throwing off ideas as usual.

I had never been an executive before, only ever been in

charge of one other person when I ran the Atticus column, but had always fancied myself running a team, enthusing them, thinking of ideas. I had had such fun as editor of *Palatinate*, our student newspaper at Durham, where most of my staff were women, and vaguely imagined that running the women's pages might be much the same.

Harry did not explain properly what was in his mind, but it appeared to be running a new section, the Look! pages, which would in effect be the women's and home section of the paper. The real reason was that he had hatched a plot to get rid of the fashion editor Ernestine Carter, a diminutive American woman in her mid-sixties, very powerful in the fashion trade, highly thought-of by shops like Harrods. He could not sack her, as she was so distinguished and had been awarded an OBE for services to fashion, but he realised she was becoming out of step with modern fashion and modern journalism and modern young readers.

This often happens in journalism and in publishing, and other forms of fashionable or creative life, and in sport. People once deemed superstars appear to have lost their touch, or are thought to have lost it, but are hard to budge because of the status and contacts they have built up. Their end is often very cruel – and of course the person doing the knifing often ends up in due course being axed themselves.

Harry's plot was quite simple. He wanted me to create some rival pages, run different sorts of family and domestic stories, the more outrageous and vulgar the better. If it upset Ernestine, who would be left only with her high-fashion page, and she threatened to resign, so much the better. He could always blame me.

The first day I arrived in the department I found two people sitting there who thought they were the editor of this new section. The first was Mark Boxer, who at one time had been editor of the Colour Mag, and was now generally hanging around. When I told him Harry had made me the boss of Look! he was more than happy to disappear. Yes, it did have an exclamation mark. Not my doing. I have gone through life hating exclamation marks, considering them the work of amateurs.

The other was Molly Parkin, who arrived one day and told me Harry had made her women's editor. When I looked into this, it turned out that Harry meant her just to be fashion editor of the Look! pages, doing modern, young fashion, while I was the editor in charge of her and the new section. Molly accepted this, which was just as well. She could not type, had very little editing experience, but was a larger than life character, wore outrageous clothes, and seemed to be in touch with all the new young designers. She had gone to art college, been a painter, then moved into fashion, working for a while with Barbara Hulanicki at Biba and Mary Quant, then did some fashion editing for *Nova* and *Harpers and Queen*. She was in her late thirties, four years older than me, and had been married to a posh, public school- and Oxford-educated gallery owner called Michael Parkin. After five years of a stormy marriage, Molly had walked out. When she left their Chelsea home, Molly used some spray paint to delete the G on a local NO PARKING sign.

Molly was now fancy free, despite having two young daughters, and every day kept the office in hysterics about her love life, telling us the most intimate details of her various blokes, some of them very well known such as two eminent playwrights.

I also inherited a new columnist called Jilly Cooper, a failed secretary, who had written a funny piece in the Magazine which Harry had liked and so he'd hired her. I took her out to lunch and discovered her husband Leo had been married before. I encouraged her to write a personal piece, about being a second wife, and to be more serious now and again.

Jilly became the most popular writer on the whole paper – much to the astonishment of the Insight team. They thought readers bought the paper for Insight.

When I joined the *Sunday Times* in 1960 the star names were Cyril Connolly, Harold Hobson and Dilys Powell. Now it had become Jilly. The paper had not promoted her at this stage, nor was she appearing on radio or TV, yet she had acquired this enormous following – all on her own. She had had no experience of newspapers or of writing columns. So, what made her successful?

Women had written newspaper columns for decades on so-called women's pages of the national newspaper and magazines, but they were ever so sensible, giving sensible advice. Jilly played it mainly for laughs – but she was also revealing herself, telling true, personal stories.

After writing about being a second wife, there were few personal subjects she would not consider, such as sex, marriage, class, but all done amusingly, without hurting anyone. On sex, which she has written about constantly since in her bestselling books, she doesn't really write sexily, not in the erotic or smutty sense. It's ever so wholesome, and fun.

I used to try to cut out her puns, many of which were

excruciating, and try to keep her concentrating on herself and her husband Leo.

People think it's easy, writing that sort of column, because it is made to look easy. But you have to have a likeable persona and a distinctive voice – and enormous discipline, to keep it up, week after week. Jilly was always totally professional.

When I meet her today she turns to other people and says, 'He was the best editor I ever had, isn't he wonderful, isn't he marvellous.' Then a waitress approaches and she says, 'Darling, you are so wonderful, the best waitress in the world.' Or she meets someone from her publishers. 'Darling, you are so sweet, I owe everything to you.'

Is she being cynical? Not in the least. She loves everybody and everybody loves Jilly.

After a couple of months editing the Look! pages, the readers' letters were streaming in. I did my best to annoy Ernestine with series like 'Me and My Vasectomy' and also a feature on what happens when men's underpants go yellow. That did have Ernestine yelping.

I only did it for six months, leaving Harry to gently and gracefully ease out Ernestine, but looking back, my time on Look! was the most fun I ever had in journalism – since my days editing *Palatinate*. Apart from Jilly and Molly, there was also Lucia van der Post and Lesley Garner on the staff of Look!, both excellent, who went on to greater things. Ian Jack, who was the chief sub, was also a close friend, later editor of *Granta* and *Guardian* columnist. Oh, the lunches we had, went on for days, in hysterics all the time.

\*

Early on in my spell on Look!, I created a novel, *I Knew Daisy Smuten*, written along with my friends on the paper, partly as a bonding exercise for the new Look! department.

In the novel, Daisy was a photographer who has suddenly got engaged to Prince Charles and everyone wanted to know who she was. I had an unofficial staff meeting, for the whole paper, or at least my friends, the ones I considered were half-decent writers. I gave them all some brief biog information about Daisy, which they would have to stick to, then asked for volunteers. Hands up who would like to sleep with her? I also asked who would like to write about having been in her class at school, had married her, had been her boss, had been her accountant, anything really, as long as they had known her at some stage in her life and could throw some insight on her.

They each then wrote their memories of the Daisy Smuten each of them had known, and I knocked the book into shape, tried to give it a narrative and consistency.

The name Daisy Smuten was an anagram of *Sunday Times*. We even sold the film rights. It was the first time in print in a book for Jilly and most of the other contributors.

It was thanks to my friend Tony Godwin, still then the editorial boss at Weidenfeld and Nicolson, that we got it commissioned. He did like unusual, new and daft ideas. When it was all finished, and everyone at the publishers liked it, he persuaded George Weidenfeld to hold a Daisy Smuten launch party – at George's private house. He must have been potty. I invited all the contributors, and their partners, friends in publishing, friends in newspapers, assorted hacks, plus there were dozens of uninvited gatecrashers.

It was the most chaotic, drunken, awful yet incredible party. A lot of George's carpets and furniture got wrecked and a valuable painting disappeared – later recovered.

For about a year, it was still being talked about in Bloomsbury. That was how we used to describe the publishing world, just as the newspaper world was known as Fleet Street. George never gave a party like that again in his own house.

During the 1970s, I came back several times to the paper, at Harry's request, when he had a problem, or a new idea, such as editing a new section called Scene. That was not such fun. It was an attempt to bring all the vaguely environmental columns and features together, including Travel, but it had no real focal point, or a proper team, unlike the Look! pages. It didn't last long. In a way Harry was too forward thinking, creating environment pages before the general public was really ready for them.

In 1975 I was asked by Harry to return once again, this time to edit the *Sunday Times Magazine*.

After that slow start, with Mrs Woodcock binning the first edition, it had quickly become successful, rich, powerful, attracting the best photographers and star writers. The staff, especially the art department, were a law unto themselves, able to operate as a separate entity, get away with stuff that normal reporters and departments on the main paper could never do, spending fortunes on stories – and on parties. Harry himself was worried it was becoming too much of a separate empire.

The Mag, at the time I joined, was fortunate in having separate and rather sumptuous offices at the top of the *Sunday*

*Times* building in 200 Gray's Inn Road, with access to a roof garden and private suite. This had originally been created by Roy Thomson when he bought Kemsley newspapers in 1959. He had even built his own lift, to take him up to his penthouse. But then he had changed his plans and it was hardly ever used. So the Mag had taken it over. It was great for parties and entertainments. It was also good fun to be able to go up to the Magazine editor's office in my private lift.

But I didn't really enjoy my two years editing the mag. I never got on with the art department who resented me arriving from the paper and they hated the changes that Harry wanted me to make.

One of the things Harry wanted done was to open up the end of the Mag. Readers were moaning that the last twenty or so pages were all adverts. I therefore had to find some sort of regular editorial to fill the inside back page. On the opposite page we could charge double advertising rates.

I was looking for a self-contained, one-page column, with a simple photo, of general interest to all readers. First of all I tried a series called Home Town in which we took well-known people back to their birthplace. I took Eric Morecambe to Morecambe and Ted Heath to Broadstairs. But it quickly got too time-consuming. Then I started a column called Sacred Cows in which writers could praise or rubbish. It got too samey.

I then had a much simpler idea – 'A Life in the Day'. I had used the title, reversing the order of the old cliché, A Day in the Life, and a similar format in a column I had written when editing *Palatinate*, the Durham student newspaper. It had been the first column I ever wrote, so a big event in my life. Twenty years later, I pinched the title from myself. The Beatles, with their 1967 song, 'A Day in the Life', stuck to the original cliché. The idea was that inside everyone's day, and life, there is another life, the trivial, mundane, routine stuff, such as when they get up, how they decide what clothes to wear, what they have for breakfast.

I mentioned the idea at a Magazine staff meeting, with all the assistant editors, and they all groaned, saying it was corny, pathetic and would be boring. At random, I picked on the chief sub, called Patrick, and asked him about his day. When I asked him how he decided what to wear, his answer amazed everyone. As far as we all had been aware, Patrick wore the same dull suit every day to work. But in his reply, he explained that before getting dressed, he always consulted his diary. In it he recorded what he wore every day. He aimed to have on a different shirt and a different tie every day for a month. No one had ever noticed. We were so surprised we all agreed the series was worth a try.

'A Life in the Day' is still going strong – having appeared every week in the Mag since 1975, the longest-running column in the *Sunday Times*. Perhaps in any paper. I like to think I will be remembered for that.

When there was no specific editing job required by Harry, in my six months back on the pay roll, I amused myself by calling myself chief feature writer again, a title I had formerly had, and interviewing famous people.

One of the famous people I did after our year abroad was Noël Coward. He was not promoting a play or a show, which is usually the case. When they are promoting something, there is usually a PR there as well and you have to keep asking about the film, play or book as if you care. In 1969 I had noticed that Coward's seventieth birthday was coming up. I wrote to him, persuaded him to give an interview – the only one he decided to give.

I got invited to his home in Switzerland, and was naturally thrilled. Getting into people's homes always provides the best copy. I booked into a hotel near his house, the Montreux Palace hotel, and had checked in and was ready to go up to Coward's house, when a call came from his assistant Cole Leslie. Originally his name was Leslie Cole, but Coward had made him change it.

Cole Leslie was ringing to say that The Master – which was how he referred to him – was cancelling dinner. The Master was not well. I thought oh bugger, all this way. However Cole Leslie assured me I could come the next night instead. But it meant I then had twenty-four hours to put in, stuck in this posh but empty hotel – empty because it was out of season.

Next morning, hanging around the reception desk, I realised there was a wing of the hotel where permanent guests stayed. I managed to read upside down the names of some of the residents – and noticed one was called V. Nabokov. Could it be him?

I memorised his room number, went back to my room, and I dialled him. I asked if he was Vladimir Nabokov. At first he would not admit it. Instead he cross-examined me, suspecting I was not really from the *Sunday Times*, which was what I had told him. He asked if I knew Alan Brien, who had a column in the paper at the time. I said I did know Alan, in fact he lived in the next street and his daughter Jane Brien was a friend of my daughter Caitlin's.

It was interesting that he was a *Sunday Times* reader, or at least had heard of one of our columnists. He agreed to meet me in an hour in a certain café in town, where he was going for his morning coffee – on condition that I did not write anything about meeting him.

After the first coffee, we walked round the town, went in various bars and cafés and he told me gossip about local people, shopkeepers and butchers whom he suspected were having affairs. He would not talk about himself, or what he was working on, but he was interested in me, when I told him about my books and life at the *Sunday Times*.

I didn't even make notes afterwards, back in my hotel room. I should have done, while all his chat was still fresh in my mind.

That evening, I got a taxi up to Château Coward. As I arrived and was shown in, there was some argument going on between Coward and Cole Leslie. One of them had farted but was denying it, blaming the other. Cole was ordered to get an air freshener. He started spraying the room which sent Coward into hysterics. 'It now smells like a fucking Turkish brothel in here!'

Coward swore all the time, usually the f word, though of course we never used such language in a newspaper. Nor did I mention the farting. But I did describe how there had been a smell of fresh paint when I arrived and Cole Leslie had been sent to get a deodorant, with a lot of cursing from Coward.

Over dinner, Coward was full of stories, amusing incidents that had happened to him, people he had met. We got on to the Beatles and he was very caustic, pretending he did not know their names, referring to John McCartney and Paul Lennon.

He told a story about going to see them perform in Rome. Afterwards, he decided he would go backstage, so a message was sent to their dressing room that Mr Noël Coward would like to meet the Beatles. The message came back saying that the Beatles did not want to meet him. He was so furious he marched into their dressing room and berated them.

'If you are a star, you have to behave like one. I always have. I believe in good manners.'

I then got on to one of his hobbies. In New York and in London, he was apparently in the habit of going into a hospital to watch operations. In each place, he had a friendly surgeon who let him know when anything interesting was happening. He had recently seen a hysterectomy, an ovariectomy, a birth and death.

I found this weird and horrific, but fascinating, and felt it gave an unusual insight into his real character. But I must have appeared too interested, or too appalled, wanting to know too many details, how he had reacted. He suddenly changed the subject, realising he had given too much away.

After coffee and brandy, and stuffing my face with food and wine – he was very hospitable, though he ate very little himself – I apologised for having stayed too long, and asked perhaps too many personal questions.

'Not at all, dear boy. I am fascinated by the subject.'

Which made a good ending to my interview. I wrote it up at length, about 5,000 words, and it made the front page of the Review section.

Another person I wrote about, in 1970, was Christy Brown. The connection came through Margaret. He had been her pen pal for over six years, without ever her meeting him. He had a written a book called *My Left Foot* sixteen years earlier, in 1954, which sold very few copies. He was published by Secker and Warburg, Margaret's publisher. He had seen her photo in their catalogue one day and asked her editor if he could write to her. Margaret agreed, as she loved writing to people, just as much as she hated meeting people. His letters to her were wonderful, even more so because he was typing them with just the toes of one foot. That was the only part of his anatomy he had any control over.

Christy was one of twenty-two siblings, living in Dublin, and was born with cerebral palsy. He rubbished his first book, saying he had done it to get published, knowing people would like a heart-rending book about a happy cripple. For the last sixteen years he had been working on the book he really wanted to write, *Down All the Days*.

In 1970 he had at last got it accepted. Foreign publishers were bidding for it and he was coming to London, desperate to meet Margaret. He pleaded with her in his letters, but she refused. I said I would like to meet him. It might make a piece for the paper.

I went to a lodging house in Shepherd's Bush, full of Irishmen. His condition was worse than I expected. One of his brothers was carrying him around the crowded room while another poured Guinness down his throat. He implored me to let him meet Margaret, going on and on, so I agreed to take him home in my car, saying it would have to be a very quick visit. He got bundled into my car along with a nephew Joe who would act as interpreter, as it was almost impossible to work out what Christy was saying.

In the car I told him I had recently met Nabokov.

'Nabokov's tragedy is too much language and not enough feeling,' replied Christy. His words came out as a series of grunts, but were translated for me by Joe, who had no idea what it meant.

When we got home, and Joe carried him into our house, I introduced him to Margaret who had been sitting reading. They talked for a bit, after a fashion, and then Christy was sick. The noise and commotion woke up Jake, aged four, who came downstairs and stared in fascination at this shaking, slavering body.

Christy didn't stay long. Joe and I soon bundled him back in my car and we took him back to Shepherd's Bush.

Margaret never forgave me. I remember driving back home on my own across London, knowing I was going to be for it. She was in bed, her back turned to me, refusing to speak. Next day she was still furious. Had she not specifically told me on no account to bring him home? I knew full well she wanted their relationship to be on paper, not face to face, which was nothing to do with his condition, but how she wanted it with everyone.

I did a long piece about Christy for the *Sunday Times*. *Down All the Days* became a massive international seller, making him £70,000, enough to buy his own house in Dublin. And then later, he got married. Christy never saw the film of *My Left Foot*, as he died eight years before it was released.

I still have all the letters he wrote to Margaret, typed with that one toe, as well as some letters to me. They are so full of life and fun, wit and wisdom, exuberance and erudition. I wish I could write letters as well as Christy Brown did.

# 12

# FOOTBALL MANIA

I was there at Wembley on Saturday, 30 July 1966, and have my ticket as well as my programme to prove it. My seat cost £5, one of the best in the house. Probably cost you £2,000 today. I got it through my friend James Bredin, now dead, who was the boss of Border TV, a thriving, thrusting little regional ITV station, now also deceased. So it goes.

Oh, it was so exciting, even though the game passed in a flash. I was never aware of the Soviet linesman allowing Geoff Hurst's second goal, nor the Germans going mad, but it didn't matter anyway as Geoff then got a third. Did we call him Geoff in 1966? Seems overly familiar. Perhaps we all shouted: 'Come on Mr Hurst', or 'Please hit the ball, sir'.

But we were all so carried away we were not thinking normally that day, or the next, or that year, or the next, or that decade, or the next. There was pride, of course, the first time we'd ever won the World Cup, but also allied with smugness and superiority. Had we not invented the game? Had we not taught these foreign Johnnies all they knew? It was only our right, our entitlement.

Naturally, we thought that was it. No need to worry about these funny foreign ways any more, with their strange formations, silly defences, strange tactics. When I first heard of *catenaccio*, I really did think it was some sort of Italian frothy coffee.

I went home that summer Saturday in 1966, glowing with pride, thinking that it was just the beginning. We'd go on to win loads of World Cups, dominate world football, show them how to do it. I now can't see it happening again. Not in my lifetime. What's left of it.

I was cheering on England that day, even though all my childhood was spent cheering on Scotland, sitting nervously with my ears glued to the radio, willing Scotland on to win. But it was football I loved, the game itself, playing it most of all, and then watching it.

I loved the years when I played football every Sunday morning on the Heath, calling ourselves Dartmouth Park United, a group of doddering dads, hardly able to run, but I played till I was fifty, despite a cartilage operation, which was really silly.

When I first came to London, I started looking for a local team to support. Obviously getting to Carlisle United's home games was going to be hard from now on, living 300 miles away. We were equidistant from Arsenal and from Spurs, but in 1960, Spurs was the more glamorous team, winning things, going places. I threw my devotion in their direction, covered them in kisses, and have continued, all these decades later.

For a few games, I took Margaret. In the early sixties, the crowds at White Hart Lane were enormous, with patient and well-behaved queues all down the High Road, as you mainly paid at the turnstiles. When it said House Full, she would want to give up. I would say, let's go round the Paxton End, there might be a turnstile still open. She would say don't be stupid, House Full clearly means the ground is full. I would say, just let's try.

This was a good example of our different characters. I rarely take no for an answer, am not put off by refusals, ignore no-entry signs, maintaining they are for other people, not for me. I am always convinced there will be a way, will be a chance, or that something might turn up.

Margaret, logically, was right. Signs are there for a reason. So you are wasting your time and energy ignoring them. But almost always at Spurs, we did get in. There was usually a turnstile still open.

Despite her forthright and strong and immediate opinions on almost any subject, Margaret was extremely law-abiding, unlike me. She accepted it when experts, doctors, lawyers, teachers, said or advised something. I suspect almost all experts. I always think their wisdom is little better than the rest of us, they are on autopilot, equally likely to say the opposite to the next person. And deep down, most of them don't really care. Listen to their knowledge, such as it is, but you don't have to always obey everything they say. In the end, we are all on our own, responsible for our decisions.

Margaret never went again to games, after our first few months in London, but on the sports pages she read all the profiles and interviews with the main characters in cricket, rugby, athletics as well as football. I only ever read about football. Football is my first and only love. I have no room in my brain or time in my life to entertain any other sports.

Going back to the *Sunday Times* for different spells during the 1970s, I did try to get jobs on the sports pages, but rarely managed it. They were a close-knit body while I was a knock-about feature writer or small-scale editor, having worked on a different part of the paper, with no experience of reporting about football.

I did eventually persuade the sports editor to let me cover the occasional match – and it was a nightmare, far harder than I had imagined. It was like being back in Manchester again, in my first months as a so-called graduate trainee journalist: being sent out to cover a road accident or fire or murder and not knowing how to do it. I would spend ages painfully writing out my reports in longhand behind the telephone box, before finally phoning it through – and getting a bollocking for being late, missing three editions.

Covering football matches in the 1970s, there were of course no computers, laptops, mobile phones, but at least you were under cover in the press box and there was a phone line booked for you.

You hand-wrote your report as the game was going on, hoping that nothing dramatic happened in the last few minutes to make a nonsense of what you had written, for you had to start dictating at the final whistle. The leading papers all had designated phones in the press box, but you had to find them, they did not always work and in smaller grounds there were not enough to go round.

The copy-takers were a long-suffering, cynical, bored bunch who sat in little booths in the bowels of the newspaper building, earphones glued to their head, a keyboard in front of them, bashing out the pearls, or otherwise, being hurled at them from somewhere in a noisy stadium.

'Is there much more of this?'

This was their most dispiriting reaction. You had probably only just started dictating, thought it was going well, but they clearly thought it was total rubbish. They hated it when you chopped and changed as you dictated your well-chosen words. As you read out your words, as clearly as possible, you had to spell out punctuation – saying New Par, or Cap Letter, or Point, which meant a full stop.

Professional copy-takers no longer exist. A career which had gone on for decades, for a hundred years since football reports began, is now no more.

I never enjoyed doing football reporting, and never got the hang of it. I was always late, struggling to think of something amusing or colourful. I like to think when I have a typewriter in front of me, and can see my words, I can usually write something readable and personal, but when you have to do it in rough handwriting to a deadline, it is hard not to fall into clichés. My match reports rarely sounded like me.

I had to do a lot of away games in the provinces, as the star reporters, like Brian Glanville, got the big glamorous London games. It always took ages to get back as you usually missed the last fast train to London. You wasted an hour messing around with your report, you went to the press bar and drank free whisky and ate meat pies, then probably hung around the car park to get a word with the players as they came out of the players' tunnel. They almost always did stop for a word, though they had their favourites, the ones they could trust, who would have their home phone numbers as well, often meet them socially. As an outsider, they didn't know me, but if I did pick up a half-decent quote, I would phone it over from the railway station.

There were no formal press conferences after the game, but at many grounds, the manager would allow the chosen hacks into his office – his actual office, where he worked during the week, where he kept his private dossiers.

He would sit at his desk while we all piled in and stood around in front of him, asking questions, writing down the gems he was kind enough to give us.

I remember once at Upton Park, home of West Ham, when Ron Greenwood, later the England manager, was in charge. We all went into his office after the game. Jimmy Hill, then working for TV, commandeered Greenwood's own chair, sitting at Greenwood's desk, forcing him to stand around with the rest of us. Jimmy Hill then took over, telling us precisely what he thought of the game and why West Ham had lost. Greenwood just smiled.

One reason I was trying to do as many football reports as they would allow me was not just for my own interest, as a football fan, but because I had got this idea for a football book – a year in the life of a top football club, from the inside.

I discussed with Brian Glanville, and other experienced reporters, what the chances were of getting into Spurs. They all said hopeless. The chairman was a dull snob and the manager a dour Yorkshireman. The whole ethos and tradition of Spurs was anti-publicity. They were above all that. They didn't need it.

It is hard to believe it now, but in the 1970s both Arsenal and Spurs had no advertising in their programmes, or in the grounds and least of all on their shirts. They were against anything that smacked of commercial interest. They were a pure football club, nothing else.

Like most football directors of the time, they had inherited their shares, and their directorships, and did not take any salary or payments. They planned to hand on their positions in due course to their sons or sons-in-law. At Spurs and at Arsenal, they were brought up to keep the image of their ancient club unsullied by any nasty modern commercial or merchandising methods.

I was told that the Chelsea board, controlled by the Mears family, was much friendlier, more modern, so I got an appointment with their chairman. I explained my idea and he seemed interested. I then wrote a letter, going over my project. And I never got a reply.

I decided if I was going to do such a book, I might as well try it with Spurs, a club I did follow, did know about, having been watching them play for over ten years. But how could I get in, as an outsider, not a regular football writer whom the players and manager would have come across?

During one of my six-month spells on the paper, I suggested to Harry Evans a feature about Spurs, an inside story of a top First Division club. It would give me a chance to see what they were like, how they would cooperate, then if it went well, I might then go on to suggest the book project. Harry liked the idea.

I spent a few weeks with Frank Herrmann, my friend the photographer, watching Spurs training, mainly at Cheshunt, which was their training ground at the time, in rural Herts. I had never been there before and was astounded by how much space they had, so many pitches, a proper restaurant, gym, a little stadium where the young players performed. Locals around Cheshunt were allowed to come into the training ground with their dogs for morning walks, stand around and watch training going on.

I did a couple of features, which got a good show in the paper. I did not appear to have upset the club, at least there were no objections, so I discussed the book idea with my agent, Richard Simon, and with Tony Godwin at Weidenfeld. They were all for it – though neither had any personal interest in football.

I went to see the Spurs chairman Sidney Wale. I said I would like to spend a whole year following the club in order to write a book. I gave the impression that Bill Nicholson, the manager, had no objections. Which was an exaggeration, if not quite a grave downright lie. Then I went to see Bill and said that the chairman had no objections, which by then was true, more or less.

I presented myself at the Spurs training ground on 15 July 1971, for the first day of pre-season training. It always starts in what is still the middle of summer, when normal fans have not yet begun to think about the season.

I hung around, watching from the sidelines, on that first day. Then next day I got there early and went straight into the dressing room. Uninvited. The players were getting changed to go for a cross-country run, which they all hated doing. To my surprise, Bill Nicholson threw me a top, an official Spurs training top. I put it on. After the run, I got in the shower with the rest of the players. And that is how I continued. I insinuated myself into their working lives. I was only thirty-six at the time, about the same age as one or two of the senior players, and reasonably fit, as I was playing Sunday morning football.

After a few weeks, I had managed to talk to all the members of the first-team pool and explained who I was and my project. I said they would be allowed to read any quotes or bits about themselves before publication, and so would Bill and the chairman.

I then got carried away and I said I would split all proceeds with the first-team pool, plus Bill and Eddie Baily, his assistant manager. So the players and coaches would all gain from the book, if it did well.

When I told Richard my agent that all proceeds were going to be halved, with one half being split between nineteen people, he had hysterics. I had not discussed it with him, so he moaned about the paperwork, said the accounts department would go mad. It was then agreed that cheques would not go out to each of the nineteen if they were only small sums, but would be added up later.

I then signed a publishing contract with Tony at Weidenfeld for the book, which Richard had negotiated. I think once again it was for a £3,000 advance, with a third down on signing, a third on the finished manuscript being accepted and a third on publication, which is still roughly the norm in publishing today. But I had no contract with the club, no contract with the board, with the manager or with any of the players. It was all done verbally. All I did was follow up with a personal letter to each, so they knew what we had agreed.

Not one of them had an agent, accountant or lawyer. No such animals had yet entered the world of football. The nearest to it was that if a club got into a big event, like the Cup final, the captain or one of the senior players, or a friend of one of the team, would create a Cup final pool in which all the bits and pieces of extra earnings, from newspaper interviews, corny photographs, appearances at supermarkets, product endorsements, would be divvied up and shared among the first-team pool. It rarely amounted to more than £100 or so each. During the season, about the only perk they got was selling their spare tickets, especially to big games, to the touts, for cash in brown envelopes, which of course they were not supposed to do.

In 1971–72, the normal First Division player was on £200 a week, even the big stars. Spurs had several England inter-nationals, such as Martin Peters, who had been a World Cup star, plus Martin Chivers and Alan Mullery, and also a well-known, well-loved Scottish player, Alan Gilzean, and the famous Irish goalkeeper, Pat Jennings.

The average earnings for an average First Division player at the time was little more than double what a good carpenter or plumber was earning, or a minor office manager. They lived in £20,0000 semi-detached mock Tudor houses on new estates and drove modest Vauxhall or Ford cars. Only the top stars had a Jaguar.

I went to all their homes, met their wives, and got invited to their parties, but the biggest excitement for me was getting into the dressing room, before and after games. During the games, I sat on the bench with the coaches.

When they played abroad, and they were in the Uefa Cup

that year, it was assumed by the foreign club I was a proper, authorised member of the Spurs party, not just a hanger-on. In some foreign papers, in photos of the Spurs stars trying out the pitch the day before, I am described as one of the Tottenham players. Oh bliss.

I knew at the time I had wangled the most amazing access, and of course boasted about it to my friends. One of the players in my Sunday morning football team, my neighbour Dr John Carrier, a lecturer at LSE, suggested I do some proper surveys, getting every player to answer not just questions about football, but about their social and domestic life, wives, cars, houses, politics, holidays, superstitions, hopes and ambitions. He said it was so unusual to be able to do any personal research on a group of top sporting people, so I must make the most of it.

I did all the surveys face to face, asking all the personal questions when I was with them alone, as opposed to asking them to write down answers. Which of course rarely works. Some people never answer all the questions, or just muck around, giving very brief or silly answers. Doing them face to face, I could also do follow-up questions when anything unusual emerged.

One day in the dressing room at half-time, cups started flying. Bill Nicholson was furious with Martin Chivers for missing an open goal. I knew from private conversations with him that he was convinced Chivers was not working enough – in fact he felt all the England stars tried harder for England than they did with Spurs.

The flying cup was not in fact aimed at Chivers. It was just one that Bill had thrown to the floor in anger, but it skidded across the dressing room towards the naked Chivers. The other players were cowering, not wishing to be in the firing line. I retreated into a corner, trying to look invisible.

I immediately thought of a similar situation a few years earlier when I had been in the studio at Abbey Road during the *Sergeant Pepper* sessions. I had insinuated myself into actually sitting with them, while they worked, whereas normal visitors, such as wives and friends, sat up in the gallery with George Martin and the technicians. I knew how privileged I was, but sometimes I worried that one day, if there was a row between John and Paul, which was never far away by that time, they might turn on me, as a stranger, an interloper, and say Out, You, Gerr'out.

I remember thinking that day in the dressing with Spurs, as I had done with the Beatles, that if I do get chucked out from the inner sanctum, if my face does not fit any more for whatever reason, and I never get to finish the book, then I will still have had this unique experience. I will have seen from the inside, at first hand, my heroes at work.

Fortunately for me, I did not come a cropper. But I had a mild panic when *The Glory Game* was published and got serialised by two papers at the same time. The *Sunday Times*, surprisingly, still ran pieces from the book, despite having had a feature on Spurs the year before, and so did the *People*. They focused on the more sensational stuff, such as the bad language and various players drinking Bacardi all the way home after a game.

This upset some of the club's directors, believing it brought the club into disrepute. I got a legal letter from Goodman Derrick, the firm of Lord Goodman, one of the most feared lawyers of the day.

I was very worried, and so was the publisher. Lord Goodman might well get the book withdrawn while corrections were made. I managed to dig out copies of the finished typescript and discovered some pencil marks on the copy I had sent the chairman. As promised, I had let him see it in advance. I doubt if he had read it word for word, probably just the bits about himself, but I had proof that it had been submitted it to him as chairman and that he had raised no objections. I never heard from the lawyer again.

*The Glory Game* is still in print, all these decades later, in the UK and the USA. It was also published in Norway and Denmark. In some ways it is dreadfully out of date, with the players wearing flares, living in such humble houses, having no agents, but the surveys have proved endlessly fascinating. I have had countless requests from university students all over the world doing social studies degrees or sports science degrees who want to use my surveys in their theses. They always hope to be able to compare them with modern teams. No chance.

I went on to do many other football books, three on football history, a football novel, and for a while I did a sequence of ghosted football biographies.

I am trying not to jump too far ahead in this exciting narrative of my life, but on the subject of football, I find it hard not to think about a more recent book I did about a top player, and compare it with the lives of top players during the time of *The Glory Game* in 1971–72.

Over forty years later, in 2006, I read one day that Wayne Rooney's life story had been bought for £5 million, five books, to cover the rest of his playing life. Yet he was at the time only nineteen. I did a mocking piece in my *New Statesman* football column, which I have been writing since 1996, saying it was mad. Mozart or Shakespeare, nobody was publishing their memoirs when they were nineteen, the football world has gone potty.

On the Monday I got a call from HarperCollins saying I was on their shortlist to ghost Wayne's book – would I like to meet him? Brilliant idea, I immediately said, long overdue, should have been done ages ago.

I turned up at the HarperCollins boardroom where there was a row of suits, all impressive, with impressive titles – manager, accountant, lawyer, publicity and even a woman in a suit who turned out to be his brand manager, whatever that meant. There was also a hunk at the door, also in a suit, an ex-cop who was his personal bodyguard.

Wayne eventually arrived in his hoodie and trackie bottoms. He was endlessly polite and courteous. I explained how I would do the book, how I would want honesty, no lying, but I promised he could read it before anyone else, so if he felt something was going to hurt his mum or his aunty, he could change it. I asked if he had any memorabilia – and had to explain what that was.

I spent eight months interviewing him, going up to his lovely house, meeting the lovely Coleen. He was hard to do, in that I had to drag everything out of him. He was not stupid, just too young, not reflective, not at that stage in his life. It was mad, doing the biog of someone his age. And the book bombed. It was angled to a World Cup, and Wayne was injured and England were useless, as usual. All together I think it sold about 40,000 copies – whereas my Gazza biog has sold 400,000. But Gazza had had a lifetime of experience, not all of it wonderful, had retired from playing and was willing to tell everything.

I never heard Wayne swear, not in my presence. He did not call me Sir, but that was his attitude. I think as a child his mother would have given him a slap if he had ever been rude to an older person. Both he and Coleen come from strong, traditional Catholic families.

When I did the Beatles book, I asked all their mothers if they had any school reports or certificates. Only Ringo's mother could find a school report. With Gazza, Mrs Gazza thought she had a swimming certificate Paul had won aged eight. I said that would be gold dust. I pushed her into the loft but she never found it.

Mrs Rooney, on the day I went to see her at home, appeared in her uniform, having just finished her shift as a dinner lady at the comprehensive Wayne used to attend. She had laid out for me two piles, in order, in neat plastic folders. One contained all Wayne's school reports from the age of four at nursery onwards. Even more interesting, she had carefully kept every letter from Everton from the age of eight.

All top clubs are very secretive about their Academies and Centres of Excellence, so to get all his reports, instructions, timetables, personal assessments from eight to sixteen was most revealing. Well, it was to me. Even though the book failed, I like to think some of the memorabilia was fascinating for all football fans. Which I still am.

Football has given me such pleasure in life, playing it for so long, till I was fifty, which was silly, and watching it even longer, but also being able to write about it so often, getting away with turning my personal interests into professional work.

My hope for the future is that I will always have the strength to be able to turn the TV on every night of the week and watch a live game, while drinking Beaujolais.

# 13

# MARGARET

It was while I was editing the *Sunday Times Magazine* in 1975 that life suddenly stopped still.

I was being driven to work each day in a chauffeur-driven car, and then to the West End for lunch, dealing with all these famous photographers, such as Donald McCullin and Tony Snowdon. The well-known features writers included Bruce Chatwin and Jeffrey Bernard. Both of whom I let go. One because I didn't want any more purple prose and the other because he never handed in any sodding copy.

I had a big budget, a brilliant staff, we were the brand leader in our field, and even though I never got to grips with the art department, I was feeling quite a hell of a feller, rushing around, being busy. And then Margaret got cancer.

I can't now remember which day it was she first told me. Or what she said. Or what I said in reply. I do tend to shove bad things quickly out of my mind, put my head in the sand, hope it will not be true and will all go away.

It emerged that she had found a lump in her left breast. She did not admit it at first, until I discovered she had made an appointment to see our GP, Micky Day. She had been our friend now for fifteen years, always invited us to her election evening party, a northern lass we felt we had grown up with.

I then forced Margaret to reveal what she had found, and of course she was sure it was nothing, she had probably just imagined the lump.

Micky said at once that she had to go to the Royal Free to have it checked. The results came back quickly, too quickly, that it was malignant. The recommendation was a total mastectomy of her left breast.

Margaret was strangely, quietly, worryingly resigned. She had always felt something awful like this would happen one day. We had been too lucky in life. Three lovely children, a whole house and a nice garden to ourselves, country cottage, successful writing careers.

I had always been irrationally optimistic about almost everything. I saw only good things ahead. Even when logic suggested the opposite might well happen, or even was happening, I was ever hopeful. A state of irrational optimism is vital for a football fan, especially a fan of the England team, but in real, personal life it is probably best to be more realistic.

Margaret always saw the worst ahead, could imagine herself into a state when something awful had happened. She had always been able to put herself in that position, so when it did happen, it was as if she had been there already. This, she argued, put herself in a better position to cope, if and when it did. Unlike those with their silly, empty heads in the sand.

When it was decided surgery was the only way to treat it, I wanted to fight it, to argue the toss, get another opinion. It seemed so sudden and dramatic. Surely there must be other treatments. Just slice off a little bit, the offending bit, then wait and see what happens. Wouldn't that be best?

Margaret trusted the opinion and advice of the Royal Free medics. They knew best, it was their considered professional judgement, even though we had both instantly disliked the surgeon who was to do the operation. She seemed to me cold and brutal, a bit like that woman doctor who had thrown me around on our honeymoon when I had a boil.

In the hospital, this surgeon strode around with her team behind her like a drill sergeant major. In front of a group of her cowed students, she explained loudly, so the whole ward could hear, that Margaret was an unlikely candidate for breast cancer. She was only thirty-six, had breastfed three children for nine months each, had never smoked, and was otherwise fit and well and healthy. Yes, most unusual.

Which was not exactly reassuring. In fact it was like being damned and doomed. It suggested that Margaret was right; her good luck in life had run out.

Margaret was insistent that I carried on working. She would not be in hospital long. From having been deeply pessimistic when the news first broke, she was now being organised and realistic. She had already thought it all through, long before it happened. Which proved her theories worked. She would be back at home soon, running the house, looking after the children again, as she had always done.

Margaret had never had help in the house, of any sort, not even a cleaner. She hated the idea of telling some woman, who might be the age of her mother, to clean or dust. She preferred to do it on her own, despite having a big house, three children, and a writing life which many would have considered a full-time occupation, turning out a novel almost every year. Margaret, of course, did not regard her writing as a job. She was just playing. Her children came first.

Caitlin was by now eleven, Jake nine and Flora three. I normally took the older two to school each morning, before I went to work, leaving Flora with Margaret, but when she went into the Royal Free for the operation, we hired a nanny. Not a proper, trained one, but Janet, the daughter of the man who was now our builder, George Wilson, who had become our family friend. Janet was calm and sensible and agreed to come for a few weeks, look after Flora, pick the older ones up from school, do some gentle housework, till I got home from work. Margaret would return soon and be able to take on the full domestic and maternal load once again.

Just before Margaret was due to go under the knife, we heard the good news that Caitlin had got into Camden School for Girls. In 1975, there was still the eleven-plus in our borough, Camden, even though comprehensives had come in elsewhere in London, such as in Haringey. We knew it was coming soon to Camden, but in 1975 the dreaded eleven-plus hung over all local children in their last year at primary school. I had suffered from it, not getting into Carlisle Grammar School till I was sixteen.

After the operation, the surgeon declared that it was in fact not such a high-grade tumour. Having one breast off should now do the trick. Margaret probably would not need radiotherapy or chemotherapy. Whatever they were. All these were new terms to me. While in the Royal Free, by a piece of luck, without asking, Margaret was put into a room on her own after her operation. Nobody else had wanted it. She was able to make it as cheerful and homely as possible, with the children's drawings on the wall, her books, pen and ink and paper beside her. As soon as she had the strength, she started writing letters and notes.

When a nurse discovered she was writing in pen and ink, Margaret was told off, warned that ink would get onto the sheets. So Margaret was reduced to a biro. It was the first time she had ever written with a biro. She had always been snobbish about them, dismissing them as ugly, unattractive and messy.

As Janet helped out only during the day, I was responsible for our evening meals. Did I moan, never having cooked a thing in my life, not since I was about ten and cooked for my young brothers and sisters when my mother was in hospital. This was in 1946 and my speciality was potatoes and mince and lots of toast. In 1975 I moved on to the Hunter's Special, which all three of my children grew to hate. It consisted of ham and cheese on toast, with a poached egg on top. Yum, yum. Well I thought so.

When Margaret eventually came out, after three or so weeks, she was offered a breast reconstruction. Everyone had it, she was told. There were modern prostheses which were excellent, so they said. Margaret refused. The most she agreed to was some slight extra padding of her left bra, so that she did not feel unbalanced while dressing or walking.

She never discussed all these options or her decisions with me. But of course I observed her slightly padded bra and knew what she had done.

We had never anyway discussed personal things, especially of an intimate sexual nature. I would have done, given half a chance. I love going over my problems and ailments of any sort, from funny spots on my willy to backache.

It was part of her pride, her strength, not wanting to reveal weaknesses or worries. She preferred to keep private and personal things to herself. She had never believed the old cliché that a problem shared was a problem halved. She felt a problem was doubled, by sharing it. Other people would now know and one of them was bound to go on about it, ask about it, when she did not want to talk about it any more. What she really wanted, above all, was privacy.

Our love-making had always been in the dark, so truly, honestly, her lack of one breast did not put me off, did not distract me, or revolt me. But of course it did to her. She was convinced I would find her revolting and ugly and repellent. So it took a few months before she agreed. I told her I loved her just the same, and in the same way, as I had always done.

When I said this to her, hesitant and stumbling, scared to use the wrong words and upset her, her reaction was to snort, dismissing my protestations. I was lying, she said. She maintained she was now a horror show, how could anyone want to make love to her. She could not bear her own body any more, so how could anyone else?

But gradually, slowly, delicately, tenderly, we did return to a sort of normal married life.

Margaret started another book, a biography of Thackeray, and got a modest advance out of her publisher, Tom Rosenthal at Secker. With novels, she never took an advance, but with non-fiction, it entails a lot of time and research, so best to get some money up front.

I also did a biography, of George Stephenson the Railway King, and then a sequence of walking books – walking Hadrian's Wall, walking the Lake District.

Because of this we decided to buy a cottage in Cumbria. We had quickly sold our Oxfordshire weekend cottage when Margaret fell ill. We had enough to think about. But now after two or three years, she appeared fit and well again, back to normal, worrying more about her own parents and their health than her own. We started going up and down to Carlisle to see Margaret's parents, and also my mother. Taking our three children with us wasn't much fun, and a dreadful squash when staying with Margaret's mother or at my mother's house.

A few year earlier, they had moved out of their respective council houses when we bought them each a bungalow – next door to each other, which was pure chance. They happened to come up for sale, one after the other. We thought it would be handy when we were visiting them – handy for us, rather than them. I don't think they actually liked living next door to each other, being such different characters. Margaret's father Arthur was very abrupt and organised, neat and tidy, and he kept his garden immaculate, whereas my mother was the opposite, preferring to sit in her summer house reading Dickens with endless cups of tea rather than worry about the weeds.

We bought a small cottage at Park End near Caldbeck in 1977, just twenty minutes from Carlisle, within easy reach of going to see them. It was an eighteenth-century cottage, once part of the family home of John Peel, very small, two up and two down, rather dark, rather damp, but awfully atmospheric. It felt like being out in the wilds, surrounded by open fells. We went up there during all half terms and school holidays.

Halfway through Margaret's Thackeray biography, she happened to tell Tom, her publisher, that she had decided to do it in an unusual way. She was writing it in the first person. She would pretend that Thackeray himself was writing it, writing his own autobiography, but she would stick to the facts, stick to his language, his jokes and style and mannerisms, and use period drawings from his various books. A reader, not knowing, might well suppose Thackeray had really written it himself.

For over a year, Margaret had read every word Thackeray had ever written, books as well as letters and journalism. Before we had left Wardington, in Oxfordshire, she had bought a whole set of Thackeray's books from Lord Wardington, who was a neighbour. I had also bought some railway books from him for my George Stephenson book. (Lord Wardington was a Pease, a member of the Quaker family who had backed Stephenson and the early railways.)

When Margaret told Tom how she doing the Thackeray biog, Tom was very upset. This was not what he had commissioned. He wanted a normal, third-person biography. How would the trade describe it? How would the bookshops file it? As fact or fiction? I thought Tom was being silly, petty, and short-sighted. Seemed a brilliant idea, awfully avant garde. She should ignore him.

But Margaret did not even pause to argue. The moment Tom raised his first objections, and started moaning, she immediately said don't worry, I will give you back your advance, just forget it, sorry I spoke.

Which she did. Paying back the money she had already taken, sending off a cheque at once, without telling me or her agent, which naturally did not please him, as the paperwork got complicated.

I told her she was silly. But she was even sillier when a year later she had finally finished the book, doing it her way – and then offered it first to Tom. He of course jumped at it. I thought he had shown a total lack of confidence and support for his author, so she should have gone elsewhere.

It got good reviews. The critics understood and admired what she had done. Lit critics do tend to have degrees in English Lit, or similar, and are always reading the same biogs of the same old figures, so doing a biog in a different way appealed to them. It was not, however, a particularly good seller. So Tom's fears on that score proved correct.

In 1976, as a break from my northern-based books, I decided I would like to do something about comprehensive schools. Caitlin had started at Camden, which soon became comprehensive. In 1977, Jake started at William Ellis, formerly a grammar school, in the first year of their comprehensive intake. I had gone to lots of local meetings and was a supporter of the campaign for comprehensives – and even chaired one. I had a struggle to contain Fay Weldon, the author, and mother of three boys at local schools. She was on the speaking panel, and went on and on talking, all very amusing, but not quite relevant and I had a long agenda to work through.

I had at the time been looking for another Year in the Life of project, having done *The Glory Game*, which was the year in the life of a football team. The walking books had been essentially year-in-the-lives, walking for example Hadrian's Wall over the span of a year. What subject or place could I use as the setting for another year in a life?

I was a qualified teacher, oh yes, having got a postgraduate Diploma of Education at Durham, mainly to get out of national service. I was legally qualified to teach, but had only done a few weeks of teaching practice – and was useless. Unlike Margaret, who was an excellent teacher. No one messed with her.

I decided to find a true comprehensive, i.e. one which had been comprehensive for seven years, so all the pupils knew only the comprehensive system. Camden had only just begun, but Haringey, the next borough, was fully comprehensive.

I approached Creighton School in Muswell Hill, without knowing any of the staff. It turned out they had just acquired a new head teacher, but it was agreed I could follow the life of the school for a year, and also do some teaching.

The new head was Molly Hattersley, whom I had never met, the wife of Roy Hattersley, the Labour Cabinet Minister. It was pretty brave of her to allow me in, when she was still getting to grips with the school herself.

I enjoyed the year, found it all fascinating, liked the staff and the pupils, following their lives through a school year. I only did a few history lessons, which confirmed how useless I was. The big problem in all such books is how to shape it. You start off with the idea of covering a whole year, which sounds easy, as if it will write itself, but you end up with a mass of material, interviews, assorted and disconnected research notes. You have to form it into a narrative, so readers will read on, which of course academics don't have to bother about. So some people I had interviewed got dumped, some events were built up, as I tried to work up the running stories of the year.

I secured a very impressive introduction to the book written by a real academic educationalist, Maurice Peston, a London University professor – later Lord Peston, and father of the TV presenter, Robert Peston. He happened to be a close friend of Roy Hattersley's, which helped.

I was so impressed by the school, and the comprehensive system, that I decided to give away all proceeds from the book to the school itself. The copyright of the book is therefore the Creighton School Association.

Today, forty years later, the school is no more; at least it has changed its name and structure. It is now called Fortismere School. As Creighton has gone, it means that technically Haringey Council inherited the rights to the book. So if Hollywood comes along and wants to make a film of it, and stranger things have happened, then Haringey Council will get the money, not the school.

Margaret was soon as fit and well as she had always been, going on long walks, climbing high fells. With so many distractions, what with her books and my books, buying a Cumbrian cottage, the two older children starting secondary school, life had got busy and buoyant and beautiful again and the subject of cancer was never mentioned.

It never came up, in the house or with the children, for the simple reason that we had not told them. Margaret had not revealed it either to her parents, nor told my mother. When she had been in the Royal Free for those few weeks in 1975, we had simply told the children and our parents that Margaret was having an appendix out.

Our closest neighbours in the street knew, as of course we had needed their help at various times, and so did Margaret's sister, Pauline, and my sisters, Marion and Annabelle. But otherwise, Margaret did not want to talk about it to anyone, refer to it in any way, and as for writing about it, the very idea made her nauseous.

We never for one moment thought she had it beaten. She always knew there was no cure. All you can hope for was a remission, for months, or for years, if you were lucky.

Several articles in newspapers, then and now, do suggest people can bring cancer upon themselves, which of course is rubbish. People go on about 'fighting it', which is also non-sense. Margaret particularly hated all talk of it being a fight. Of course it isn't. It is a one-sided attack. You cannot fight it. You just have to live with it, be sensible, hope for the best.

The most depressing cancer stories to read in the newspaper are about people announcing they have 'been cured', closely followed by news of the latest miracle breakthroughs. When cancer comes into a family, you suddenly notice all these cancer stories which you had not been aware of before. The most depressing of all is when they produce statistics to prove that with all the different types of cancer, the success rate in the UK is rubbish, usually around the twentieth position in a list of thirty European countries, miles behind Scandinavia and even Eastern Europe. In the end, we decided to give up reading them all.

*

In late 1977, Margaret's cancer returned. This time it was in her right breast. The prognosis was more serious. There was no talk this time of how unusual it was for it to happen to such a healthy person. The cancer had spread to lymph glands so there was no alternative but another mastectomy.

Micky Day, our GP, had been on holiday when the final decisions were being made for the first mastectomy. But when she heard about Margaret's experience with the Royal Free, she said that Margaret had to go into the Marsden, the specialist cancer hospital, situated in the Fulham Road, in Chelsea.

I moaned a bit, after I looked at the map, realising how hard it was going to be, for appointments and visits, and then getting back for the children. But from the very beginning, Margaret loved her surgeon, Mr McKinna, and was willing to put up with any inconveniences. He was a small, smiley, pawky Ulsterman, gentle and kind, always exhausted-looking, but not at all off-hand or fierce, as the Royal Free surgeon had been.

I went with Margaret for the initial appointments and he did not give her any false hopes, explaining how serious it was, surgery might not work, the cancer might return again quite soon. She would need at least six months of chemotherapy after the operation.

Conditions at the Marsden were far less pleasant than the Royal Free. Building work was going on, some wards were closed, there were queues everywhere. She was not in a room on her own but shoved into a large cancer ward where people were lying with their faces half cut away, some were screaming in pain, some were dying, and the whole situation was a nightmare, just what you don't want when you are going through your own nightmares. But throughout it, Margaret had total faith and perhaps even took pleasure in Mr McKinna's gentle touch and calmness.

I have just found some notes I wrote each day in January 1978, while Margaret was in the Marsden. They are full of details of the endless delays, the blood tests, the biopsies, results getting lost, waiting in agony, trying to work out what it all means, what we should do.

The descriptions of the other patients were even more horrific than I had remembered – patients screaming, coughing up blood, nurses shouting at them to shut up.

I had also forgotten how long drawn out it had been before the actual operation. There had been endless tests and delays and discussions during the whole of December. Then of course nothing happened during the Christmas holidays, which at least meant we could have as normal a Christmas as possible, without ruining it for the children.

On 3 January, I wrote in my diary notes that M seems so well and fit and healthy, as if she was waiting to go in for a voluntary op, one that was not strictly necessary. But on the other hand, after almost three years since the last one, we were now back to square one. And now she did know what to expect.

I did mention the word mastectomy one day in talking to Margaret. She was quite upset. She thought she had banned that word from my lips or her lips. 'It was a glimpse of her being worried,' so I wrote, 'but trying to convince herself there might be hope.'

On 11 January 1978, she had the right breast removed. So now she had had a double mastectomy.

I took Caitlin, aged thirteen, Jake, aged eleven, and Flora, five, into the Marsden to see her. How can I have done that, when the place was a nightmare? I assume I wanted to prove to them that Margaret was alive and well, that she did exist, that it was just another routine op and she would be out soon.

When I arrived, Margaret slipped me a handwritten note – telling me on no account to make any comments about how she looked, which of course was awful.

I took Flora a second time, as she was harder to leave at home, and she was fascinated by all the machinery and all the drains. Jake declined. He could not bear to go again.

On 18 January, I went to see Margaret on my own, and wrote down what was happening.

M still worried that lab reports had not arrived, but looking better for once, sleeping more, thanks to strong sleeping pills and Brenda (the woman in the next bed who screamed) had been quietened.

That night McKinna himself rang me at home. Some good and some not good news. Out of the 20 lymph glands he took out, two are bad with secondaries in them. So bad news. It means it's spreading. But he says the rest are ok and shows her body is fighting. So better news. She will go on chemo for six months to stop the spread.

She's to take pills for six month. They will decide which pills 'by taking them out of a hat'. His actual words. They are trying out various types of drugs for people at this stage, to find which works best. Sounds appalling and scary. I ask how on earth they will they know which has worked. We

Margaret and I got married on 11 June 1960, in Oxford. Just two other people were there – Mike Thornhill and Theo Parfit, standing behind. The wedding snaps were taken in the back garden of Theo's family home.

Also in 1960 I joined the *Sunday Times*, eventually running the Atticus column. I gave it up in 1967 and had my photo taken with others who had written the column. Left to right: Philip Oakes, me, Robert Robinson, Godfrey Smith, Sacheverell Sitwell.

With the Beatles, 29 August 1967, on the train to Bangor with the Maharishi. It was the weekend that Brian Epstein died. Left to right: me, Paul, Ringo, John, the Maharishi, plus the back of George's head.

Paul McCartney and his new girlfriend, Linda, came to stay with us in Portugal in December 1968. Left to right: me, our son Jake in arms, Linda, Paul, Margaret. Note her Vidal Sassoon-style haircut. Linda's daughter, Heather, is in front and our daughter Caitlin.

Ace *Sunday Times* journalist H. Davies, left, on some exciting job in the Sixties with friend and photographer Frank Herrmann.

Some of the authors of the novel I created, *I Knew Daisy Smuten*, all on the *Sunday Times* in 1970, when I was women's editor. I am kneeling. Behind me is Jilly Cooper.

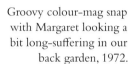

Margaret and me at the swings on Hampstead Heath, 1968. Spot Caitlin, aged four, and Jake, aged two, in the pipe.

No, it's not George Best, it's me taking the children to school, 1970.

Groovy colour-mag snap with Margaret looking a bit long-suffering in our back garden, 1972.

Dartmouth Park United, the Sunday morning Dads' team I helped to found, 1975. I am in front row, fourth left. My son Jake, aged ten, is standing rather squashed at the back. Two of our stars later became lords – Melvyn Bragg, back row, fourth from right, and Bernard Donoughue, back row, second on left.

Happy Family snaps – Caitlin, me, Margaret, Jake, 1970.

Wardington Cycling Club, 1974, where we had for a while a country cottage – me, Caitlin, Flora, Margaret, Jake in front.

Our Christmas card, 1972, taken by Frank Herrmann, with us pretending to wear Edwardian clothes. Flora, on Margaret's lap, had just been born. Me, standing, with Jake, left, and Caitlin.

The children grown up, 1990, posing beautifully to please Mummy and Daddy – Jake standing, left, then me; Flora sitting left, Margaret and Caitlin.

Margaret looking pensive on a broken dry stone wall at our Lakeland house, 1989.

Me on Hadrian's Wall, 1974, working on a book and a TV film about walking the wall.

Our Lakeland house at Loweswater, which we had from 1987 to 2016. We lived and worked there half of each year.

We treated ourselves to the West Indies for my fiftieth birthday, in 1986. Never realised at the time that me and Margaret were wearing matching tops. Such co-ordination.

With two of our four granddaughters – Ruby, left, and Amelia, on a family holiday in Crete, 2006.

Famous people meeting me, sorry I mean the other way round. With former prime minister Tony Blair, on his election battle bus, 2001. He just happens to be holding up one of my excellent books, which I just happened to have given him.

With Wayne Rooney, my literary colleague, working on his autobiography, 2006.

The Queen, about to graciously give me an OBE, 2014.

Outside Buckingham Palace with Flora, Jake and Caitlin. Margaret refused to come.

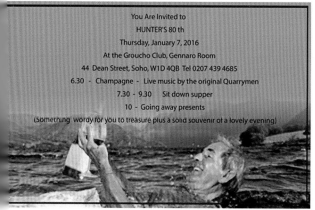

You Are Invited to
HUNTER'S 80 th
Thursday, January 7, 2016
At the Groucho Club, Gennaro Room
44 Dean Street, Soho, W1D 4QB Tel 0207 439 4685
6.30 - Champagne - Live music by the original Quarrymen
7.30 - 9.30    Sit down supper
10 - Going away presents
(Something wordy for you to treasure plus a solid souvenir of a lovely evening)

Margaret was still alive, if only just, for my eightieth birthday party at the Groucho Club in 2016. Not that she would have gone to such a boring, showing-off event anyway . . .

One of the last photos of Margaret, taken in 2015 at Loweswater, in our garden with the matching rhodies.

Margaret's gravestone with snowdrops, in Loweswater churchyard, taken on the first anniversary of her death, 8 February 2017.

Me, that same day, on our memorial seat on Hampstead Heath. We had it erected with an inscription on 11 June 1985 to mark our twenty-fifth wedding anniversary, choosing the spot carefully and amusingly – with a silver birch behind.

get into slight hassle as he tries to explain to me what it means, which I can't follow.

Margaret is going straight on the drugs tomorrow and, if ok, will come out on Friday. The drugs will have side effects, but not much of her hair should fall out.

I am in tears after the phone call. For once I felt utterly broken. We had got used to this awful new stage, having to have another mastectomy, got our minds accustomed to it, had all the bad news, assimilated it, learned almost to live with it, thinking once this is over and she is out and gets fit, life can carry on.

Now I know it just goes on. Life could not be worse. How could it be worse? Apart from being dead. The next butchery can only be worse than the two so far.

Later M rings. She has been told what McKinna told me. She sounds awful. She is ringing because she said she would. She has nothing to say. So there is silence. I try to chatter, saying the source of the primary has now gone, the bad glands cut out, so surely there is nowhere it can come from next time ...? But I am not very convincing. It is clear to both of us that it is spreading, and going to spread, whatever happens. M is dreading the chemo.

Somehow I go straight to sleep, but wake at 5, feel awful, get up and make tea, eventually get back to bed, but never get back to sleep.

Flora is the only nice thing in the whole world that I can think about. But I worry that when she and Caitlin are older, the same will happen to our two daughters. Despite myself, and our vows, I have read all the stories about breast cancer running in families.

Sometime after the operation, Margaret was given an appointment again to see the prosthesis people, to get fitted it up with, well, whatever they might suggest.

This time, she decided to have nothing, not even a padded bra. Having two breasts off, it meant she was balanced. So why pretend. She took to wearing long loose jumpers and in bed a loose night shirt, which she never took off.

Six weeks after the operation, and before she started on the chemotherapy, we went up to Caldbeck, to open up the cottage, now that some building work had been finished. It was just the two of us, me and Margaret, staying at the cottage for a few days. My sister Marion had agreed to stay in our house and look after the children for a long weekend.

We explored all the walks around and over the Caldbeck fells, most of which we did not know. We did nothing too energetic, and slowly Margaret did appear to be getting her strength back.

Back in London, the chemo lasted nine months, not six. Her white blood cells fell, which meant delays and endless blood checks. Her hair did not fall out, despite the threat of it, but she felt sick and tired most of the time. But, as she kept on saying to anyone who commented, you do feel tired most of the time with three young children. As before, we did not tell the children the truth about what had happened, or her parents, or most people.

It was only many years later that Caitlin, our oldest, revealed to us that aged eleven, a kind girl in her class had said to her one day, 'Your mum's got cancer, that's why she's in hospital.'

Caitlin did not believe it, she said, and so ignored it, so she said. But the fact that she did not tell us about it at the time suggests she might have been worried that there was some truth in it, but did not want to know the truth. A bit like me really.

As the months and then years went by, I grew to believe it wasn't true either. I wiped it from my mind. Margaret seemed so healthy and fit again, just as she used to be, much fitter than me, climbing all the fells, waiting on the tops for me to come up, panting. Once again she would carry our little rucksack on our long walks, except when going past houses. Then I would carry it, just for show, trying not to look like a wimp.

She would stride away, her back straight, her gait perfect, slim and athletic-looking with her marvellous skin and healthy glow, compared with me, all hunched, shambling, moaning and groaning, how long to go, Marg, are we nearly there yet, Marg? In the next few years, no stranger, seeing her striding over the fells, would ever have guessed what had happened to her.

It was all history. Something that happened to another person, in another life. That's how I saw it, that's how I coped.

According to Margaret, I was in denial. What's wrong with that, I would say. I have wiped it from my mind. Which I had.

And that's how it went on. Year after year. There was no sudden recurrence this time. The double mastectomy seemed to have sorted it. So we settled down, got back to our living and working and family routines, while I, as ever, looked forward to many more years of married bliss and happiness.

# 14

# Family Affairs

When you are the oldest in a family, you don't really spend much time thinking or worrying about your younger brothers and sisters. They are just there, hanging about, getting in the way, or so you often think. You are expected to look after them, look out for them, so your parents or teachers might tell you, or people assume, but you try to ignore that.

They look up to you, and also in the sense of looking forward, to what you are doing now and what they might be doing at your age, yet knowing you will always be older than them, ahead of them. But you don't really look back to them. You are too concerned with your own self, your own life.

In my case, I was off and away at the age of eighteen to university, and never returned. When I did, I was a different person from the one I had been, doing different things, with a different life, with very little in common with my family any more. So I thought.

The twins, Marion and Annabelle, three years younger than me, had to share the burden of my father as he got more and more ill, and worse tempered, throwing his food around till he died, in 1958, aged fifty-three.

Their lives, and my mother's life, began to change for the better after that. In the 1960s, there was eventually a phone in the house, a washing machine, an immersion heater so we had hot water and could have a bath, all things we never had when I was growing up there in the forties and fifties.

The twins both left school in Carlisle, the Margaret Sewell, aged fifteen, with no qualifications. The school did do GCE O-levels, at sixteen, as my school did, but they were not put in for it, not being in the A stream. Annabelle left and went into a bookmaker's office. Marion went into a tyre factory.

Marion then announced she was emigrating to Australia as a £10 emigrant with another girl, which upset my mother. She had a fantasy that now my father was dead, her girls would be her best friends in life and never leave home. She often slept with them, even as teenagers and young adults. They did love her of course, felt sorry for her, but it must have become uncomfortable and cloying, hence Marion wanting to get away.

Marion got all the emigration papers but at the last minute her friend met somebody and wanted to get married. Marion did not fancy going to Australia on her own, so lost her £10.

She then met Jeff, a male nurse, and they got married and moved to a very nice house in St Aidan's Road, near the river and near the football ground. Jeff had gone to a sec mod but started taking courses, often staying with us in London while attending some college. He eventually qualified as a sister tutor, teaching nursing to nurses.

Annabelle had already moved to London, getting a job in the Guildhall in the City of London, and shared a very smart flat with three others girls in Chelsea. She then met and married Roger, a Yorkshireman, who had gone to grammar school and then into the civil service. He didn't have a degree, so it took him a while to advance, but then he began to move up the civil service grades. For a time he was working for Shirley Williams in the House of Commons in the 1970s, when she was a Minister in Harold Wilson's Government. He was her private secretary, preparing answers for her on trade matters.

He then got posted to California, a really glamorous appointment, something you do not expect to fall into the lap of a humble civil servant. He was made the UK commercial consul in San Francisco, spending two years setting up a British trade fair which Princess Alexandra came to open.

Afterwards, back in England, back in Whitehall, he became unwell, staggering and shaking, all the symptoms my father had displayed all those decades ago. After endless tests and treatments, it was confirmed that he had multiple sclerosis, just as my father did. So my sister Annabelle twice in her life had to witness a loved one suffering the same awful disease.

Roger struggled on for years, going by train from their home in Leighton Buzzard in a wheelchair, travelling in the guard's van, where he was often left if the message had not got through to the station staff about which train he was on. He ran a campaign for his Whitehall office to install ramps, to accommodate disabled workers like him.

He was honoured with an OBE and retired not long afterwards. He was confined to a wheelchair at home, unable to move himself, but he still managed to study for an Open University degree. I never had anything but awe and admiration for him and how he coped. And also for my sister

Annabelle. She used to come on holiday with us, and her two children, Ross and Lindsey, when Roger could get into a care home for a week. Annabelle, who had long given up office work, somehow managed to retrain as a teacher. She then got a job in a large comprehensive, teaching office studies and typing.

Marion meanwhile remained in Carlisle but she too decided to get some qualifications. It was being presented at work with an ornamental tyre, to mark her ten years working in Tyre Services, that made her think, what I am doing with my life, there must be more to life than this.

So she started studying for A-levels at the local tech, after work each day. She and Jeff had no children. She had helped him while he had retrained, going off to college in London, now it was his turn to support and encourage her.

She got through her A-levels and then some union official at work suggested she should try for Oxford – and blow me, she got in, to study social sciences at Ruskin College. This is the trade union college, mainly for mature students, but still a proper part of Oxford University. She hoped her studies, if she passed, would lead her to become a social worker.

Meanwhile Johnny, my little brother, five years younger, had left school and become an apprentice electrician. At twenty-one, when he was qualified, he got paid off. He then got a job for the Carlisle State Management, which owned all the public houses in the region. From there he got a job in a local approved school, looking after the boys.

Johnny was very blond when young, and always big and

strapping, unlike me, so the boys in the home did not mess him around. Part of his job was to teach them basic electrical work. He did it so well, enjoyed it so much, that it was suggested he should have proper training. By this time he was married to Marjorie and they had two children, Simon and Clare. So off he went to study at Newcastle Polytechnic, now part of Newcastle University, in order to become a residential social worker, never in his working life till then having written anything apart from his time sheet.

So, by the end of the 1970s, my two sisters and my brother, with none of the fast-track educational advantages I supposedly had had in life, had all become mature students and were now doing useful jobs, which society needed, helping the community. Compared with me, a jobbing author and hack, writing so-called funny columns or books about football, which the world was not exactly crying out for. I was contributing very little to the general good of society. Unlike them.

When Marion was at Oxford, she was seduced by a female tutor. She had not realised till then she was a lesbian. She immediately told all her friends, and her husband, proud to be gay and out. But she did not tell our mother. That would have been a step too far. My mother's general health was deteriorating and this would have worried and confused her, when she was already becoming highly confused.

Marion returned to Carlisle after Oxford, working as a social worker, but Carlisle in the 1970s, like most other small provincial towns, was a bit limited in its facilities or venues for lesbians to meet each other. It meant she had to go to places like Newcastle to mix with like-minded people.

So she decided to come to London. She applied to Camden and got a job as a social worker, soon rising to become a team leader.

Margaret and I had encouraged her to come to London, assuring her she would be bound to have a better social and personal life and a working life. We said that she could stay with us for a few weeks, till she found somewhere to live and got sorted. Which of course was not easy, even in the 1970s.

I then did something which made Margaret absolutely furious. I bought another house in our street. Not quite as nice as ours, as the garden was smaller and it did not have a garage or exit at the back, but all the same, a similar three-storey mid Victorian house in what had become a very desirable street. It came with two lots of sitting tenants, with only the ground floor vacant, and was a bargain. So much of a bargain I have now forgotten how much I paid, but I think about £20,000.

Margaret said I was stupid, taking on sitting tenants, when our own tenant, Mrs Hall, had driven me mad for so many years. And also by offering Marion the ground floor flat we were influencing her decision about coming to London.

It seemed to me a perfect solution, the best way to help her out, give her independence yet be near us. I remembered how fraught my early months in London had been, sleeping on people's sofas, not knowing anyone, or my way around in London. Margaret had never had to do that, being able to live with me in my flat, however much she criticised it, the moment she left Oxford.

I was also attracted by the price. Local house prices were shooting up all the time and I could see no sign of them coming down, ever. It seemed an obvious bargain.

There is, hidden not far away inside me, an entrepreneur wanting to get out, to do deals, snap up bargains. The reason why I had done that novel about Jake Sullivan was that I was fascinated by property developers. There were even more of them now, springing up all over London, buying and developing houses and blocks, ducking and diving, using rents to pay the mortgage on the next acquisition.

I was not going to borrow, or get a mortgage. I had spent little of the Beatles income during the seven years after we returned to London, but gradually I had started spending. There had been a bungalow each for the parents, then our cottage in Cumbria, always paying cash in order to get the best price.

I have never had any interest in shares or unit trusts or any of the other obvious investments which people with spare cash go for and which so-called experts advise. I reckoned that bricks and mortar would always be a good buy. Secondly, I wanted to be in total control of my own investments, not have someone else creaming off percentages, or playing with my money. If this meant headaches, as Margaret predicted, having to mend leaks, having tenants moaning, then I would just have to cope. So I merrily, hopefully, wilfully imagined.

Margaret never had any interest in money or investments or buying stuff, least of all buying another house, when we already had more than enough. Forgot to mention we had our Portuguese house which we had bought in 1970, the year after we came back, a small, new-built terrace cottage in Porto de Mos, which Alison our friend had taken us to see and said, look, you must buy it at once, just look at that wonderful beach down below. So we did. Cost us £4,000.

I had gone rather mad, carried away by a passion for property. It seemed such an obvious and sensible thing, if you had the money, but I did not tell many people about buying the other house in our street, nor did Margaret, who was embarrassed if not ashamed of me as a landlord and property owner. My argument was that we didn't have pensions, as I had long left the *Sunday Times* staff. Margaret never had one, as she was never properly employed (when teaching, she was a supply teacher). I felt that if we ever fell on hard times, and nobody wanted our books – or even more likely, one of us might be ill for years and need constant care, which after the double mastectomy seemed a bit more likely – well then, we would sell one or all of the properties and live on that. It was our security for the future, for us and our little family. I was just being a good sensible husband and father. Margaret was not convinced.

I have forgotten to mention the flat in Swain's Lane, which Mrs Hall was still living in. That had gone up in value, so I was no longer regretting having to buy it. So in total, counting the bungalows where our parents lived, I was the owner of seven different properties. What a capitalist pig.

The house I bought further down our street had only one floor vacant, which Marion moved into. Above her, I had two old ladies, sisters, and they did drive me mad with constant complaints about sink problems and leaks and dodgy ceilings. On the top floor was a single man, a parky on the Heath, who looked after the men's open-air pool. He was very nice, never moaned or complained or demanded. He agreed, after a few years, to accept a lump sum to go, give up his sitting tenancy. It was his suggestion. He had found a small place of his own to buy. So I did him a good turn, enabling him to pay a deposit and become a property owner.

Marion eventually moved out to Crouch End, buying a flat of her own, and I helped her with the deposit. And then she met someone and they lived together from then on.

But then the most surprising thing happened. After several years as a team leader for Camden Social Services, she suddenly started writing about being a team leader. I never knew she had aspirations to be a journalist or a writer, had seen nothing she had ever written, or any evidence that she had been trying.

She suddenly appeared as a weekly columnist in the *Guardian*, in their Society supplement, writing a very funny column called Leader of the Pack, by Mary Black. I didn't even know about it, till she had had it accepted. She had sent off three columns, on spec, out of the blue, with no contacts, which they accepted and started using every week.

During the three years she did the column, from 1991–4, she never met anyone from the *Guardian*. No one from the paper told her that last week's column was good. No one asked what her column would be about next week. No one said come and have lunch. She never even knew if her column, which she posted each week, had arrived, till she saw it in the paper.

The style of the column was staccato, short sentences, flat, but very effective. It was based on her real experiences as a team leader, dealing with the members of her team as well as the clients and their problems. All names were changed; nobody could be identified, least of all herself. She had chosen the name Mary Black because that was the maiden name of our grandmother, our mother's mother. Mary Black also turned out to be the name of a well-known Irish singer, which Marion didn't know when she began. She had to use a pseudonym because Camden Social Services would not of course have allowed her to write anything about her work.

I once went to see Glenys Kinnock, wife of Neil, then leader of the Labour Party, at their semi-detached house in Ealing. When I arrived, Glenys was sitting reading the *Guardian* – and by chance had it open at the Society section, on the page with Leader of the Pack, by Mary Black.

I asked her if she had read that column and she said oh yes, she always did. I told her it was my sister, and explained about her life and career – working in the factory, then Ruskin, and how now, aged nearly fifty, she had suddenly emerged as a journalist.

I would have gone mad, writing a column for three years with no encouragement or interest from the office. I need recognition and encouragement if not applause, even when I have just written my name at the top of the page. She had of course come to it as an outsider, late in life, from another world, not knowing what to expect in the wonderful world of journalism. So she just accepted being ignored.

I remember a few years earlier, about 1983, being at a supper party at Joan Bakewell's house when James Cameron was one of the guests. Born 1911, he was one of the most distinguished foreign correspondents and broadcasters of the post-war years. He worked for many years on the *Daily Express*, covering Vietnam and other major wars, then joined the BBC and became an award-winning documentary maker and presenter. In 1957, he had been one of the founder members of CND – the Campaign for Nuclear Disarmament – along with Bertrand Russell, J. B. Priestley and Canon Collins, which had enormous influence in the UK and all over the world, being the beginning of an international peace movement.

By the time I met him, in the early 1980s, Cameron was getting on a bit but was still working, writing a regular column in the *Guardian*, which was much liked by the paper's readers and admired by other journalists. At the supper, I was surprised when he started moaning about the *Guardian*, saying nobody ever contacted him, nobody said his column was good. I was amazed at the time, that someone so distinguished should be treated like this – and also surprised that someone who had done so much, achieved so much, should care so much. From then on I always used to tell younger journalists that as long as it gets in the paper, that means they like it. Don't expect telegrams.

When James Cameron died, in 1985, the *Guardian* cleared the pages, devoting acres of space to saying how marvellous he had been, how proud they were to have had him as a columnist.

So Marion's treatment, just a few years later, was clearly typical of the *Guardian*, even with a newcomer, a total beginner, treating them as if they didn't exist.

After three years of doing her team leader column in the *Guardian*, Marion decided that next she would do a lesbian column, a funny one. I encouraged her, but wondered if the world was ready yet for such a column, even in the *Guardian*.

She had also written a stage play, which got put on at the ICA and later became a BBC radio play, with a very good director, Claire Grove. While doing her column and her play, she was still working every day as a social worker.

I do like it when people take hold of their lives, change direction, do something totally different. I often used to think there must be something else I can do in life, apart from shifting words, something I should try, before it is too late. Apart from being a mini property magnate.

The other house I bought in our street, which had an empty flat when Marion moved out to live with her partner in Crouch End, ended up being very useful, despite what Margaret had predicted.

For about ten years, my mother had clearly begun to wander, mentally and physically, getting lost every time she went into town in Carlisle. She had always had a poor sense of direction. Just like me.

Once while visiting us in London, when Caitlin was little, my mother insisted on taking Caitlin to the Heath in the pram. She went off – and just disappeared. She had gone for hours, so we rang the police. She had wandered off in completely the wrong direction. She was eventually found lost and confused in the back streets of Archway.

I rang her up once, at her bungalow in Carlisle, and said, 'Hi Mum, it's me, Hunter.'

'Oh, Hunter doesn't live here any more,' she replied. And hung up.

We had had a sequence of local carers in Carlisle coming in to look after her in her bungalow, till we realised she was becoming a danger to herself. So we decided she would be better off in London, with us, or near us. We could not very well accommodate her in our house, with three children still at home. So the ground floor of our other house down the street, once Marion had moved out, proved perfect for her. And us. We could just pop along at any time and see how she was.

As her Alzheimer's got worse, we had a sequence of round-the-clock carers, going in night and day to look after her. One of those on the night shift was a Sister from La Sainte Union Convent round the corner on Highgate Road, a lay worker, but she wore a nun's habit. She was Irish and very kind and willing, if a bit slow.

She had answered an advert I had put in the window of the local newsagent, and naturally I was surprised when a nun turned up. When she began, she insisted I had to pay her in cash and not to tell anyone at the Convent that she had a wee job, or that she got paid in cash. I never found out if she was spending the cash at the bookies or on Guinness or sending it back to Ireland.

So buying the house turned out to have been a useful thing to do, as it helped not just my sister Marion but my mother. My mother's deteriorating condition, which we were now observing at first hand, also provided something else. It gave Margaret the basis for a novel, *Have the Men Had Enough?*

The novel was about a woman with Alzheimer's, at a time when such people were rarely written about in fiction. Margaret seldom, if ever, based any of her novels on real-life events or real people, as opposed to her non-fiction.

It got good reviews and won some awards. I always thought it was one of the best and most moving novels Margaret ever wrote. And also funny.

Margaret could be witty in real life, and in her letters she always managed to find some amusing story or funny dialogue, even if she made some of it up, but in her serious fiction, she rarely allowed herself any comedy. She left that to the Davies side of the family, to me and to Marion, who despite being a late starter had turned out to be a witty writer. Well, we both thought we were funny . . .

## 15

# NOW FOR SOMETHING DIFFERENT

And then I became a publisher. Among other things.

Being a publisher was one of several new projects and amusements I first took on in the 1980s. I suppose I could have bought a fast car, moved to a posh house in Hampstead, started a proper property company, or even bought some decent clothes, the sort of supposedly modern gear I often acquired in the sixties, but I didn't fancy any of that.

I gave up my regular *Sunday Times* work around 1980, the one I had been doing roughly six months of each year during the seventies, and soon hankered after doing something else, now and again, instead of just sitting at my desk writing books.

When I finished on the *Sunday Times Magazine*, I was so relieved not to have to go to an office ever again, not to have to waste all that time travelling, listening to people chuntering on, moaning about their secretary, their expenses, the size of their office, their dopey ideas for an amazing story which would mean them flying to Cuba this very afternoon.

But after a few months at home, writing away every day, all on my own, I began to realise there was one thing I missed – lunch.

I was moaning on about this when Margaret said why not organise your own lunches? I had already organised my own football team, Dartmouth Park United, which played only a few hundred yards away on the Heath, at a time of my convenience, with me as captain, picking my own team. I think they allowed me to score all the goals as well.

I sat down and in thirty minutes had made a list of forty writers I either knew or knew of who lived within two miles, all of whom were working from home and probably, like me, interested in a regular lunch with fellow hacks, at which we could rubbish agents and publishers.

Only two out of the forty said definitely no. One was A. J. P. Taylor, the eminent historian, who lived two streets away. He said if I was organising a regular dinner, he would come, but he no longer ate lunch. David Cornwell (John le Carré) said he would rather meet his fellow writers in the next world, not this world.

I booked a room in a cheapo Greek restaurant at Camden Town, near the Tube, which I thought would be handy for most people. The idea was that once invited, you were invited forever, on the last Wednesday of every month, even if you never showed up for months or even years. And you could bring another writer.

The first lunch, on 30 March 1983, was packed, with lots of drinking and shouting and eating. Those attending included Margaret Drabble, Joan Bakewell, Kingsley Amis, Eva Figes, John Hillaby. Later writers who attended included Martin Amis, Julian Barnes, Salman Rushdie. One of the visiting writers was Jessica Mitford, over from the USA.

After the first lunch, I got a distraught phone call from a young novelist, who had just had her first novel out to great acclaim, to say she would not be coming to the next lunch. She could only afford £5 a week to keep herself alive – and she had spent it all on that one meal.

I had decided at the first meal that we would divide the whole bill exactly by the number of people. Just to keep it simple. What I had not realised was that Kingsley Amis had drunk whisky all the way through, practically doubling the drinks bill. From then on, only the food was divvied up. You had to pay for your own drinks.

The lunches went on every month for several years – though it later moved to a Hampstead restaurant in the High Street called Fagin's. The hardcore members by then were mainly Hampstead-based, and mainly women, such as Bernice Rubens. I had given up attending by then. A new job I had acquired, at about the same time as I started the lit lunches, had suddenly changed its timetable and I could no longer go on Wednesdays from then on. That was our recording day. The lunches fizzled out after about ten years.

This new job was on the radio, presenting BBC Radio Four's *Bookshelf* programme. In 1983, out of the blue, the producer in charge of it, Helen Fry, rang up and said I was on their shortlist to present it, would I come for an audition.

Margaret and I had always listened to *Bookshelf*. Then, as well as now, regular programmes about books were few and far between, so if books are your main occupation in life, you would obviously want to listen to them. And *Bookshelf* was the best, a programme totally devoted to books. Frank Delaney, who had a wonderful Irish voice, and was so fluent, was giving up presenting *Bookshelf* to do more TV work.

I had been on the programme once or twice when I had a new book coming out and had enjoyed it, but never thought I was very good at it, not being fluent enough, going off at tangents, not being able to act. I had always gone through life thinking I had a rotten voice. Not just the accent, but a tendency to gabble, speak too quickly, which is what the editor of the *Cumberland News* had told me when he turned me down for a job when I was a student.

My Carlisle accent had faded, after all these years in London, not deliberately losing it, as Joan Bakewell ditched her northern accent when she went to Cambridge, but it just disappeared with time. I was still taken, and still am, for a northerner, but no one can ever identify the original location.

In my Durham days, even when I became Senior Man of the Junior Common Room, and conducted JCR meetings, I envied all those people, usually public schoolboys, who were such natural, effortless talkers. At the *Sunday Times*, it was full of very plausible, immensely fluent people, many of whom I dismissed as chancers, but they were impressive.

At home, Margaret was always telling me I was mumbling, asking me to repeat things, which was very annoying. Or saying to me, please, can you just not talk for ten minutes. Stop chuntering on. Let's have some peace and quiet.

So I was surprised when Helen Fry was interested in me. And presumably my voice. I was given a sound test, and then offered the job, but she made it clear it would take time to knock me into shape.

In the early weeks of interviewing authors, one of the things all the producers did, while sitting behind the glass panel, would be to put their hands to their faces and open their mouths wide. This was to indicate that I should smile, especially when I was reading stuff out. I never realised how just the act of smiling, in a studio, where you are not seen, does affect the way the words come out. Listening to radio now, I can always tell when presenters are putting on their phoney smiles, to sound, well, smiley. Mariella Frostrup, though an excellent broadcaster, does seem to me to overdo the smiling, till I find myself screaming at her STOP SMILING!

I also had a terrible habit of interrupting people, or going hmmm, yeh, hmm, when they were talking, waiting for them to pause, so I could get my oar in, which you should never do as an interviewer. You can nod and smile at an interviewee, but you must not make any mumbling sounds.

I presented *Bookshelf* for three years, from 1983–6, and worked with some excellent, creative producers, such as Simon Elms, though he did drive me mad at times as he was so thorough. Unlike me. We did a feature once about Arthur Ransome and Simon insisted we rowed across Lake Coniston to an island, just to get the real sound of rowing across Coniston to get to an island. I said must we? Surely you can dub on the sound effects afterwards? But he insisted.

I went with Simon to the USA where we did several good features, such as one about the Harry Ransom Center in Texas, which has one of the world's best collections of literary manuscripts. And also locks of hair from famous authors.

Back in the 1980s, BBC Radio could afford to take great pains with even the simplest little radio feature. There was a large staff in our department, which was called Archive Features, and producers were given lots of time and facilities to get things right.

I would spend a whole day once a week interviewing three authors, usually in the studio, sometimes out on location. I liked to take at least forty minutes talking to each of them, as I was always so interested in their lives and work, which left the poor old producer with the task of getting each piece down to a maximum of ten minutes, or less, if they were adding archive footage.

Then I would be sent a roughcut of the programme and had to write a script to go round the clips, which I did at home. Then another day was spent at BH, recording the programme. So roughly it took up at least half the week, more if there was any travelling involved.

These days, when a BBC presenter comes to interview me at home, he or she is on her own, working the gear, with no producer present. The tape recorder is of course much smaller today, carried in a handbag, whereas in the old days you needed a Pickfords lorry. They also tend only to record what they know they are going to use, i.e. five minutes' worth, and then they are off, rushing to the next appointment.

It was a bit of faff and labour intensive at the time I did *Bookshelf*, in those good old radio days, when such care and time was always taken, but on the other hand, the quality did show, the depth and richness was apparent. I was so proud to work there, and have a proper BBC pass, which allowed you cheap food in the canteen and cheap wine in the BBC club which was over the road in Portland Place, now a posh hotel. For years after I had left *Bookshelf* I used to flash my BBC card when I was at football matches or abroad, hoping to get into the press box, carefully putting my finger over it so they could not see it was now years out of date.

I hugely prefer radio to TV. In the seventies, I did do three or four TV documentaries, usually tied in with a book I was doing, such as walking along Hadrian's Wall or George Stephenson or Beatrix Potter. I did it really to please the publisher, knowing they would be thrilled that I had secured a tie-in with a TV company, which would be great publicity for the book, but oh God, the time it used to take. For a two-part TV series on walking Hadrian's Wall it took eight weeks, with a crew of eight. I became so bored, walking a walk I had already done and talking to people I had talked to. TV, in theory, is considered more important, attractive, more glamorous, but to me it is the more pointless, less fun, less illuminating. You are asking questions to which you already know the answers, going to places you have already been to, or the researchers have been there first and told you everything. On radio, you move more quickly, waste less time, and get more out of people.

I loved being involved with *Bookshelf*, and liked all the producers. As presenter, I also had input into the programme, suggesting authors and features. The book world, after all, was one I had come to know pretty well, after all those years of being published.

I left of my own volition. It had just become so time-consuming. I wanted to concentrate on my own books, which is my real pleasure in life. *Bookshelf* was a heavy commitment. I had to sign a contract each year to do the programme for thirty-three weeks, so it was hard to make other plans or other arrangements.

By the end of the third year, I was, to my surprise, sometimes being recognised by my voice. I would be talking on the phone to a total stranger, such as complaining to someone at BT or HSBC, and they would suddenly say heh, don't I know your voice? Are you on the radio? I was always charmed.

I can so easily imagine the hell and inconvenience and annoyance of what it is like to be really well known, recognised by sight, rather than by your voice, which is much more subtle and discreet. I have been with enough famous people in my life, from the Beatles to star footballers, and being out with them in the street or a restaurant is horrendous. People staring, people coming up, people stopping you, people making personal comments, wanting autographs, wanting selfies, treating you like public property. The nice people, the true fans, hold back. It is almost always the nasties who push themselves upon the well known.

The accents of my own children are interesting. Obviously, being born and brought up in London, they are Londoners, but only one of them, Caitlin, has what you might call a middle-class, BBC accent. While she was a student, I was always encouraging her to work on the campus radio, with her lovely voice, have a go, pet, but she never did. The other two sound more north London. I think it was because they went to fully comprehensive schools whereas Caitlin at Camden had best friends, all the way through, who were more middle-class, from the same middle-class background as hers.

In our minds, having moved into the middle classes, we liked to think in our attitudes and beliefs we had not changed, we had not become right-wing and Tory, hangers and floggers, would never on principle send our children to fee-paying schools or pay for private medicine, certainly not.

We had also retained a lot of our background in other ways. Growing up in the same far northern town, same sort of estate, same sort of families, same sort of school, at the same sort of period, Margaret and I always had so much in common, which of course our children did not have. They were in many ways foreigners to us.

When they were young, and if we did not want them to understand what we were saying, we would use 1950s Carlisle slang, the sort of words we had used when growing up, such as *scran* for food, *gadgie* for bloke, *bewer* for girl, *marra* for mate, *cushty* for good, *shan* for being embarrassed. I don't think in fact anyone in Carlisle actually uses these expressions any more, but they lived on in our awfully nice middle-class house in London, NW5, best part.

My career as a publisher began in 1984. I had been writing quite a few children's books and one of them came out in a paperback with fourteen pages blank. It was not a mistake, just how they had done it, fitting it into a certain length of book, with fourteen pages totally empty. I was furious. What a waste. All those pages going through the printing process, with nothing on them. If I had known in advance, I could have filled it with words, jokes, smart remarks. It made me think how dopey publishers could be.

I had at the time been thinking of doing a guide book to Lakeland, now that we were going up there all the holidays, walking all the Caldbeck fells. Jake and Flora loved being there as well, especially when we converted the barn into a playroom and bedroom. Caitlin by this time was a moody teenager, so not excited by the thought of being stuck miles from anywhere in the remote countryside. She much preferred staying in London.

I was sure I could get a publisher for a Lakeland guide book, but it was seeing all those blank pages that made me think I might do it myself. Why let publishers muck it around? I had written enough books by now to know there is no mystery. Both Wainwright and Beatrix Potter insisted on being published their way, with no one telling them what to do. Both started off their careers by self-publishing.

I wanted to give a rating for everything and everywhere – not just for restaurants and hotels, which is the norm in guide books. I wanted to give stars for lakes, mountains, views, towns, scenery, which I was sure most publishers would not be keen on, thinking it silly or impossible. I also wanted lots of jokes, cartoons, quizzes, and of course every page would be filled. No gaps, no waste.

Lying awake at night, excited by my own excitement, I thought why not a whole series of opinionated guide books? They would be all in the same style and format, covering the whole world. Brilliant! I would hire a team of researchers and writers, brief them personally, to do each book on the lines I dictated. Never been done before, as far as I was aware, not in the way I would do them.

After *The Good Guide to the Lakes*, I will do *The Good Guide to London*, then New York, Paris, the whole world. I talked to my old friend Michael Bateman about this. He said yes, great idea. He would like to do the Paris one.

I immediately started on *The Good Guide to the Lakes*, to create the format, the template for the whole series to come. I knew the northern Lakes pretty well by now, as Margaret and

I had explored everywhere with the children, but I did not know the southern Lakes as well. I hired a researcher called Colin Shelbourn, a young York University graduate based in Windermere. He would do the South Lakes, at my direction, in my style, which he did excellently. He also turned out to be a very good cartoonist.

When I had most of the material written and ready, I went round the local Cumbrian printers, determined that the book would be wholly written, printed and published in Cumbria. None of this nonsense of sending it off to Hong Kong or Italy to be printed, which so many of the big publishers had started to do. I got estimates for printing 10,000 books from several local printers.

But what about distributing and selling the book? Hmm. I needed to get the books into the bookshops, which I could not possibly do without help.

I heard that Anthony Cheetham was beginning a brand-new publishing firm called Century. I had met him when he was still at school at Eton. Along with Derek Parfit, the brother of Margaret's best friend Theo from Oxford, Anthony Cheetham had produced a magazine. They had doorstepped me one day at my *Sunday Times* office, arriving with copies of their magazine. I admired their cheek and did a story about them in Atticus.

After Oxford, Anthony had gone into publishing and was now starting a new firm, along with Gail Rebuck, ex-Sussex University, whom I also happened to know. She had been a young editor at a publishing house called Hamlyn, for whom I did a book of British Lists in 1980. She struck me as a bit bossy, but highly efficient and enthusiastic and I had listened to and obeyed all her suggestions. I did three books for her, which all sold well.

I went to see Anthony and Gail in an upstairs room in Greek Street, Soho, where they were setting up Century. I told them about my publishing venture, not just *The Good Guide to the Lakes*, but how it was number one in a series which was going to cover the world. I did not want them to put up any money. Oh no. No need. I would be paying for everything – writing, researching, printing and publishing. All I wanted from them was distribution. The advantage to them, as a young firm just starting, was that they would have my title on their first list, in their catalogue, without actually spending a penny.

The deal Anthony offered me was that they would take 20 per cent of the net returns. Their reps would take orders, distribute the book to the shops, collect the money, then pay me my whack every month. All I had to do was get my books from my printer in Cumbria to their warehouse in Colchester. They would do the rest.

I got 11,000 copies printed of the first edition – can't remember now why I ordered that number – by Frank Peters, a printer in Windermere who charged me £6,923. It was rather a large first print for a brand-new book. Normal Lakeland books rarely sold more than two to three thousand.

I had also told Century I would do some marketing, despite not knowing what that meant. I approached a well-known maker of Kendal mint cake, Romney's, who were mentioned in the book, along with the other main Kendal mint cake makers, and talked them into giving me 1,000 free bars. I said it would be good publicity for them. The idea was that the first 1,000 buyers of the book in Lakeland would get a free bar of mint cake.

I went in one day to a bookshop in Ambleside to find a customer had just stormed out. He had bought the book, been given a free bar of Kendal mint cake, which he had thrown on the floor in disgust. The assistant had run after him, explaining it was a free gift. And he then explained that he was a dentist. It made a good story, when I went round promoting the book.

What I didn't know was that giving inducements for sale, even just a free bar of mint cake, was against the publishing trade rules. At the time, you could not even give discounts on books. You had to stick to the price on the cover. The Net Book Agreement, as it was called, has fortunately long since gone.

All 11,000 copies were sold – even before I had the official launch party, which was held at Brockhole, the National Park Centre in Windermere, inviting all the Cumbrian media, all the book sellers and the main tourist attractions mentioned in the *Good Guide*. That first edition of the book reprinted three times and in the end sold 32,000. My little company, Forster Davies Ltd, had a turnover that first year of £24,000.

Forster was after my wife's surname, but she had nothing to do with the publishing. In fact she thought it was potty. It was just me plus my chief researcher Colin. I had already created a company called Forster Davies during that year we went abroad, to collect any UK incomes we might earn. I had kept it going, for no real reason, forgetting about it really, but it proved handy, already having a registered company, which was now needed when I was becoming a proper publisher.

I went on to do many new editions of *The Good Guide to*

*the Lakes* over the next twenty years, selling over 100,000 copies. It did so well, I decided to give some of the money away, such as £1,000 to the Cumbria Tourist Board to run an annual award for the Best Lakeland Book of the Year, which is still going strong today. I also gave £1,000 to my old college at Durham to give a prize for the best bit of journalism each year in *Palatinate*. Showing off, it's called.

Because *The Good Guide to the Lakes* had done so well, in its various editions, I then got a bit carried away with being a publisher and produced some other books, such as a *Quiz Book to the Lakes*, and one to London, and then a book about the towns and villages of Lakeland. They did not sell as well. Eventually, the sales of the *Good Guide* tapered off. Updating prices and all the new telephone numbers when regional codes came in, that all became really annoying and expensive. So in the end, after twenty years, I packed it all in. I sold the *Good Guide to the Lakes* title, for a modest sum, to a proper publishing company, Frances Lincoln, and then wound up my own company, Forster Davies Ltd. Though I still have the headed notepaper. Somewhere.

Michael Bateman never did get round to writing his *Good Guide to Paris*. And I never published any other city guides, except to London, so I let down Anthony Cheetham and Gail Rebuck, having boasted I would cover the world.

What I didn't know was that roughly around the same time, other people were beginning similar series of opinionated guidebooks, such as the *Rough Guides*, which went on to become hugely successful.

In the heady years when every edition of *The Good Guide to the Lakes* was flying off the shelves, I ordered yet another updated edition, without first checking sales with Random House. (Which is where Century ended up, with Anthony and then Gail as the big boss.) I had assumed, for some reason, all the copies had gone. It turned out there were still 3,000 copies of the old edition in the warehouse, yet I had printed 10,000 copies of a brand-new edition. I was told by Random House's sales department that the old 3,000 would have to be pulped.

No chance, I said, they are my flesh and blood. I will not pulp them. Which is how I ended up with 3,000 copies in our side passage, much to Margaret's annoyance, as it blocked the side entrance to our back garden. They are mostly still there. I gave some away, the rats and the mice got a lot, but there must be around 2,000 still in the side passage, all mouldering away. But they are mine all mine, a souvenir of a happy stage in my life when I imagined I was about to begin a new career as international publisher.

# 16

## BACK TO BOOKS

I have always been all over the place in books, hardly seeming to stick to one type or one publisher. It means that you don't quite build up a following, because readers don't quite know where to place you. They might enjoy a book about Lakeland but have no interest in football, or absolutely adore collecting stamps but hate the Beatles.

What has usually happened, over these last fifty or so years, is that I fall in love with a subject, start off with almost total ignorance, then hope to con – I mean persuade – a publisher to advance me some money to write a book about it. Sometimes the money is piddling, and the publisher minor, but that does not really matter – just getting a commission is what matters, getting someone to show faith in my self-created project.

When the National Lottery began in 1994 I was reading about one of the very early winners, an Asian man living in Blackburn, who, after years of humble work in a factory, since coming to this country twenty years earlier, had only recently bought his own semi-detached house. I wondered if winning £18 million had ruined his satisfaction and pleasure in all those years of saving and scrimping, becoming rich just by chance and luck, making a nonsense of his previous efforts. And how would it change his life?

I had actually bought a ticket in the very first lottery, on 19 November 1994, not to win anything, as obviously I did not want or need the money. I won the lottery in life when I met Margaret. As I always said, while Margaret rolled her eyes, but I always meant it. I wanted the ticket as memorabilia, to add the first-day lottery ticket to my various dopey collections, such as first editions of newspapers and magazines.

But on that first day in 1994, it made me think of all the ordinary, unknown people, in the years ahead, whose lives were going to be changed by this new creation, the National Lottery – and also society as a whole. There was great play made with the fact that billions were being promised to good causes, culture and sport.

I wondered if I could somehow follow ten or so winners over the first year of their win, see how their lives changed. I rang Camelot, found out who their publicity director was, and told him my brilliant idea. Only to find other writers had already thought of it. But I managed to get a meeting with him – and Camelot eventually agreed to help me.

They could not provide any winners. That would be up to me. But if I attended a press conference when a winner had decided to go public, and was being unveiled, they would allow me to meet him or her. It would then be up to me to persuade him or her into letting me follow them for a year.

I slowly persuaded Camelot that I was trustworthy, would not publish stuff about any winners without their permission, and that I had written lots of books they could look up. I eventually managed to extract two more vital things from Camelot.

One was access to their staff, to the so-called winners' advisers, who go to the homes of the big winners, tell them the news, and offer advice. Even more important, Camelot agreed that even when a winner wanted no publicity, and had ticked the appropriate box, if a winner's adviser decided, after a few weeks, that the winner might just possibly be willing to be interviewed by me, a letter from me would be passed on to them. I would not know their name or anything about them.

In my letter, I explained who I was, how serious a project it was, how Camelot was helping, how they would read every word about themselves, how I would disguise their identity, not reveal their jobs or families. I explained it was how they themselves felt, how their lives and attitudes, desires and ambitions had changed over the year, that was what I was most interested in. Which was true. I have always been fascinated by money and the effects it has on people. And on myself.

In the end, I was able to follow ten jackpot winners, half of them known, half not known to the public. There were in fact around twenty individuals I followed, as some were in partnerships or syndicates.

By a sequence of events, I had no agent at the time. My first agent, Richard Simon, who had done so much to get me going, had retired and moved to Scotland. I personally contacted several publishers with whom I had done books before. The first one to jump at the idea was Alan Samson, then working at Little, Brown.

I don't know how it happened, but in the contract I kept control of the serial rights, which is not normally the case. Usually the publisher handles it, and the income goes against the advance.

When I had finished the manuscript, the National Lottery was an even bigger story than when I had begun, with the big winners dominating the TV news and all the tabloids. The *Sun* had even appointed a Lottery reporter, Lenny Lottery, making him change his name by deed poll.

So I knew that all the papers, broadsheet and tabloids, would be interested in taking bits from the book. I also knew how newspaper serialisation works – there is one person in each main paper, whose name is not known to outsiders, whose job it is to buy and gut books for serialisation.

I found the names of the right person on three papers, got them interested, then worried about sending them copies of the manuscript. There was one paper in particular I did not quite trust. If they did not acquire the rights, they might well leak the names and details of my winners to their newsroom, and therefore bugger up the coverage of whichever paper did buy the rights.

So I made each of the three come in person to my house. I gave them a certain time, and then allowed them two hours each to read the manuscript, but not to copy anything or write down any notes. Then I allowed them two days to make an offer.

They all did and I chose the *Sunday Times*. From memory, they paid £100,000. Can I have made that up? The days of silly money for serials have all gone. Even the richest papers, like the *Daily Mail*, rarely pay more than £5,000 for book rights nowadays.

In the book, I did lots of surveys, questions and answers, for each of my twenty assorted winners, just as I had done with the Spurs footballers in *The Glory Game*. I realised I had access to people in unusual circumstances, in this case lottery winners, so I wanted to record everything about their lives, likes and dislikes, before and after winning.

One of the interesting revelations was that what people say and promise before their win very rarely comes to pass. On a Saturday evening, when they are queuing up at the corner shop to buy a ticket, they tell themselves that if they win, you won't see me for dust, I will be out of this place, off, off and away to some sunny island and sunny beach. And if I win, I will help poor people, oh yes, I will give a huge amount to charity, help cure cancer, help the homeless.

My surveys showed that in 90 per cent of cases, none of this happened. After a year, not one had moved abroad and almost all of them were still living in the same area as before, though perhaps in a slightly bigger house. They had given between 10 and 20 per cent of their wins to their immediate family and friends, but hardly anything altruistically, i.e. to a charity. Only two out of the twenty had given to charity, though several others said they would do in the future.

The big cliché about lottery winners, in the public minds, and encouraged by the tabloids, is that winners waste their money on cars and drink and drugs, and that it will all end in tears. This is a compensatory myth – to make up for the rest of us not winning. Money, so many like to believe, does not make you happy.

I did try to gauge their happiness and only one out of twenty was *less* happy a year after their win. I always knew this, but it seemed to come as a surprise to many of the newspapers. The most common source of everyday arguments and distress in most households is about money – not having enough to pay the rent, pay bills, feed their families. So if this is eliminated, one major source of unhappiness has gone.

If of course you have problems in your marriage or your relationships, or in your personality, suddenly having money might well make everything worse. But the average person copes well with money. The average person is sensible and prudent.

Of my twenty, the only one who thought he was marginally happier before he won was a single man who worked in the kitchens of a college at Durham. Despite his win, the single most happy moment in his life was not his win but securing a job, some time before his win, after several years of unhappiness at being unemployed.

I like to think my book, *Living on the Lottery*, was social history, a human dimension to one of the biggest innovations of the nineties. It is now being said that it was John Major's greatest achievement as Prime Minister. Theatre, music and the arts generally up and down the country have been helped while our sport has been transformed. Would we have won so many gold medals in London 2012 and Rio in 2016 but for the Lottery money?

Social history? Perhaps that is getting carried away. But looking back, I do seem to have done quite a few books with a social dimension, starting with *The Other Half*, in 1966, about the new poor and new rich. I never did *The Class of '66*, about university students, but I did do *The Creighton Report*, about comprehensives. *Born 1900* was about people and institutions born in that year. I also did a book about adoption, *Relative Strangers*, about triplets adopted very young who then meet again after seventy years. This was an idea from Alan Samson, one of the few times a publisher has come to me with an idea, rather than me badgering them.

I have done quite a few books which dear Margaret always dismissed as non-books, such as the *Book of Lists*, or collections of newspaper columns. And I have put up dozens if not a hundred book ideas over the years, which have been turned down flat by every publisher. In the old days, they did reply nicely and fairly quckly. The response tends these days to be one of total silence. That's when you know it is not a runner.

One of my failed projects was a biography of Canon Rawnsley, co-founder of the National Trust, and a great friend of Beatrix Potter. I always thought he was worth a proper biography, but I got fed up with every publisher saying no (quite recently a religious publishing house in Oxford did contact me, out of the blue, about a Rawnsley biog, but I had too much on – and still have).

I did for a while specialise in biographies, and have done ten overall, not counting the football ones. They include biogs of Wordsworth, George Stephenson, Beatrix Potter, the Beatles, Alfred Wainwright, the Grades, Eddie Stobart, Robert Louis Stevenson, and Christopher Columbus.

The Wordsworth biog, which first came out in 1980, is still in print, but what a slog it was. He lived till he was eighty, still writing away, and it took me practically a whole year just to read all his poetry, plus his letters and other writings. I always told myself that if I did another literary biog, I would go for someone like Keats or Shelley who died young. But I never did.

Two of those biogs were about travellers, about Robert Louis Stevenson and Columbus, going back to the places associated with them. In alternate chapters, I told their life story, and then visited places associated with them, so there were past and present stories. Total pleasure to write and research them, but they did not sell well. I think people who like biographies like proper ones, in straight chronological order, not mixed up with the present day.

The majority of my books are now out of print, bastards, but this is the nature of publishing today. There are just too many new books coming out. You could of course be lucky and find one or two in a charity shop.

But at least three have remained constantly in print since the day they first appeared, now almost fifty years ago: the Beatles biog, *The Glory Game* and *A Walk Around the Lakes*. There are a few others which go out of print and then someone wants to reissue them, such as George Stephenson and Wordsworth.

For about forty years I turned down ideas and suggestions from various publishers for another Beatles book, and ideas for other pop music biogs.

I did not want to be seen as a pop music writer. So in the forty years after 1968 I did around forty other books, none of them about the Beatles, but then in 2012 I did *The John Lennon Letters*, followed two years later by *The Beatles Lyrics*, both published by my old friend Alan Samson at Weidenfeld, a publishing house I used to be with many years ago. I like to think those two Beatles books were original pieces of research, with material no one had seen before, not just another rehash of the same old story. Though yes, I know, I have done endless rehashing in my writing life.

How many books have I written? When asked this, I have to say I don't know, which sounds like boasting, inverted snobbery, which of course it is. When people say they don't know how much they earn, or how much they are worth, or how many houses they have, everyone always scoffs and sneers, but I can understand that some people might not know these things, being too busy or not really all that interested in counting up their possessions.

The first problem is – what is a book? Does it mean any book which has my name on, even books I have edited? Should I include books which are anthologies of columns, or are new editions of old books? The Beatles biog, even though I never did a completely new one, has emerged over the years in different editions, such as an illustrated version. Do they count as different books if they are from a different publisher, in a different format, with extra material and with a different ISBN number? Or is that cheating, just to get the numbers?

And what about all the children's books I have done? For about twenty years I did one if not two every year, particularly about a little girl called Flossie Teacake, aged eight, who by a piece of magic becomes sixteen. Then I did a series for Penguin called *STARS*, set in a comprehensive sixth form, one of them coming out every month for a year. Should I include them as well?

Oh God, I haven't got the time to tot them all up. I can't even guess what the total might be. When I have finished writing this book, I will sit down and make a list and put it in the appendix, unless Iain MacGregor, the publisher of this book, says oh no, too boring, are you an egomaniac or what?

# 17

# My Life in Columns

My life as a columnist has continued to this day, which is surprising. Columnists tend to have strong opinions, and can come out with instant judgements and thoughts, criticisms and comments. In normal life, I don't have that facility. In fact I rarely know what I think. I agree with the last person, or anyone who sounds sensible. I need to sit down and start writing a column, to find out what I really think or feel.

Margaret was excellent when it came to opinions, whether asked or not, yet the last thing she ever would have wanted to do, or ever did, was write a newspaper column.

Over a meal, when we were discussing topics of the day, she would come out with some biting, original angle I had not thought of, and I would say there is a thousand words in that, pet, shall I ring the *Sunday Times*? Don't you dare, she would reply. I won't answer the phone.

Almost from the beginning of my journalistic career, back on the student newspaper in the 1950s, I have been writing columns. And they have almost always been on the same topic, myself. Well it is what I know best, what I am expert on. My thinking is that if I have felt or observed something, however apparently trivial, other people will have done so as well. My job is then to make it amusing or interesting. And possibly informative. I can't do that all that well verbally, as I get lost, ramble, lose my thread, but I seem to be able to do it better on paper, though I always overwrite, at great speed, and then have to boil everything down later.

The minute I went to fathers' classes, over fifty years ago now, or had my vasectomy, or had a child who never slept till he was five, or last week when I fractured my finger, I immediately thought, hmm, there must be a thousand words in that.

Is it showing off, in that I think somehow my ordinary experience and my thoughts are better, more interesting than other people's? Not really. I want to share. Just as when I was a little boy aged four in Scotland, I stood at the gate in Johnstone and told everyone in the street, total strangers, passing by, exactly what my parents were doing, that very moment.

You have of course to develop or create a style, find a voice which people will recognise. They might hate it, and I know my silly phrases and slang and style have annoyed many readers over the years – and also my own friends and family. Hard luck. If the editor still wants to print it, that's what matters.

When you have a regular column or several, you are thinking about them all the time, all week long, looking for something to happen, something overheard, seen or thought, which somehow can be used and turned into a column. It's the reason I always carry a pen round my neck, ready to write down possible material.

One of my heroes as a columnist was Miles Kington, who died in 2008. He did a daily column in the *Independent* which was always funny, creative, imaginative, never hurtful, never boastful, always wry, and always wise.

People used to ask him how he managed it – and he said it was what he had done, all his life. In his days on the staff of *Punch*, he would come in every day and have to write something amusing. So in his later life, as a freelance, it was a daily rhythm he had got into, a pattern of life, just doing the job he had always done.

I first met Miles in 1979 when I too joined *Punch*, not on the staff but as a weekly contributor, one of the most enjoyable and interesting jobs I ever had.

It was Alan Coren's idea. I think he had invited me to one of their weekly lunches and I was going on about my three children, how when you work at home, people think you don't have a proper job, or actually do anything, so you get asked to do stuff, like take other people's children to school. He suggested I write a family, domestic column, purely from the father's point of view.

From the beginning of mass-market newspapers and magazines in the early nineteenth century, there have of course been domestic columns, advice for cooking or child rearing, but rarely have they ever been written by men. In the 1970s there was a new batch of domestic columns, this time with feminist overtones, in publications like the *Guardian* and *Observer*. Alan's idea was that it was about time a man answered back – not in the sense of giving his views, but from his perspective, on his day-to-day experiences of being a dad.

The column was called Father's Day. From the very beginning I made an awful mistake which later rebounded on me. I did not want to call my children by soppy names, which was what some women columnists were doing, such as calling their children Little Treasure and Big Treasure. I wanted my column to be real, so I decided to use their real names – Caitlin, Jake and Flora. They were quite young at the time. Flora was only seven, so was not going to object, and their friends would not be reading *Punch* anyway.

With this sort of family, domestic column, on the lines of the one by Tim Dowling in the *Guardian Weekend* magazine, you flam up things, exaggerate, put incidents and experiences together, spin things out, but basically you don't lie, don't totally make up things. It's just that there are other truths you don't reveal. You play to the character you have created in the column. I wrote about stuff that had happened, sort of, but I did not write about bad or sad things which happen in all families.

After about five years doing the Father's Day column every week, Jake started complaining. At his comprehensive, there were several teachers who read *Punch* and they had started making jocular remarks in passing in the corridor to him, commenting on something I had said he had done. He got furious. He did not know what I had written, and what I had written was probably not quite true anyway. But he certainly did not want attention drawn to himself. Least of all by teachers. He said he didn't want his name in the column any more.

If I had given my children soppy names from the beginning, I could have kept them at the same age forever, just as Just William was the same age forever. They would not have been identified or ever complained. But by making them real, they grew up, changed attitudes, and went through different stages.

I didn't want to give up the column, as I loved doing it so much, and it was doing well, so to keep Jake happy, for a while

I changed his name to Jimmy. Till he forgot about it. Didn't really fool anyone.

With Margaret, I decided from the beginning not to use her real name. Instead I referred to her as the Old Trout, which was silly and yucky, demeaning and sexist, so corny, so amateurish. I don't know why I did it. It was what I had disliked in other people's columns. When I started referring to her as the Old Trout, I did tell Margaret. She sighed, but had no objections. Eventually letters from readers started coming in complaining about me calling her the Old Trout. She did enjoy that.

She did criticise the column now and again when I made what I thought were funny remarks but she thought were hurtful. Just a joke, I replied, a tease, surely they can see that. Oh, you always think that, she replied.

I have noticed over the years that you can't tell the real character of a columnist or a writer from his or her words. I had a friend on the *Sunday Times* called Philip Oakes, who was also a poet and novelist. In real life, he was always vitriolic, rubbishing everyone, moaning and groaning, with intense hatreds and jealousies of others, but when he put pen to paper, in a review for example, none of this came out. He was measured and kind. Auberon Waugh was the opposite. He could be a pig on paper, really hurtful, but in real life, in all the times I met him or had meals with him, he was the gentlest, nicest, kindest, and most charming of men.

I can understand what happens to some people when they pick up the pen. You are trying to draw attention to yourself, amuse or annoy people, have a go at the icons of the day, so you can get carried away. You often come out with remarks and ridicule you don't actually believe in, or care either way, just for the effects. Usually it is a sign of youth – wanting to make a mark.

I eventually got invited to join the *Punch* table. This was an honour in itself. The *Punch* office, just off Fleet Street, had their own dining room and a huge, ancient wooden table, going back to its beginnings in the 1840s. Over the decades, distinguished writers and contributors, such as Thackeray, had carved their initials on the table. In his case, WMT. When Alan invited someone to be a member of the *Punch* Table, you not only got a free slap-up meal with loads of wine once a month on a Friday, but you got to carve your initials on the table. So I got to carve HD. Wasn't going to make it EHD, was I, and give away my real first name.

There were usually about twenty people at the lunches, most of them regular staff and columnists, but there were always two or three eminent outside guests, invited by Alan.

The two funniest people I have met in my lifetime, listened to with admiration and guffaws and amazement, were Peter Cook and Alan Coren. They were so inventive, so clever, so funny. When they were on a roll, letting their imagination spin, creating a verbal fantasy, making up stories and scenes which appeared to be all over the place but always had an ending, you wondered how one small brain could be so fertile. Peter did comic voices as well, which Alan did not do. Alan was more literary, more intellectual. I was in awe of both of them, wished I could be as verbally amusing. Peter's life was tragic in the end, wasting his talents by drinking. Alan, deep down, so I always believed, really wanted to be a novelist, or possibly a TV personality. He never quite managed either – but as a humorist, a columnist and an editor, he was exceptional. Alan died in 2007, due to cancer. Were he alive today, I know he would be immensely proud of his two children who have become media stars in their own fields – Giles Coren and Victoria Coren Mitchell.

My Father's Day column acquired a fairly large following in staff rooms, junior common rooms, sixth forms. I would get invited all the time to address college unions, but rarely went.

Three collections of the columns appeared in book form. Even more surprising, they became a TV series. When the rights were bought, I thought it was dopey; no one could turn silly little articles into a TV series. So I refused to do the scripts. Instead they got one of the star TV writers of the time, Peter Spence, who had just had a big success with writing *To the Manor Born*.

By a strange coincidence, the actor who played the part of me in the series, which ran for two years, was John Alderton. He was the actor whom Tony Palmer and I had chosen to be the lead in our film of *The Rise and Fall of Jake Sullivan*. Which never got made. In the TV series of *Father's Day*, one of John Alderton's own children acted the part of one of his daughters.

The series ran in *Punch* for ten years, by which time the magazine was coming towards its end, its sales and influence diminishing. It finally closed in 2002. It had been for so long a great publication, a national institution with a great history and the most incredible archive of cartoons, illustrations and articles.

One of the reasons I finally gave up was that I was beginning to run out of copy. By using their real names and real lives, I had done myself out of a job, which I might have kept going forever if I had kept them ageless. One by one they grew up and eventually left home. You can't really write about your children if you haven't got children around you any more.

I had another column, about the same time, which also ran for almost ten years. Very few people read it at the time – and probably won't even remember it now. It was in *Stamp News*.

When my Sunday-morning football career was coming to an end, on getting towards fifty, I could still play football but no longer recover from playing football. I was knackered or injured all the time. I started looking around for another weekend activity, to use up my energy and act as a distraction. So I became a born-again stamp collector. Didn't need a lot of energy, but it did get me out of the house.

Once I started, haunting all the stamp fairs and stalls, I began writing in *Stamp News*. They used to boast it was the world's only humour column about stamps. Not a great deal of competition. It came out as a book with my friend and neighbour, Wally Fawkes (cartoonist, clarinet player and creator of Fluke in the *Daily Mail*), doing the cover drawing.

For a couple of years I was a football columnist on the *Independent* and also had a personal column in the *Independent on Sunday*. The editor at the time was Ian Jack, an old friend of mine from our *Sunday Times* days.

He arrived at our house very early one Sunday morning, before the *Independent on Sunday* had arrived, and stood there nervous and hesitant. I invited him in, gave him a cup of coffee. He said he was sorry I was not in the paper.

'Oh really,' I replied. 'Not seen the paper yet.'

These things happen in newspapers, so I wasn't too worried by what he had just said. If papers suddenly lose adverts and lose pages, or something big happens, columns can get chucked out.

'In fact I am afraid you won't be appearing in the paper again . . .'

I had been sacked. Obviously my column was not quite good enough, but I never quite found out the specific reason why it had happened then, though Ian did mumble something about the women on the staff complaining there were too many male columnists. Ian seemed more upset than I was, having to sack an old friend. I thanked him for coming to tell me personally, and being so civilised, and we remained friends.

I also got the sack from the *Evening Standard*. I had been doing a column there for about two years. They had a different columnist every evening, one of whom was Beryl Bainbridge. I think she did Wednesday and I did Tuesday. She often rang me saying what shall I write about, you know how to do these columns, I am a novelist, you are a proper journalist, I don't know what to write, help me please.

So I would talk to her, find out what she had been doing that week, and suggest a topic. Not that she always used it, but it did get her thinking.

Then blow me, I got the sack. And Beryl didn't.

I never got to the bottom of that sacking either. I thought perhaps it was to do with the fact that two weeks running I wrote about comprehensives. I was meant to keep off anything political.

*

The strangest sacking I ever experienced happened when we were in the Lake District. We were up there for the summer when I got a call from the *Mail on Sunday*. It was Jocelyn Targett, the editor of the section where I was writing about TV. He was the one who had hired me, rung me out of the blue in 1993 and asked me to be the paper's TV critic. I said I didn't watch TV, just the football. He said perfect, that's what I want, a fresh view.

I did not actually have to sit down and watch TV. I got posted, several weeks in advance, videos of upcoming pro-grammes, or I could ask for programmes to be sent to me. I could therefore watch at my leisure and convenience, and only go for those I felt I would write something amusing about. So it was easy and fun to do. For about a year it seemed to have gone well.

That week I happened to say in the column that I had been watching *EastEnders* – for the first time ever. The editor in chief of the *Mail*, David English, was so annoyed by this, appalled that his TV critic should never have seen *EastEnders*, that he ordered Jocelyn to sack me.

Jocelyn had recently sacked someone else. It had turned very awkward and embarrassing because this person had found out he was going to be sacked before Jocelyn had actually told him. He stormed into Jocelyn's office, complained about the awful way he had been treated, others knowing he was going to be fired.

Jocelyn had vowed to himself, there and then, that if he ever had to sack anyone again, he would make sure no one else knew until he had told the person concerned, face to face. When he rang me, wanting to see me, face to face, he did not know of course that I was in the Lake District. He was a bit taken aback, paused for a bit, then said don't worry, I will come and see you tomorrow.

I said oh don't come all this way, surely you can tell me on the phone, whatever it is you want to say. He said no, he had to see me, it was urgent.

I began to think, hmm, must be something exciting, if he is prepared to come 300 miles to tell me. Perhaps I am going to be offered a really fab job.

Next day he arrived in his chauffeur-driven Jaguar, which was steaming as the driver went the wrong way and got stuck in all the tourist hot spots. Jocelyn stepped out. I introduced Margaret to him. He said he did not want to speak in front of her, so could we go somewhere. We walked down to the lake, he said he was sacking me, got back in the car and was driven the 300 miles back to London.

I was totally stunned. At the time, he gave me no reason. It was only some time later I heard about the background, about never having seen *EastEnders*, and the big boss demanding I got the sack.

When you are being sacked, I always feel it is bad form to ask why. It makes you appear pitiful and pleading, as if asking for mercy. By not asking, or complaining, you don't get into arguments, which you can't win. The reason for getting rid of you is not always logical anyway, especially in journalism. Your face or your tone does not fit. They have someone better or cheaper in mind. Just accept it. You are not going to be able to change the decision. Better to feel sorry for the person having to sack you – and then think their turn will come. And when it happens to them, they probably won't have other sources, other outlets, as I had, poor sods, they'll learn.

I did get the push from the *Guardian* once, but at least they explained why. I did a column every week for a year in their Saturday *Weekend* magazine about my various collections. It got a good display, I was so pleased with it, a whole page, with a nice photo of one of my treasures. My line editor was a friend of mine who lived locally and had gone to school with my sister's children in Leighton Buzzard. We had got on so well.

Alas, the editor of the mag, whom I had never met, said that's it Hunt, your time is up, thank you and goodbye. The reason she gave made sense. She had to lose £100,000 from her budget and ten pages. One of her economies was to sack two of the better paid contributors, which were me and Stephen Fry. He had been doing a techy column, on new gadgets. It was a satisfying, soothing, explanation, whether the real truth or not. Didn't suggest I was rubbish or the readers had gone off me.

As I write, I have got three regular columns. Although of course I might have been sacked from all of them by the time I finish this book. Or even finished this sentence. Two have been going for twenty years and one for almost ten years, so I hope they will be civilised when the time comes to have cuts and send me on my way. Which happens all the time these days, in all walks of life. Not like the sixties, eh. We assumed then we had a job for life, whatever it was.

It was in 1996 I started doing a football column called The Fan in the *New Statesman*. Since then, I have done it every week in the football season. These days the football season lasts almost the whole year, especially if there is a World Cup that year or a Euro. Despite having done it for over twenty years, I still meet people who are surprised. They assume that the *NS* is mainly a political mag, not aware of its arts and culture coverage.

As with all my columns, it is personal, as much about me as the football itself. I like to think I have a theme each week, from haircuts to football history, but I muck around, till I get to whatever point I am trying to make. Often, when I read it in the mag on a Friday, I think, what is he on about?

Spurs is still my team, but I also go to Arsenal. I have lots of friends and neighbours with Arsenal season tickets who usually have one spare. I also watch every game possible on TV, having subscriptions to every known football channel.

I write the column on a Sunday, after the last game of the weekend, and send it in on Monday morning. It doesn't appear in the shops or through letterboxes till Friday, which means I can't really do anything too topical. By Friday, everything can have changed, my predictions looking really stupid.

I have had four different *NS* editors, three of whom were not really interested in football, just thought it should be covered as a subject. The middle-class professionals and intellectuals love footer these days, far more than they ever did in the past. I am always surprised by how many QCs I find myself sitting beside at Arsenal.

The present editor, Jason Cowley, as I write, is a football fan and has written a lot about the game which is useful and he sends me nice notes when he likes something, which none of the other editors did. On the other hand, he knows when I am talking bollocks.

\*

My *Sunday Times* column in the Money section has been running since 1998. It now gets a good postbag, with readers saying they read it every week. Funny how people get these things wrong. It appears only once every four weeks.

I don't do Twitter or have a blog or log in to see what readers are saying, but I know without knowing it that most people who write in reply to newspaper columns don't read them properly. They jump on things out of context, imagine opinions and language you never used, or confuse you with someone writing in a totally different publication.

Writing about money was a total departure for me, a subject I have always been interested in but about which I know very little, not in the technical sense, never having invested in shares. Twenty years ago I wrote a piece in the *Evening Standard* rubbishing pension funds, saying annuities were a con. I had just discovered that my large, self-funded pension pot with the Equitable Life would disappear totally when I died. My fault, not realising. Much better to invest in property, which is what I was advising my children to do, if they ever got any spare money.

The then editor of the *Sunday Times*, John Witherow, then asked if I could do some personal pieces for the Money section. I said I would only do it monthly, as I feared I would not find enough topics for a weekly column. It was called Me and My Money at first but one day, phoning it in, which shows you how long it has been running, a sub editor misheard and thought I had said Mean With Money. He made that the heading on the column that week. Which fitted it much better.

My running theme is how mean I am, how I love bargains and cheap fruit from street stalls, even when I have to wipe the mould off. All true. But of course not the real truth. I am of course amazingly generous and spendthrift – when it comes to big sums or big treats for myself.

During the twenty years, I have had five different editors of the Money section. Some of whom, I suspect, have not been fans of the column. They think everything in Money should be useful and helpful, written by experts. My column was often held over, if space was tight, which made me livid and mucked up my working life. I have every deadline for a year ahead written in bold in my diary and I like to think I am never late.

The present editor, Becky Barrow, as I write, which you always have to say, is a total professional, a real journalist, and a real enthusiast. She will also suggest topics, which previous editors never did. As an old hack, I am more than willing to oblige.

My third current column is also a monthly column. It appears in *Cumbria Life*, a very high-class, glossy, excellent county magazine. I began writing that in 2008. Again, it is personal, but of course it always in some way has to be connected with Cumbria.

I am surprised the three columns have been running for so long, though I know at any moment I could be surplus to requirements. I also do around six travel pieces a year for the *Mail on Sunday*, and have done so for about twenty years. The travel editor, Frank Barrett, is an old friend of mine. It does pay have to friends.

I write my three columns at the weekend, on Saturdays and Sundays, while Monday to Friday I am always working on a book. I don't have weekends, in the normal sense. Every day is a writing day. Which is what I love. Having a month off, or a week off, even an hour spare between books or columns, I get bored or frustrated.

When I am feeling rotten, with a cold or flu, or fed up and moaning, or had too much to eat and drink at supper, I find writing energising. I often drag myself up to my desk feeling I can't face it, I'll watch telly instead, but when I sit at my computer, something always comes. Afterwards, I feel so much better.

It is a bit like when I had asthma as a boy, lying in bed, wheezing, feeling miserable. If I dragged out my stamp album or my football scrapbooks, slowly turning the pages, studying them, getting absorbed, my asthma would miraculously lift. Work is distraction. It takes you out and away from yourself. Distracts you from the often rotten, depressing, unfair business of living.

I cheat a lot of course, in order to fill these three regular columns. And all the books. With age, I am more than ever recycling topics I have covered in the past. Not exactly the same, at least I hope not, but similar themes keep coming up. When the section editor in charge of you is only thirteen, or so it often seems, they can't possibly remember what you wrote in the past, as they were still at school, so when they say I hear you were at the 1966 World Cup final, amazing, or did you really meet the Beatles, wow, then naturally I try to oblige and knock out a thousand words on the subject. Again.

Many years ago, when we had our cottage at Caldbeck, I met an old countryman called Charles Norman de Percy Parry living locally in a caravan. He had been writing a column for *Horse and Hound* for fifty-three years. He had started it in 1925 and in 1978, when I talked him, he was still doing it, by which time he was then aged seventy-eight. It was said to be the longest-running column in any magazine.

At the time, I was totally amazed. How could anyone ever keep up the same column for fifty years? So he told me his secret.

'The public's memory is only five years long, so never throw away old copy. After five years, you can start to repeat things. I couldn't have lasted this long, if I had been unable to repeat old stories.'

I suppose writing about country matters makes it a bit easier, as the same seasons always come around. You have the same old things to react to every year.

Writing about myself, I do have the same thoughts recurring. Different events and stimuli trigger them, present-day happenings throw them up, but then I find myself going back to the same old stories and observations, topics and events, from my long-legged life. Another plus to being old. You have more to write about.

# 18

# Loweswater

In 1987, we decided we should look for another house in the Lake District. The object was very simple. To change our lives.

For several years we had become fed up charging up and down the motorway five or six times a year, for half terms and holidays, to stay at our little cottage near Caldbeck. It was lovely when we were there, and the house was pretty enough, but small and dark and cold and very uncomfortable and cheerless in bad weather.

Wouldn't it be nice, we used to say to each other on the long journey, to have a proper Lakeland house, you know, with lakes around, as we didn't have any at Caldbeck, perhaps on a little hill, with views and light and space, big enough to have a room each to work in. A place we could live in – as opposed to visiting, rushing in and out.

But we felt we could not do it for some time, perhaps forever. Margaret's father Arthur was still alive, aged eighty-seven. It's always easy to remember his age, as he was born in 1900 (one of the inspirations for the book I did, *Born 1900*). He was a widower, as Margaret's mother Lily had died in 1981, but in incredible fettle for his age, digging his garden, having several pints at the weekend at his Conservative Working Men's Club. He had learned to cook, which he had never done in his life. He was always occupied. We went to visit him regularly enough and he would often just grunt when he let us in, saying he was busy, had his spuds to put in, had the sweet peas to weed, the grass to cut, though usually he was waiting for the racing to start on TV to see if any of his horses had won.

Flora was only fifteen still, at school, so too soon to leave her for months on end on her own, but the older ones were as good as off and away. Jake was about to graduate, so he had left home, while Caitlin had not only graduated but flown the country, in America doing graduate work.

But the more we thought about it, the more we felt we should start looking now for our Dream Lakeland Home, even if for the first two or three years, till Flora left home, we would just use it as we had done with Caldbeck, during the school holidays, not to live there.

After looking for quite some time, we found what we thought was almost our ideal fantasy house, at Loweswater, seven miles from the town of Cockermouth. It had three lakes within walking distance – Crummock Water, Loweswater and Buttermere – at the end of a stunning valley, surrounded by wonderful hills. It was on its own, surrounded by fields, but there were other houses not far away. Loweswater is not a village as such, though it looks it on the map, and from the signposts. There are no shops or streets, just a cluster of farm houses, but it does have a church, a village hall and best of all a wonderful pub, the Kirkstile Inn.

The house was on a slight hill, which was something else on our list, and with a mature garden with yew trees and lots of rhododendrons. There was a high hedge at the front, which ensured privacy and a yew bower over the wooden front gate, through which you entered. Then you walked up a little hill to the front porch.

The front was the same as the back, each with a porch, and there were large windows all the way round, letting in loads of light, even on the darkest day. Just two storeys, Victorian, from 1860. Not listed, so we should not be having too many problems with the Lakeland Planning Board. It was so symmetrical, front and back, it was like a child's drawing of a country cottage.

It had originally been the house of the village carpenter and all the floors were in the finest wood, in sparkling condition. His actual workshop was next door, but that had been converted into a small and separate house, lived in by the retired Vicar of Loweswater and his wife Joan, whose family owned both houses, and a lot else beside it.

You never get all that you want, when you play these fantasy house games, but there was only one thing missing – it did not have a lake view. But I told myself that in winter, when the leaves are down, if I lean out and stretch I am sure I will get a glimpse of Crummock Water, just half a mile away.

It was being sold on 7 May 1987 by auction, at the Globe Hotel in Cockermouth. Robert Louis Stevenson once stayed at the hotel, according to the plaque outside, which was a good sign. We had not been properly inside the house, just had a little look on a quick trip with Flora, most of which we spent sitting outside on the grassy, sloping lawn imagining ourselves living here. We had not done a survey either. We just both decided it had Spoken To Us.

I decided to go up from London for the day on my own for the auction, arranging for my brother Johnny to pick me up in Carlisle and drive me to the hotel where the auction was being held. If I failed to get it, I would come back that evening. If I got it, I would stay overnight somewhere, and ogle it.

It was the only house being auctioned that day by the estate agents, Smiths Gore. An elderly estate agent had come out from semi-retirement to conduct the sale and started by saying that in his opinion, after decades of selling Lakeland houses, this house had the finest situation of any he had auctioned. I thought oh God, I'd better go home now. The price will go mad.

I had been told by the agent that the guide price was £80,000. I promised Margaret, when I left for Euston that morning, I would not go beyond £90,000.

I started the bidding thinking I might frighten others off, hoping they would assume some slick stranger, probably from London, must have loads of money. But it rapidly got to £90,000. Despite the vow to Margaret, I thought I can't stop now, having come all this way. I got it for £92,000.

What I didn't know then was that there was a rival bidder, much richer than me, a London solicitor, who would easily have paid more – but he wasn't there. He had sent his clerk with instructions not to go above £90,000. No mobile phone in those days, so he couldn't ring his boss and bid more. The solicitor later told me he would have bid more, but in the end he bought another house in Loweswater, right on Loweswater Lake, and we became good friends.

I stayed the night at Scale Hill, an ancient coaching inn in Loweswater, quite near the house, and went back to London the next day.

For three years we only used the house during the school holidays. Then in 1990 we began to live there for roughly half of each year, from May till October. We each had a study where we worked every day, just as in London, then walked every afternoon, just as in London. Except of course the Lakeland walks were a bit different from our London walks.

All the local walks were far better, far more extensive and far more stunning than we had imagined when we first saw the house. It was possible to walk for hours and hours, in total isolation, up and over fells, round lakes, without crossing any roads and seeing no one. When we left Caldbeck, where we had been for ten years, one of our local friends there had said that Loweswater was becoming trendy. 'It's attracting all the yuppies.' That was a new phrase in 1987, a new smear. But it wasn't true. Buttermere can be a tourist trap on bank holidays, but Crummock and Loweswater never get overrun.

Crummock Water was reached down a country lane, almost opposite the house. Perfect for swimming. No one could believe that when I told them, back in London. But every year for almost the next thirty years I have swum in the lake in July and August. Not every day, and some years only half a dozen times, but the average was about twenty swims every summer. I know because we kept a cottage diary. In it we recorded how many days we stayed, how many swims, how many perfect sunny days, what day we picked the first black-currants, gooseberries and apples. Perfect days were defined by Margaret with complicated codes on the wall calendar.

The garden was big enough, with three lawns which took me almost two hours to mow, but then I also bought five fields, some fourteen acres, around the house. In the smallest field, little more than a paddock, I created an orchard. I got a local nurseryman to plant twenty apple trees, both eating and cooking apples, insisting I wanted them all three-quarter trees, as I did not want them to grow so high you would need ladders. They all survived and went on to give us thirty years of lovely fruit – but I forgot one thing. They all ripen at the same time so we have a glut. That was mistake.

In the orchard, I later built a tree house, using recycled wood and planks and old telegraph poles. Oh the fun I had. And we had.

From the beginning, we made a vow never to go to London while we were in Loweswater. We were up here, properly living here, for five to six months at a time, and would avoid all invitations or temptations to go to London. We were rural people.

I came in from the garden once and heard Margaret on the telephone, saying sorry, we can't come, we are in Lakeland.

I said who was that? She said Number Ten. I said Number Ten where? Downing Street, she said, some party, but it's next month so we can't come, we'll still be here, we agreed we would never go to London while we are up here.

This was in 1997, during Tony Blair's first premiership, and he was having trendy parties of so-called cool Britannia media people.

I picked up the phone and got through to Downing Street. I said, err, someone was just talking to my wife about a reception, we will be back in London in November, err, should there be another similar reception. Which there was. Margaret even agreed to go with me, after I twisted her arm. It turned out that Cherie Blair was a fan of Margaret's books.

Some time later, I got a call from a tabloid picture desk saying they had a topless photo of Cherie in some villa in Italy reading a book. They gave me the name of the book, and I recognised it as one of Margaret's. I added that we knew Cherie was a fan. They had worried slightly that it might not be Cherie, but someone else, so this was a clue it could be genuine.

In the end, they never used the photo of a topless Cherie. Probably scared of a total bollocking from Alastair Campbell, Blair's press officer.

The thing about living at Loweswater for the next thirty years was that it was like living twice. We had a rural life and an urban life, totally separate, totally different. By living there for up to six months at a time, you become totally settled, totally into the routine, as if you have never been anywhere else. Meeting people in the street in Cockermouth, they would not realise you had been to London for the winter, thinking they just had not seen you for a while.

When people did say to me, 'Enjoying your holiday?', I would go mad, explaining we lived up here, do you mind, we are locals.

I liked to think I became part of the community, attending village events, joining groups, giving little talks, manning stalls at Loweswater fairs, entering for the Loweswater Show. I like to think I got to know everybody in the Loweswater area, partly because I was part of a newspaper delivery syndicate for many years. One or two of the people we delivered to were housebound, so it was social work, as well as a chance to catch up on local chat.

I drove around the little lanes and up farm tracks delivering the newspapers in my old Jaguar, which was a bit daft, bashing into hedges, getting awful scratches, using so much petrol. When we moved to Loweswater, we had so much to carry up and down each time that I had bought this ten-year-old Jaguar. I have no interest in cars, but it was so spacious and comfortable to drive. I used to say it was gliding, not driving. Till it fell apart.

Margaret was not as sociable. She was constantly asked to give talks locally, to the Women's Institute or Cockermouth School, as I did, but she always refused. She did not feel any obligation, to her publisher or the community. I looked back to my own school days in Carlisle, which of course Margaret had experienced as well, when no authors ever came to our schools, unlike schools in the London area. I said it was part of the duty of being an author up here, to help local worthy bodies when asked, especially in remote areas. She said I just liked showing off.

But Margaret always went to the Loweswater Show, which she loved. She was the judge one year of a children's handwriting competition – and donated a prize. She always had wonderful, immaculate, bold handwriting.

Margaret loved the fact that we were cut off in Loweswater. No one door-stepped us, no door-to-door salesmen or Jehovah's Witnesses. No friends or neighbours knocked at the door out of the blue, uninvited, though we made good friends and neighbours who would help if we wanted them, but they kept their distance, as Cumbrians do. There is an old joke about Cumbrian farmers. They winter you, they summer you, they winter you again, they summer you, they winter you again – and then they say hello. That's exactly how Margaret liked it. She didn't like all this southern phoney friendship and intimacy, kissy kissy, first names from the moment you meet. She liked to keep a distance.

I always tried to pretend I am really a Cumbrian, which is still how I think of myself, despite being born in Scotland. I was brought up in Carlisle and still look upon it as my hometown. Margaret was of course a true Cumbrian, born and bred, with a Cumbrian surname. She also had a Cumbrian character, inherited from her father. As a little girl, whenever they met anyone, he would always instruct her 'Say nowt'. It was partly a leftover from the war, when of course Hitler and the Nassies might be listening, but also to the ingrained Cumbrian character of keeping themselves to themselves.

We both did a lot of work in those thirty years at Grasmoor House. I ran my little publishing company from there, doing all those *Good Guides*, plus many other books with a Cumbrian connection, such as biographies of Wordsworth, Beatrix Potter, Wainwright and the one and only Eddie Stobart.

Margaret set several of her novels in Cumbria, or at least sections of them. One early novel, *The Bride of Lowther Fell*, published in 1980, was written while we still had our cottage at Caldbeck, and was based on a local story. Her 2016 novel, *How to Measure a Cow*, was set in Workington. In the book, Workington is a random choice, the heroine looks at the map and wants to get as far away as possible, where no one would know her. It was Margaret's joke, in a way, to send her to Workington. Not exactly the most handsome town in Cumbria.

People think that writers, real writers, meaning Margaret not me, are inspired by place and by scenery. In my experience, they are not. Writers are inspired by an idea in their head, which needs an empty room, a blank wall, no interruptions, peace and quiet in order to turn it into words on paper. They can find that, or create that, almost anywhere, if they try hard enough and concentrate, hence all these young writers today bashing away on their laptops in crowded caffs.

Inspiration can be helped by a feeling of well-being, happiness and contentment, but that comes after the work, when you relax and refuel. If you are in a beautiful or stimulating setting, there is so much to look forward to and enjoy, once you have finished for the day. But it does not necessarily inspire your work.

I found Cockermouth inspiring and stimulating, an historic Georgian gem, but not overrun by tourists, like Grasmere or Ambleside. I always went three times a week to swim in Cockermouth. In London, I have always done the same, but to Kentish Town Pool. In Cockermouth, I lunched afterwards in one of the many cafés and small restaurants, poked around the antique shops and collectors' stalls, or popped into Mitchells auction rooms. I never stopped being in love with Cockermouth.

In London, coming out of Kentish Town Pool, I can't wait to get home. Kentish Town High Road drives me mad, the crowds, the traffic, the litter, the noise, the dirt – ugh. I always looked forward to moving up to Loweswater, counting the weeks and days as soon as we got to spring. But I never looked forward to returning to London.

So why didn't we live in Loweswater full time? As writers, we could have lived anywhere. It was a question friends asked us. And we asked ourselves. People also asked which we liked best.

We usually said Loweswater, for the simple reason that our spirits rose, our hearts fluttered, every time we were driving down the Lorton valley, ticking off all our favourite spots. Our hearts did not soar when driving back to London.

There was another question we pondered. If we had to choose, forced to pick one place to live full time, where would it be? We always knew the answer would have to be London. As the years went on, that's where our three children and their families lived, that's where we have medical help on our doorstep. Both our London GP and the Royal Free Hospital are within walking distance. These things matter as you get older, even if we hoped never to have a serious illness again. In the countryside, it is advisable not to get ill. At Loweswater, any of our friends suddenly taken ill with an emergency or a complication always ended up in Newcastle or Lancaster, miles and miles away.

We never actually thought about the future, only when asked. We knew it was inevitable that we would leave, but it did not hang over us. We loved and treasured every moment of being there. It was such a wonderful combination, town and country, the best of all worlds.

'This is the life, eh, Madge,' I used to say, getting into bed after a particularly wonderful day, having met nobody, just written all morning then walked and wandered around the rest of the day, beside the lake or the fells, across the fields or in our garden.

The wording was a joke observation. Mocking myself for making such a banal remark, and also calling her Madge. Like many domestic jokes and family nicknames, which you find yourself using without thinking what they mean, you forget how they began. Or even that you are saying it. This is the life, Madge, eh. Madge would not reply. Just smile and roll over.

I think Margaret was at her happiest in Loweswater. By being there from May to October, we got the best times of the year for light and warmth, sun and the changing seasons. It also meant we were there every year for Margaret's birthday on 25 May.

On her fiftieth birthday, in 1988, she proposed to climb Red Pike before breakfast, as a treat to herself. I said great, I'll come with you, as I had never done Red Pike. By 1988, I was beginning to get awful arthritic pains in my knees, so there were days I could not manage the high stuff. But I felt pretty good at the time. However, on the morning of 25 May, I slept in.

About eight o'clock I was awakened by Margaret, bringing me a cup of tea in bed, as she did all our married life. I noticed she had her walking boots on and her hair was wet.

She had got up at six, she said, tried to wake me, but I was so sound asleep she decided to leave me. She walked round Crummock Water, climbed to the top of Red Pike, describing a lone walker she had met on the top, what he looked like, what he had said. Then on the way back along the lake, she stopped at Ling Crag, which is a little peninsula on Crummock, and had a swim in the lake. She had no swimming costume with her but as there was no one around the lake, she swam in her underclothes.

I had not heard her getting up and going out, not a thing, and was not aware she had gone, till she woke me up with my tea.

But then for years she had always been much fitter than me, effortlessly climbing to the tops of all the fells, looking so healthy and wonderful.

It became a legend in the family, what she did, on her own, on her fiftieth birthday. It was not quite as legendary as Wordsworth climbing Gable on his seventieth birthday, which makes me sick, because I always knew I would never manage that, but pretty good for fifty, doing it on her own, before breakfast.

Very recently, Jake, our son, got out the map and declared that he now thinks she was lying. She could not possibly have got from our house, up to the top of Red Pike and back in two hours, plus having a swim.

Margaret enjoyed lying. Hard to explain her lies, but they were really exaggerations. If someone asked her where she had been or what she had done or why, sometimes she could not be bothered trotting out the truth, because the truth was usually boring, and people should not have asked her, so she would make it up, not wild fantasy, more embellishments, and always convincing. If ever caught out, she would just laugh and say, 'You didn't believe, it did you?'

That walk and that swim on her fiftieth birthday could, at a pinch, jogging all the way, climbing at a trot, swimming like fury, have been done in two hours, if perhaps not quite getting to the very top of Red Pike. So I have decided that I will always accept her word that she did do it. Because that's what I like to believe.

## 19

# BLISS IN THE WEST INDIES

For my fiftieth birthday, in 1986, as a treat for me, and for ourselves, we went for the first time to the West Indies. Bit different from climbing Red Pike. Took longer and was slightly more expensive.

I had always hated having a birthday on 7 January. All those years in Carlisle it was hellish, so cold in the bedroom, trying to get dressed under the blankets, knowing if you put one bare foot on the lino you could be frozen to the floor and be stuck there till spring.

I had for years been saying oh wouldn't it be lovely on my fiftieth to wake up on a tropical island. So we did it. In January 1986 we flew to Barbados on Concorde. It was quite cramped inside, just 100 seats, two seats either side of a narrow aisle. It was like flying in a large cigar, but oh so exciting and special, especially when a sign announced we had reached Mach 2 which meant we were about to fly faster than sound (Mach 2.04 signified the speed of sound, or 1,354 mph). The food and the service were top class, but ever so discreet and tasteful. I kept all the menus and luggage labels as mementos. I always do that sort of thing, but also

256

because even at the time no one really believed supersonic flights would last. We all knew Concorde was losing money on every flight, so how could it survive? So it felt historic, even in the present.

Concorde was a joint UK and France creation, with BA and Air France running the planes. They never fell out, which has not always happened in Anglo-French relations. It was so beautifully shaped, with that bird-like swoop and elegance: a work of art as well as technology, one of the most attractive pieces of engineering to emerge in my lifetime. And then disappear. A shame it lasted only twenty-seven years. Service flights began in 1976 and ceased in 2003.

Because of the four-hour time difference between the West Indies and the UK, if you left London at nine in the morning you arrived at Bridgetown at eight. The flight itself took only three hours. So you could have two breakfasts.

We went on Concorde three times in all to Barbados. Once we had an emergency stop in the Azores. Something to do with needing to refuel, so we were told. Everyone moaned, but when we landed at a little airport on one of the islands, we were all able to get out and take photos of ourselves standing beside Concorde. Which we had not been able to do in London. Getting on the plane at Heathrow, you entered through various lounges and never actually saw the plane from the outside.

In 1986, on that first trip, I went straight into the Caribbean the moment we arrived at our hotel – and ran straight out again, screaming in agony. I had stood on a sea urchin. All my fault, going in at a rocky bit. Two waiters heard my shouts and rushed down on to the beach in their waiter's uniform. One had a lemon, which he squeezed onto the wound, while the other had a candle. He lit it with his cigarette lighter and let the candle grease drip on to the bite, then waited for it to harden. When the candle grease fell off, it removed the sting from the sea urchin. Clever, huh.

From then on, we went every year in January for my birthday to the Caribbean, always going first to Cobblers Cove hotel in Barbados. Barbados is so easy to get to, so civilised, everything works. Eventually, we decided it was a bit staid and westernised so we started island hopping, spending five or six days in other islands. In the end, over the next twenty years, I stayed at thirty-two different Caribbean islands. Naturally I got a book out of it – *A Walk Round the West Indies*. In fact two books, as I also did the Columbus biog which involved travelling to the West Indies and to Venezuela.

*A Walk Round the West Indies* had a theme, so it was not quite a travel book. In each island I went in search of two sorts of people. Firstly, I talked to expats who had come from Europe to live in the West Indies, escape to the sun, and settle in paradise, so they all said. How was it for them? In so many cases, if they were couples, they had split up. What they were usually running away from was themselves, something wrong in their lives, in their relationships.

The other sort of people I was looking for were black West Indian returnees, who had emigrated to England many years earlier, the post-*Windrush* generation who had lived in England, always saying they would go back one day. Now they had done so. So how was it for them? Most of them found it tough. They had gone back comparatively rich, because if they had worked on London Underground for thirty years, had bought a little terraced house in the sixties or seventies, they had probably sold it for a good profit. Back home, when they returned to Grenada or Antigua, they were considered dead rich. But they didn't fit in either. They missed England. The ones who had never left Grenada or Antigua felt jealous of them.

While in the West Indies one year, we also did some research for a biography Margaret was writing of Elizabeth Barrett Browning. Her family wealth came from the sugar plantations in Jamaica and she wanted to see the place where they had lived. So that was a good excuse to go there.

The thing about the West Indies is that the landscape is benign, no horrible snakes or crocodiles, no dangerous beasts that might attack you, as in Africa and elsewhere. And it is never too hot, not like the landlocked tropics, where you can't breathe during the day or step outside. In the West Indies, there is always a slight sea breeze. It does rain, but usually only for forty seconds at a time.

I did get mugged in Jamaica. I was there on my own, on the Columbus trail. I went to the museum in Kingstown to look at the Arawak exhibits. I stayed so long that when I came to leave, the door I had entered by was locked. I went out the first door I found open, and got lost, having little sense of direction. I realised I had wandered into the docks area, and found myself walking down a narrow street, clearly lost, passing blokes mending cars in the gutters.

Two youths started following me, one about eighteen, and one about fifteen. I quickened my step, and so they did, till they both passed me, saying something to each other I did not catch. The younger suddenly stopped, standing in my way. He produced a knife and lunged at me, ripping my shirt – a silk shirt, as it happened, my best favourite.

I was lucky that he did not appear to be trying to stab or injure me, just to rip open my shirt pocket where I had my passport and Visa card. He pulled them both out, holding the knife to my face. I pleaded with him to give them back to me, saying I was leaving next day. They were no use to him, he couldn't use them.

I pulled some money out of my back pocket and offered him all I had on me. It wasn't much, just a few Jamaican dollars, but he took it, roughly checked it, then slowly gave me back my passport and card.

I think, on reflection, he was just as nervous as me. Probably his first mugging, egged on by the older boy. He was probably quite pleased to have got something out of it. I lost a good shirt, which was ruined, but I did come out of it with my life and body intact.

It was all over in seconds, but at the time seemed to happen in slow motion. I had been in a dream, my own world, thinking about Columbus, and did not see the attack coming, my mind and body elsewhere. The next day I was flying to Haiti, which everyone had told me was the most dangerous island in the Caribbean. That did turn out scary, with the sound of gunshots in the street all night outside my hotel, but I never felt personally in danger.

The Caribbean island we eventually decided we both liked best of all was Bequia. This is a small island in the Grenadines, not far from Mustique, but totally different.

Mustique is manicured, like a garden suburb. Bequia is like the West Indies used to be, with real people doing real work, living real lives, not living on tourists. It has the most fantastic harbour which is always full of yachts which have crossed the Atlantic, so there are lots of ship chandlers, boat builders and little supply boats buzzing around the harbour taking water, laundry and provisions to the yachts.

Our favourite beach became Lower Bay, but the first time we stayed there, in a wonderful cottage right on the beach, the sound of the sea kept me awake all night and I moaned and groaned.

Margaret loved the Lake District, and was always happy there, but she also loved the West Indies, as we both did. We only ever went for two or three weeks a year, every January. We never for one moment ever thought of living there, as the life there is so unreal. We always knew from our first experience of living abroad, all those years earlier, that after six weeks of perfect weather you wake and say oh no, not another perfect day. But during every long winter in London, for months and months ahead, we so looked forward each year to the thought of swimming in the Caribbean.

We always knew how lucky we were, having found our fantasy house in Loweswater, as well as our London home, plus a glamorous West Indian holiday every year. We were always aware, counting our blessings, never took it all for granted, trying not to feel too smug and self-satisfied.

And most of all, we always felt lucky to have each other. Even when we were shouting at each other. We always still argued, although not as vehemently as in our teenage courting days. We never went to bed on an argument.

By argument, it was usually just Margaret telling me I was stupid, I had done something really silly, or wanted to do something really silly. Or I had forgotten to do something I had promised, left a mess somewhere, not cleaned up after doing something.

The children, at various times, were a worry, as with all families, and there is always a temptation to blame the other for what has happened or arguing about what we should do about it, now it has happened. All totally normal marital behaviour for a long-married couple.

On holiday, especially in a place like the West Indies, so far away, so different from normal domestic life, you do tend to forget all the domestic and family cares and problems back home.

Margaret always became particularly happy in the West Indies, letting herself be relaxed, almost forgetting herself, and what had happened to her, back in the 1970s.

Swimming and sunbathing all morning, then a lovely long lunch beside the sea with fresh fish, caught that morning by Cobblers' own fisherman, and a bottle of Chablis. Then we would go to our lovely bedroom all afternoon and have a long siesta, or what we called a siesta. Which of course was a euphemism.

It was about the only time in the year, when we were in the West Indies in January, that Margaret seemed able to forget or ignore that she had a double mastectomy, managing to wipe it from her conscious mind.

I had long wiped it, or ignored it, ever since 1978, but then I am a denier of anything unpleasant. In London, or Lakeland, in our normal daily lives, especially in bed, I felt she was always aware and self-conscious, if just at the back of her mind, holding back, not letting herself go or be seen. In the West Indies, however, every year for over twenty years, it was bliss.

That particular form of bliss came to a sudden end in 2007.

# 20

# THE BIG C RETURNS

After Margaret's double mastectomy in the 1970s, she did of course have regular checkups. Every three months she was tested, then six months. When it finally got to a year, I went around saying, 'Brilliant! Isn't the National Health wonderful, the magic medicine has worked!'

She would sigh, snort, give a weary smile, and tell me not to be totally stupid. 'You know there is no cure for cancer, it is always there, lurking in the background, so just shurrup making those sort of inane remarks . . .'

So for about twenty years the subject of cancer had never really come up. I forgot she had had the mastectomy, or at least wiped it from my mind. And she never talked about it. When interviewed for her books, which now and again she would be forced to do, and her health came up, she would change the subject. She never wanted to talk about it, be known and categorised as someone with cancer.

From time to time she had worries about pains in her legs or back which seemed to have no explanation or cause and sometimes would take weeks to clear up. But they always did clear up. She then assumed she must have pulled something, stretching for something in the kitchen, getting out of bed the wrong way, walking too far, and that was the only reason. When you have had cancer, regardless of how many years earlier, you are bound to think that any mysterious pain, which otherwise you would ignore, is the Big C, trying to make a return visit. She clearly feared that, without ever voicing it.

In 2002 she had pains in her ribs and hip which did seem to take an unconscionably long time to clear up, despite anti-inflammatory pills from the GP. She assumed this time it could be arthritis. In the end, she had a spine scan. It took some weeks for the results to come through as they had got lost. The GP rang to say bad news, the bone scan has shown 'hot spots'. She would be getting an appointment with an oncologist at the Royal Free. That took more weeks of waiting; meanwhile she had other X-rays and blood tests.

Hot spots sounds quite fun, as if you are going on holiday somewhere nice, but clearly it meant the cancer was back. We would have to cancel going to the West Indies, going to the Lakes. We would have to tell the children this time, as they were grown-up. We were convinced that was it. It has returned.

'Oh well then,' I said, 'I will sell the car, if we are not going to Lakeland again, so some good will come out it. I have always hated driving. Will be good not having a car.'

One evening over supper, while still waiting for the oncologist's appointment, I happened to be twitting on about what might happen if it did return, how I would have to sell up Lakeland, but the worst thing would be having to learn to cook.

'When I am gone, I am sure you will meet a young nubile woman' – she paused – 'and Flora will be furious . . .'

This was not like her, to make such a suggestive remark. I was being flippant about not cooking, but she had been cynical. And I also couldn't understand why she had dragged Flora into it, as opposed to the other two. But I said nothing. And we finished supper in silence.

I came with her to see the oncologist, which in the past I had not always done, as she was usually insistent she wanted to go alone.

He was tall and handsome and fleshy and looked like Glenn Hoddle. He was rather facetious, which doctors rarely are. Bored, irritated, stressed, not interested, overworked, all of those are normal, but you don't usually come across facetious medics.

He said the blood tests and all the other tests showed nothing, except some hot spots. He did not know what that meant, or where they were coming from, whether it was a new primary or a secondary from the breast.

I asked if it was unusual for there to be a twenty-five-year gap after a double mastectomy before a secondary appears.

'After twenty-five years, most mastectomy patients are dead.'

Cheerful, bloody bastard.

His considered opinion was – do nothing. His advice was to go away, get on with life, and see what happens. Double bastard.

But I took it as good news. I was enormously relieved that there was not going to be any new treatment. Margaret was less sanguine. It was what she had always believed and expected. It was still there. It would come back. It would get her in the end.

But we did get on with our lovely life for the next five years, having wonderful times in Lakeland and the West Indies. And then in 2007 it did come back.

Once again there were mysterious pains in her back and ribs that did not clear up. One of the GPs looked at her old wounds, the breast scars where the mastectomy had taken place, decided there was some eruption, a discharge or infection or something had happened, and booked her into the Royal Free to see a dermatologist. Dermatologist? Even I could see that was stupid. A dermatologist was not going to stop her internal pains.

But, as ever, she accepted the wisdom of the medics. She patiently waited for a dermatology appointment which, when it came, was for four weeks ahead.

By which time she was in total agony. The main area of pain seemed to be in her back. She had, when younger, had a slipped disc, so we thought it might be something to do with that.

There is a joke that if you are over sixty and you meet someone over sixty, you just have to say, 'How's the back?' And they won't stop talking for an hour.

One of my many boasts was that even in my seventies I still did not have a bad back, but, oh lord, I had had twenty years of arthritis. My joints got all swollen, I was screaming in agony at night in bed wanting someone to come and cut off my toes and my hands.

Over the years, I had had the usual drugs for arthritis – sulphasalazine, methotrexate, plus steroids when it got unbearable. They had each worked for a while, then they ceased to be effective. But I had an excellent rheumatologist at the Royal Free, Huw Beynon, who had put me on some good drugs with the trade name of Humira. I had to inject it into my tummy every two weeks – and the result was brilliant. All the joints calmed down. The agony had gone. Amazing.

One Friday, at the height of Margaret's pains, as she still waited to see the dermatologist, I was due in Dr Beynon's clinic for a checkup. I happened to tell him about Margaret – her appalling backache, and her cancer history.

Unlike Margaret, I have always gone out of my way to develop personal relations with all medics who are treating me – creeping and arse licking, it is called. I even had Dr Beynon's personal mobile. When I was in total agony, I would ring him. He would then say come at once, no need for an appointment, go to his next clinic and he would give me a steroid injection.

He had never met Margaret, knew nothing about her history, she was not his patient, but he said it sounded bad. She could come to his Royal Free clinic now, at once, and he would see her at the end of his surgery. I said how kind, but you are a rheumatologist not an oncologist.

'I am also a surgeon. I will be able to give a quick response to how serious it might be.'

I was so pleased that I rushed out of the Royal Free and jumped into a black cab – something I never do, being mean. I told him to race to our house and wait outside, to hell with the clock ticking over, I knew there was only half an hour before Dr Beynon finished his surgery, though it always ran late.

I ran upstairs to Margaret's office where she had propped herself up, trying to write, but clearly in awful discomfort.

I said quick, get your coat and shoes, I have a cab outside, my Dr Beynon will see you now.

'He's not a cancer specialist,' she said.

I explained that as a surgeon, he was trained and experienced enough to know the signs of something dodgy when he saw it.

'No, I am not going. I do not like the idea of jumping his queue.'

'Don't be daft. It is his idea, not mine. I didn't ask him. By the time you see the stupid dermatology department, anything could have happened . . .'

She still refused. I knew there was no point arguing when she said no to something, so I went outside and paid off the black cab.

I rang Dr Beynon's mobile. I left a voicemail, saying how kind he had been, but Margaret would not be coming – a message which he would probably not pick up for days.

That night, Margaret was in even worse agony. I thought she was going to pass out with the pain. So in the morning I rang Dr Beynon on his mobile again, asking if there was some way he could have a quick look at her. It was now Saturday, so he was not at the Royal Free. He rang back to say he had a private surgery in a private hospital in Barnet, whose address he gave me. He could see her there in an hour. Then he hung up. He was always brisk and decisive, which I like.

We had never used private medicine, ever, or had any private health insurance, even though we could afford it, just as we had never sent our children to fee-paying schools. We always believed we should support the state system, for health and education.

In his waiting room, at this private hospital, there was a tourist board woman I had met in the West Indies. She started a long banal conversation about our favourite West Indian islands, going on and on, while Margaret sat there in agony.

When Dr Beynon examined Margaret, he immediately said the problem was in her spine. It was serious. She should be treated at once, but first she would need an MRI. He would not be able to arrange one at the Royal Free till Monday. She could wait till then, or go now, on Saturday morning, and have it done privately.

I said immediately we would pay. Margaret, for once, agreed.

Dr Beynon made a few calls then gave us an address of a private hospital in St John's Wood where he had booked her an appointment. We got in the car and raced like mad to St John's Wood, to a posh hospital near Lord's Cricket ground.

They took down Margaret's details, and said yes she could have an MRI, but before having her MRI, we would have to pay for it. What? I could not believe it. Why would anyone want to go through with an MRI then do a runner when the bill came in?

By chance I had my Visa card on me, which was fortunate, as we had rushed out of the house in a panic that morning without taking any cash. The cost came to around £1,500, which luckily was the limit of my credit.

We paid, the card said transaction completed, and she had the scan. We got the result in our hand, in about half an hour, as Dr Beynon said we would. Then we drove like mad again back to Barnet. He studied the scan and said yes, it was what he feared. There was a tumour on the spine.

He told Margaret to go first thing on Monday to the Royal Free A&E and check in. I sighed heavily. A&E on a Monday morning at the Royal Free, or any hospital, is heaving with the weekend accidents. You can sit there for hours. It's a nightmare. Dr Beynon said it was the only way to be checked into a ward quickly. The oncologist on duty would come down and see her. Margaret would then be admitted into the ward. He would ring the chief consultant, Alison Jones, a friend and colleague of his, so they would know she was coming and the details.

Getting through Saturday and Sunday was awful. Margaret could not speak for the pain, but did not want to speak anyway.

Waiting in A&E was the normal nightmare. I was convinced no one from oncology would see her, or have her details, or know anything about her. And that all Dr Beynon's arrangements and efficiency and kindness would be wasted. But after about an hour's wait, she was seen by a nurse, then a duty oncologist came and finally she was admitted into the cancer ward.

She was in hospital for two weeks, having endless tests, by which time her legs had suddenly gone. The tumour in the spine was enormous and pressing on various vital organs. No surgery could be done, because of the delicate position, so she was put on a series of heavy-duty cancer drugs, all the names of which I used to know, but most of which I have forgotten.

Arimidex was one and Exemestane, which I think was a drug on trial.

When she came home, she still could not walk, could not get upstairs to bed, so I immediately got on the phone to John Lewis, Margaret's favourite shop, which I normally refused to use saying it was too expensive. What about Curry's, I would say, they have the same brands. Or Pound Stretchers. They are really cheap.

I ordered the best, most comfortable single bed and mattress John Lewis had. It came the next day.

Margaret spent the next six months sleeping downstairs. We have a lavatory downstairs, but our bathroom is upstairs, so she could not wash herself properly. I at once rang builders and plumbers about installing a shower, asking them to come and estimate. Margaret went potty when they started arriving. She wanted no more work done, ever, in the house. She could not face it, the disruption, the dust, the noise. She would manage fine without a shower.

After a few weeks, palliative care nurses came from the Royal Free, all very nice and pleasant. They arranged physiotherapy at the Marie Curie Cancer Hospice in Hampstead. So for a month or so I drove her across several times a week and she did exercises in their gym on the top floor.

She was then given a zimmer frame on which she laboriously learned to stagger around the garden. You don't realise, till you have any of these awful devices, that you have to be taught how to use them, which is not easy.

I was surprised and delighted how mobile she was becoming, yet how much effort it was taking. I caught her on my video camera one day, and of course she was furious. She did all her lessons and exercises, being a very obedient girl. I would have said they were stupid and given up, and would have taken twice as long to recover, At the end of six months, her legs were strong enough for her to get up the stairs and sleep in our bedroom. Very slowly, after about a year, normal life returned. She was back to walking enormous distances round the Heath, far further than I ever did.

She was still of course on constant heavy drugs, packets of them in straw baskets all over the house, neatly labelled, with times and dates ticked off. But there were awful side-effects, such as sickness and always feeling tired.

We managed the next year to get up to Loweswater. In the car she had her back propped up with orthopaedic cushions and we had lots of stops. We stayed for about three months, then she had to come back for tests. It did seem as if life would slowly get back to some sort of normality.

But her back was constantly painful. She could not be touched there, or anywhere round that area. It meant that from then on, from 2007, I could not touch her. The slightest contact made her wince. In bed, I had to make sure I did not go near her. Holding hands was about the most she could manage, without experiencing the most searing pain.

One thing which really upset her was that she could not play with our two new grandchildren. She could not pick them up, hold them, the way she had with our two older grandchildren. The older ones had stayed with us a lot. Margaret had looked after them, while their parents had holidays. Now she could do nothing with them. It made her feel useless, and a failure.

Because of her back, she could not manage any aeroplanes

or airports. She could not go to the West Indies. But she insisted I went on my own. She did not want her problems to ruin my life. She could manage fine on her own at home for two weeks. So from then on, from 2007 onwards, for the next eight years, I went every January on my birthday to Cobblers Cove, the same hotel, the same time of the year, usually staying in the same bedroom, in which we had so many happy years. Having gone for so long at the same time, and knowing all the regular guests, the hotel had become like a club. Many of the guests knew Margaret, and knew what was happening to her, and why I was on my own.

One other effect of all the heavy drugs she was now permanently on was that she lost her taste for alcohol. The drugs had somehow ruined her taste buds. We had gone through our married life having a bottle of wine with our evening meal, arguing about who had had most. I often marked the bottle in pencil every time she had a glass, to make sure she did not have more than me.

So from then on, I drank for her. Which is why I was soon on a bottle of wine a day. It crept up to two small glasses at lunch and three in the evening. Okay then, I limited myself to a litre a day. Tops.

Stupid, I know, and not good for one's health, but bugger it. I have got to have some simple pleasures in life, so I told myself, even if poor Margaret can't.

# 21

# FAMILY MATTERS

Caitlin, our oldest and tallest, which is what she always says, is today so sensible, so organised, so hard working, so reliable, so prudent, and so caring.

Which she was as a little girl, she was always neat and tidy, doing what Mummy said, wearing the clothes Mummy laid out for her, always obedient, excellent at school, loved by all the teachers, a paragon of all the virtues, really. This lasted right up until, well, about the age of fifteen.

What happens to them? Hormones kick in, so they always say, they suddenly want to rebel, go against whatever grains they have been given or fed, but there again it does not happen to all teenagers. And also when it does happen, it takes many forms, some serious, some just passing madnesses and idiocies.

The first signs were a teenage party at fourteen, which we allowed her to have in our house. All her friends, girls and boys she had grown up with, seemed so nice and well behaved, so we did not think for a moment things could go wrong. How stupid was that. But when it is your firstborn, who has been so well behaved, you are not wise to the world.

I did hide all my drink, just in case, and Margaret emptied the fridge, but we forgot the eggs on an egg rack. Then we went out to the cinema.

The house got wrecked and the walls covered with broken eggs, where they had fun throwing them at each other. Not Caitlin's fault of course. Uninvited guests pushed their way in. Caitlin was in tears, but she and her girlfriends worked hard to clear the place up.

We blamed each other, saying you should have stopped that, you should not have allowed it, you should have stayed in and supervised. A typical incident, a rite of passage all parents have to go through when they have teenagers. You always get caught the first time, not expecting things to go wrong or get out of hand.

We always worried about her friends taking drugs, getting drunk, especially when she started staying out late, hanging around Camden Town. I would insist on picking her up at an agreed spot, so she did not have to catch the late-night Tube or bus, but I never knew where she had really been.

In the upper sixth, aged seventeen, she left home and moved into a squat with her awful boyfriend, but she still managed to keep up her A-levels. She went to Sussex University to read American Studies. The awful boyfriend followed her down and spent all her money. I started giving her a living allowance weekly, as opposed to once a term, hoping she would not give it all to him.

Eventually he disappeared, phew, and she went off after graduating to the USA, doing research and getting another degree, and working as a TA – a teacher's assistant – at Clark University, Massachusetts where she met and fell in love with

Ronald from Botswana. He was doing a computer science degree. She qualified as a teacher back in Brighton, then joined Ronald in Botswana, worked there as a teacher, and then when they set up house in Maun, his home village, on the edge of the Okavango Delta, she became editor of the little local paper, the *Okavango Observer*. And won an award as journalist of the year.

I was so pleased when that happened. All the time at Brighton I was trying to encourage her to work on the student newspaper, as I had done, or the student radio, but she ignored me, even though I knew she was quite interested in writing. As a little girl she had often written down little scenes, things that happened, overheard conversations.

We went out to Africa to see her every two years, and she came home in between. I moaned all the time about getting there, as it took three days, with having to go to Jo'burg first in South Africa, then Gaborone in Botswana, then Maun. I was always saying oh if only she had married a West Indian, it is so handy to get there, and lovely beaches. Margaret warned me on no account to say that to Caitlin herself.

But we did make the most of her being in Africa, going on safaris, exploring the surrounding countries, such as South Africa, Zimbabwe and best of all Namibia. Made a change from the Lake District.

She was in Botswana twelve years, during which time she had started to write, and got her first book accepted, a novel, *Jamestown Blues*, published in 1996 by Penguin, which was good going, considering she was living so far away and out of the London literary swim.

But then the marriage collapsed, and various awful things happened to her, such as being brutally attacked. She also got involved in various campaigns which upset the authorities and got herself arrested. So she came back to England, with a baby, no money, no house, no husband, no job. Her daughter Ruby was then diagnosed with epilepsy, which fortunately faded after a few years.

They stayed with us for six months, upstairs in our house, back in her childhood bedroom. I hoped she would apply for a council flat. I wanted to be able to go around boasting 'Council house to council house in two generations'. Then she got a job as a teacher and found a flat just a few streets away.

After a year or so teaching, she started doing pieces for the *Independent*'s Education Supplement, which was quite a large section at the time, writing various columns. They paid badly and slowly, but they did pay. She also started writing books, novels and non-fiction.

She has now had ten books published, but none of them has made much money. Her books involve a lot of research, and take a long time, such as the history of swimming down the Thames. I think back to myself at her age, when I did a few niche books, meaning a subject which is likely to have only a specialist readership, such as a book I did about adoption, but at that time I got reasonable advances for them, about double what Caitlin gets today. Publishing is in a bad state. I read somewhere that the average professional, published author earns only £5,000 a year. How can they live on that?

Caitlin has recently been doing two days a week at the

University of Westminster, as a Fellow of the Royal Literary Fund, which pays quite well, enabling her to work the rest of the week full time on her books. As I write, she has just secured a contract for a book about the history of Holloway prison, Europe's most famous women's prison, and has secured access to all their archives. This was where the suffragettes were locked up, and lots of other female prisoners, well-known or notorious.

Ten years ago she went on an internet dating site, which alarmed Margaret and me, not understanding such things, worried where it would lead, but it turned out brilliantly for her. She has been with her partner, Nigel, ever since. He was a photographer and is now in the lay-out department of a well-known online newspaper. They live near the Holloway Road, just within walking distance.

Her daughter Ruby is now sixteen and has been at the girls' comprehensive school near us which Flora attended – and is now at a sixth form college. Ronald, Caitlin's former husband, later became an MP in Botswana.

Jake, our son, was a right pain as a young child, unlike Caitlin the paragon, never sleeping, doing really stupid things, falling over, injuring himself. You would shout at him not to kick a tin can across the road or run along the pavement with a piece of plastic pipe in his mouth – and he did, falling over, giving himself the most awful injuries. We seemed never to be away from A&E.

He was also slow at reading and learning generally. He loved football and when I was doing football books I made him do lists for me – totting up the goal scorers, away goals, penalties. He would often fall asleep with a Spurs programme still on his face. I used to maintain to Margaret that it was thanks to me getting him interested in football programmes that he eventually did learn to read.

As a teenager, unlike Caitlin, he never rebelled or caused us any worries. It was as if he had got all of that bolshie nonsense out of his system in his first seven years of driving us mad. Or perhaps boys don't generally have such troubled adolescences as girls.

It was in the sixth form that he seemed to emerge, academically. We always knew he was good at arguing, often just for the sake of it, just like his dear mother, fluent and convincing. He was also very knowledgeable on things like politics, unlike me and Margaret. After a childhood in which he had appeared a slow learner, he got into Cambridge to read History. And then blow me, got a First.

And then he did, well, nothing in particular for the next six years, so I thought, I am sure unfairly. He went off to Spain and then Italy, teaching English to foreigners in language schools, having lots of girlfriends, playing lots of football, but of course little money.

Every time he came home I would suggest to him that with his fab degree he should apply to the BBC or the Diplomatic Service, get a professional job, with a career structure. He would sigh and say he was not like me, he did not want to wear a suit, have a career, have a mortgage; he was not ambitious or interested in money.

Margaret said I had to stop nagging him. She maintained I was just jealous that Jake appeared to be enjoying himself going around Europe, which I never did. After university, I went straight to work. Gap years did not exist in my time. He did though learn Italian and Spanish.

Eventually, of course he did want to settle down. He then met someone he wanted to live with. So began endless discussions about what he might do. In the end, he decided he quite fancied being a barrister. It seemed to suit his skills and talents. His degree was in History, so he spent a year transferring to a law degree, then another year at Bar school, then another year as a pupil in chambers. So it was another three years before he was earning properly.

With Caitlin doing books and journalism, it has always been easy and interesting talking to her about her working life. We both understood what she was on about, and could join in discussions about royalties and slagging off bastard agents and stupid editors. The Bar was a totally foreign country, to both me and Margaret. We had no idea, for example, what pupilage was or how it worked.

His chambers are in the Inner Temple, prime position, ancient buildings, lovely situation beside the river. I love seeing his name, painted on the outside of their entrance. But by starting his career late, he is around eight years behind his contemporaries who went straight into the law, many of whom are now QCs. He specialises in employment law, often representing local councils. Councils have been making endless cuts and barristers generally are having a hard time, with legal aid being reduced. When they hear he is a barrister, people always think that he must be rolling in it. But the law is like football. It is only in the Premiership you make big money. The majority of barristers and lawyers earn fairly modest money, considering all the years it has taken them to qualify.

Jake is married to Rosa, who is English, but has an Italian-Irish background. She is a set designer who has worked for the Royal Shakespeare Company, the Royal Court and the Tricycle Theatre. They have a daughter, Amelia, seventeen, at a local comprehensive.

Flora, six years younger than Jake, also went to the local girls' comprehensive next to his school, which Ruby later attended. While Flora was there, the school experienced a lot of industrial actions, teachers on strike, lessons cancelled. I always thought Flora lost out by this, but she never thought so, and would not consider for a moment the idea of finding another school.

She did two A-levels and got an A in each – and refused to go to university. I think she saw the example of her older brother and sister, getting good arts degrees, then not knowing what to do. Caitlin seemed to be doing endless research and other degrees. Jake was wandering round Europe.

Flora decided she would go to London School of Printing, learn something useful, which would lead to a proper job, in this case screen printing. Afterwards, she did various jobs, none of them in screen printing. For a time, she worked as a paralegal, so we were thinking we would have two legal eagles in the family. Eventually she went into TV. She started as a lowly researcher, working her way up and eventually becoming a producer, doing several BBC documentaries.

She did that for ten years and then got married and had children. Amarisse is now nine and Sienna eight. Amarisse was born on my birthday, 7 January, so at my birthday party for my eightieth she celebrated her eighth at the same time. Flora is married to Richard, who is French-Cameroon.

Since Caitlin returned from Botswana, all three of them have lived in north London, not too far away, two within walking distance, which has been a delight, with them and their children calling in all the time.

Our four granddaughters, unlike me and Margaret, have a mixture of foreign blood and culture flowing through their veins. Between them their antecedents come from Botswana, Cameroon, France, Italy, Ireland, plus England and Scotland. Modern life, eh, especially modern London life.

I used to think, when they were little, and often driving me mad, with fury or worry, that when they got to eighteen and left home, off to college or wherever, that would be it, no more worries. They would be on their own, nothing to do with us any more, we can relax, they are grown-ups now, responsible for their own lives. But of course it does not work out like that. As long as you are alive, and they are still alive, you are still the parent, they are still your children, so you still worry about them – if they are happy, if they are well. And I suppose always will.

This did not happen with our own parents. When we each got to eighteen, we hid everything remotely worrying from our own parents, not wanting to upset them. We never told them about Margaret's mastectomy. We did not ask for their help financially when trying to buy a house, as of course they had no money. Our intimate, personal connections with them ceased, more or less, when we left home. I feel today I am in touch with all my children's lives, all the time, more or less. Which is good. Adds an extra dimension to living.

*

After several years living in our street, with an army of carers, plus of course my sister Marion and Margaret, my mother went into Friern Barnet Hospital in north London. It was a nightmare of a place, a vast Victorian mansion which looked awfully impressive from outside, with handsome wings, long driveway, extensive gardens, but inside was like a scene from Kafka, long echoing corridors, constant screams and shouts in the distance, inmates crowded like cattle into so-called recreation rooms. My mother slept in a vast open ward, beds all huddled together, a so-called Florence Nightingale ward, which looked unchanged since the Crimea.

By this time, aged seventy-eight, she had no idea where she was, or who she was. She just wanted to stay under the blankets all day. When awake and vaguely compos mentis, she was often a bit angry and bad tempered, which was not like her, accusing people of stealing things from her, as if she had anything worth stealing.

I was in Caracas in Venezuela, working on my travel biography about Columbus, when she died on 8 December 1987. I was sitting in my hotel room writing what I thought were awfully amusing postcards back home. At the top of them all I was writing the dateline 'Christmas, Caracas'.

The phone rang and it was Margaret to say my mother had died. I am supposed to have said, 'You're joking', which has been held against me ever since. I don't remember saying it, but I probably did say something like that.

I missed my mother's funeral, which Margaret and my sister Marion organised, as the next day I was on a plane to the Orinoco, trying to discover the place where Columbus first set foot on the continent of the Americas.

My mother was seventy-nine, which was remarkable, considering the hard life she had led and all her years of ill health. It meant that if I got to 7 January 2016, my eightieth birthday, I would have beaten both my mother and my father, who died aged fifty-three.

My mother left nothing of course, not a bean. I have kept safe quite a few of her letters, a lot of them sent to me in the late fifties and sixties, during my first years in journalism. She would reply to say she had safely received my £2, which I sent in an envelope, every week, in cash. It never got lost, not like today. She would tell me the latest chat about the family, my sisters and brother. Her remarks and descriptions were always amusing, caustic without being cruel or hurtful.

My brother Johnny, who was an electrician for many years, then later became a social worker, ended up running a department of Carlisle Social Services with about fifteen people. He is long retired, but still living in Carlisle with his wife Marjorie. He has two children and three grandchildren.

Annabelle, my sister who married Roger, the civil servant, who suffered from MS, is a widow and lives in Leighton Buzzard. She seems to be travelling all the time, making up for all those years spent homebound, caring for Roger.

Marion, my sister who went to Ruskin College Oxford, then became a social worker in Camden and started writing the column in the *Guardian*. She never did the column she intended to write about being a lesbian, but she did have success with her play.

Marion was working on another play when she died in 1995. She had organised in advance her own funeral service and had found a woman minister to conduct it, which was quite hard twenty-two years ago, as there were few women clerics.

Marion had been suffering from throat cancer for some time. She had had endless awful operations on her throat and nose, though she could still walk and get about at home, living with her partner Frances. She had smoked most of her life, which clearly had not helped. She spent some time at the Marie Curie Hospice in Hampstead, and then came home to die. At the end of her life, she seemed to live on ice cream, about the only thing her poor throat could tolerate.

A few weeks before she died, she wanted to be interviewed by me about her life. It was partly to pass the time, as by then she was sitting slumped all day in a chair. She hoped it might be a distraction, an amusement.

I had no plans to do anything with it, but I thought I should buy a proper, modern, professional tape recorder. For three days, I spent some time each day talking to her, taking her through her life, from working in the tyre factory, her marriage, coming out as a lesbian, trying to be a writer. But on the fourth date, she said she had had enough. It was too emotional and also upsetting. She could not remember why she had done things, or wasn't able to express her feelings the way she had wanted to. We had left it too late. It was distressing not distracting her. So I gave up.

Marion was only fifty-six when she died, just getting into her stride in her new career, and her new life with a new partner. All my children still remember and talk about her.

Margaret wrote a well-received non-fiction book in 1998 called *Precious Lives*, about the life and death of her father

Arthur and about my sister Marion, who both died about the same time. A few years earlier, she had done a book called *Hidden Lives*, about her own family history and its mysteries. Later on she did a book called *Good Lives*. This was about the wives of eminent men and their marriages, with the running theme being her own marriage.

Margaret's novel *Have the Men Had Enough?* was the one about my mother's Alzheimer's.

Is it unfair, cheating, bad taste, to use the lives and deaths, pains and pleasures, of other people in your own books? Obviously I don't think so, having written about myself and my own family all these decades. And still doing so.

In the books about her family and mine, in the way Margaret did it, it was a homage, a celebration of unknown people, such as her father, and their ordinary, unknown lives.

People often say to writers who cannibalise their own or others' lives, oh, that must have been easy, you have just lifted that from real life. You've pinched that story, stolen that drama, copied that character, and used things that I have said. Very often they get it wrong, assuming someone or something is based on them, when it is not.

One reaction is to say, go on then, you do it. If it is just a matter of lifting from real life, why don't you have a go? It has of course to be shaped, filtered, altered, used in a certain way, given a narrative and of course written with insight and style and tension, so that readers will want to read on.

Where else do writers get their thoughts and material from, except from their own lives and of those around them? But not all directly use the material. And some do it so you can never see the joins.

It often happens, with all novelists, that something from real life – a character, an incident, a thought, a reflection – sparks off a book, but when they get down to writing it, the original incident disappears, or at least becomes invisible to the reader and often the writer. It is the reaction of a novelist to the world which matters, not the facts.

Margaret in fact was a proper novelist. Almost every book was out of her head. She made up people, and then made up what they did, what they thought. I was only ever allowed to read her manuscript when it was at the proof stage, had been accepted by the publisher, but I could sometimes see where odd sentences and incidents had come from in her or our life. But most times I could not work out where the original spark had come from.

She always wrote about women. They were her main and often only characters. They almost always had families. The plots concerned ordinary domestic events and relationships. Nothing dramatic happened. She preferred not to tie up loose ends, or create happy endings, which of course don't always happen in real life anyway. Quite a big canvas, really. Which almost everyone in life can relate to.

## 22

# MARGARET'S LAST BOOKS

Despite the cancer coming back in 2007, and having to take all the dreaded medications and treatment, for most of the next eight years Margaret did get back to a normal writing routine, even if her day-to-day life and pleasures were not quite the same.

She would go to her room each morning, after she had made me a morning cup of tea, and then run my bath. Correction, she ran her own bath. She had her own bath first, and then I followed her into it. She did not like me telling the neighbours I used her old bath water, but I thought it was so sensible, so ecologically sound, and also saved me time. I hate waiting for a bath to run. And I am mean, so it saved money on hot water.

Also, slight correction on the tea. She used to in the old days, for over forty years, bring me tea in bed, plus the newspaper, latterly the *Independent*, nicely ironed. She then switched on the radio for the *Today* programme. I do find myself awfully tired when I wake up. She stopped doing that after 2007, when she was trying to conserve what strength she still had, so I installed a kettle for my tea in our bedroom. Even managed to switch it on myself. I am not totally incapable. But if she had a bath, I still got into it after her.

Over the years, many friends and folks were horrified to discover that such a strong, independent, feminist woman should be so craven, waiting hand and foot on a man, but as she always said, we had divvied up the jobs when we got married. She willingly took the domestic, cleaning, catering role, while I did, well whatever I could get away with. Not a lot really. Okay then, I always did the gardening. I looked after all financial affairs, investments and all bills, booked holidays, which of course can be terribly stressful. I also did all the driving and the odd repair jobs, in London and the Lakes. And answered the phone, which she hated doing.

Around nine o'clock each morning, she would go to her office at the top of the house, on a back extension, which was like being on a ship, looking out over all the gardens. She would sit there for one and half hours each morning, writing. She had no phone in her office, no computer, no mobile, just blank sheets of paper and her Waterman fountain pen. She never read what she had done the day before, just started each day at the top of a blank page. She never numbered the pages, but each day she would find she had written precisely ten pages.

When she had finished the novel, she would then read it through to see she had not changed the heroine's name or hair colour, numbered all the pages and send it to Gertrude, her typist for so many years. I would scream at her when I found she had posted the only manuscript, without making a copy. What if it gets lost in the post, destroyed or burned?

Your year's work will be ruined. 'Doesn't matter,' she would say, 'I am only playing.'

For each of her twenty-six published novels, she would make no notes, never talk about it, either before, during or after. If the publisher had queries or worries, she would not be too upset. Doing it was the thing. She was not interested in a book after she had written the last page, and saw no reason to help with promotion. She had an agreement with her publisher that she would not be required to do literary festivals, of which there are now over 500 in the UK, give talks or do signing sessions.

I am sure our three children, when growing up, had no idea their mother wrote books. If they came into her room, she would hide the current manuscript, drop everything and attend to whatever they wanted. She never ever talked about the novel she was working on.

Non-fiction was a bit different. She did do research, wrote lots of notes, and would talk about the person she was working on all the time, given any excuse. Daphne du Maurier or Elizabeth Barrett Browning would constantly come into her conversation.

The first book that she published after the cancer returned, while she was being treated, was a novel called *Over*, which came out in 2007. It seemed spooky, that she had chosen such a title. She did not know when she was writing it that the cancer was back. But then at home she did begin to talk about it as being her last novel.

However, the medications and drugs and radiotherapy kept her going and she continued writing. In 2010, she published *Isa and May* and in 2013 *The Unknown Bridesmaid*.

She did one final non-fiction book, *My Life in Houses*, published in 2014. I was allowed to read it in proof, not knowing what it was about, apart from the title, which I presumed gave it all away. It is indeed about the houses she lived in, from being a little girl, but as the book progresses, it is about something else – the history and treatment of her cancer. It comes up almost incidentally, in passing, so that you can miss it at first. I was in tears when I had finished the book.

But still she kept going, and somehow managed to complete another novel, despite being racked with pain and vomiting. *How to Measure a Cow* came out in April 2016.

The title was mine. I had bought a load of local memorabilia, part of the estate of a local farmer in Loweswater, containing bills and accounts and notes going back to the 1770s. Among them were handwritten notes on sheep dipping, sheep shearing, what medications he had used. One section was called How to Measure a Cow. (Apparently it is the height times the diagonal of the body, or at least that was how in nineteenth-century Loweswater they compared one cow with another.)

The wording amused Margaret, so she worked it into the book. It is only referred to once. As with *Catcher in the Rye*, the title has nothing to do with the book, being only mentioned in passing.

Margaret's heroine, who has run away, assuming a new identity for reasons which emerge, is befriended by an old lady, the widow of a farmer, who takes her in her car round the Lakes. On the way, the old woman is moaning about her life, that she has done nothing, achieved nothing. All she has learned, so she says, is How to Measure a Cow.

When the book came out, the title proved not as amusing or as memorable as we had thought. Booksellers were endlessly being asked for *How to Milk A Cow* or *How to Measure a Couch*.

Every summer, from 2007 to 2015, despite all the awful drugs Margaret was taking, and beginning to feel the side-effects of, we did manage to go up to Loweswater every year. We went in May for Margaret's birthday, when all the rhododendrons were coming out in our garden. But the time we could spend there got shorter and shorter. It had been at least five months in the old days but this became reduced to five weeks. She had to come back for scans and tests, which always exhausted her, so was unable to return.

One scan revealed some sort of new dark cloud, which they diagnosed as being a blood clot on the lung. It could burst into life at any moment and finish her off.

From then on, she had to inject herself with yet another new daily drug. She kept a long list of all her various drugs, and the time she had to take each one. She would panic if she forgot and was half an hour late. She would then put her own meal back half an hour, as she had been told to take the drug after a meal. I said it was silly. Doctors just say anything, the timings are approximate. Drugs don't know when they are taken. But she always did what she was told.

From time to time the tests and scans would be quite reassuring – the most cheerful news was 'stable', i.e. the cancer was still lurking, but not doing much, just hanging about, resting or sleeping, not bothering anybody

But then more and more of the dreaded shadows were

appearing on the scans, spots near the lungs and elsewhere were identified, contents unclear, missions not stated, but it was obvious the cancer was active again, expanding into areas where it had not been invited.

In September 2015, it was decided she should go back on chemotherapy – taken orally, as pills. The side-effects started almost at once, making her tired all the time, with no energy, making her sick. For five days, she was projectile vomiting for several hours at a time. Nothing was in her stomach, for nothing would stay there, but still the vomiting would start. Her whole body was shaken and shattered by the intensity of the vomiting. It was almost like joke vomit-ing, exaggerated and over the top, the sort the two lay-deez did at the mention of homosexuality on TV in *Little Britain*, done for laughs.

I took to sleeping upstairs in Jake's old bedroom when the vomiting was especially violent during the night. She didn't want me to be there, when she was in agony, to witness what she was going through.

Another side-effect of the chemo was constipation, which she found humiliating, never having had trouble of that sort in her whole life.

She did not want me to ring the doctor. She said the chemo had to be taken, it was all for her good, so the side-effects had to be suffered. But in the end I rang our GP's surgery and to my amazement the chief partner, Dr Stuart, arrived on his bike. He was on his way home, after a long day. Never had our doctor actually come to the house in about fifty years, not since the days of Micky Day, our first GP whom we joined in

1960. He took blood tests which I then took over next day to the Royal Free to be analysed.

Eventually, she was put on even more drugs, to counter the side-effects of the existing drugs, mainly of course the chemo pills. And there was a minor improvement or at least abatement in the downward spiral.

She still managed a short walk round the edge of the Heath after lunch, using her walking stick, the one her father had used. She usually wore her orange coat and black trousers, tucked into her boots, going very slowly, but usually getting as far as the first pond.

Later, on my own walk, for since I was fifty I have always had a siesta after lunch, I would catch up with her, or more often catch sight of her from the flanks of Parliament Hill. I would glimpse a flash of orange, recognise the walking stick, realise who it was, and then notice how small she had become. I had always looked upon her as taller than me, because she held herself so well, walked tall and erect, but during the last few years she had lost two inches and had become very slow and slightly bent.

It got harder each day for her to get up out of bed, get dressed, go downstairs, bring in the milk, fill our two bowls with her homemade muesli, make herself her one and only cup of coffee of the day. She insisted on struggling to do all this, otherwise what is the point. Then she would drag herself back to bed. She would just lie there, with her clothes on for the rest of the day, with no strength left to get up again.

She did not want to discuss what was happening, or would possibly next be happening. If I mentioned food, what can

I make her, or for myself, she would groan. The thought of food made her sick.

I started asking her to give me some notes, dictate to me how to cook certain favourite things, the sauces she made, the quiches she created. The very words made her sick. I had never cooked in all my life, except Hunter's Special when she first had cancer in 1975, which I fed to the children every evening. At least there was just the two of us to feed this time.

I did not know how to use the washing machine, or how to put on the dishwasher, which orifices needed filling with which potions. Appalling that in fifty-five years of married life I had learned so little. Not even how to make a salad dressing.

But by now she did not want or did not have the energy to tell me, or direct me, or dictate instructions to me. She did not want to think about anything like that anyway.

She eventually gave up attempting to go on the Heath and restricted her ambitions to the garden, dragging herself round it, again and again, taking forever each time, with lots of stops and sits, leaning and staring, pretending she was examining the flowers and bushes.

Earlier in the year, I had arranged for the decking in our back yard to be ripped up. It had been laid at great expense ten years earlier, when decking was all the fashion, but had proved a great mistake. The wood had started to rot, so it was dangerous to walk on it, and rats were breeding underneath. Poisons usually worked in the end, but the smell was appalling. So we had decided some months earlier to have it all up and York stone slabs put down.

Should we cancel having it done? Was it worth it at this stage in her condition? She had already vetoed my idea for a summer house at the bottom of the garden. I thought it would give a focal point, a staging post in her morning meander round the garden, somewhere to sit and stare and rest. She said certainly not, she did not want a summer house, over her dead body.

But she agreed that getting rid of the rotten decking would be worth doing, save her falling if she ever ventured out or being bitten by rats.

We got an excellent gardening man to lay the York stones. He was called Mick and was Irish, probably the first Irishman to work in the house for about fifty years. In the sixties, when we first moved in, we seemed for a while to be occupied by the Irish.

The only problem was he worked on his own and it took him five weeks. He also started very early in the morning, which upset Margaret as he worked just outside the back door, a few feet away from where she was sitting having her morning coffee. But he was kind and careful and brought with him his little dog Joey which amused us all. In the end, she was grateful the work had been done. It gave us such pleasure when the terrace was completed. The York stones were so attractive, turning different shades of colours in sun or rain. And were also easy to walk on.

In October, Margaret's hair started to fall out. After her bath there were great strands of it floating on top of the water. She rarely now had the strength to walk in the garden. There were more scans and more scans as her white blood cells had suddenly become low. Whatever that meant, for I didn't know, except that it increased the risk of infection. She therefore had to stop any of the family coming to visit if they might have the slightest cold. Yet she still insisted on trying to cook, despite her hands shaking and being unsteady on her feet. I was terrified she would fall, but she would not let me anywhere near her in her kitchen. The solution was to have very simple meals, with the minimum of preparation.

She was assigned a palliative care team, who worked at the Royal Free. Two of their nurses came to see her, a senior one and a trainee. All the trainee could say was, 'Goodness you do look well, goodness we expected you to look far worse than you are, goodness you look wonderful . . .'

That would have cheered me up, even if I had scoffed, but Margaret always hated any personal comments, of any sort, with people telling her either she looked well or she did not look well. In this case, it was of course meaningless. This trainee nurse had never seen her before and did not know how absolutely shitty Margaret was now feeling. Perhaps the hospital notes had led her to think Margaret was on her last legs. Margaret moved the conversation on smartly, asking pointedly if that was all they wanted.

Mentally she was still totally alert, though she refused to discuss the future, refusing to discuss anything more than one day ahead.

The proofs of my memoir *The Co-op's Got Bananas!* arrived, which takes our life together up to 1960 (the previous volume of the book you are now reading). She said she would like to read it.

She made a few pungent observations, pointed out I had not described how she looked and dressed when we first met as teenagers, which I added. She said that in the book, all she seemed to do was criticise me, so I altered that a bit. She asked if the scene where I describe her getting fitted with a diaphragm was really necessary. I said of course. It's social history, my darling.

On 11 November 2015 I went with her for her regular appointment at the Royal Free where she saw her oncologist, Dr Newby, whom she always liked. Alison Jones, the Royal Free oncologist she first saw in 2007, had now retired.

Dr Newby had the entire scan in front of her, and went through the usual stuff about black spots and shadows and stuff, looking suitably grim and serious.

In Dr Newby's last official letter, recording the previous meeting, she had used a strange phrase about Margaret, saying she 'had not asked any questions'.

We took this to mean that Margaret had not asked how long she had to live. So I said I would ask it straight out this time, but she said don't you dare. It is up to her. She decided she would do it elliptically, asking what 'stage' she was at. This was what one of the palliative care nurses had recently asked her.

'We don't talk in stages or in figures,' replied Dr Newby, 'but if you are asking how long might you have to live, I can give you an estimate. If you would like that?'

We both nodded.

'You can never be sure. It is only an estimate, but I would say it is months not years. Asked to guess how many months, I would say between three months and nine months.'

We both sat, silent.

She said some more radiotherapy might possibly help, and she called in the consultant radiologist, another doctor whom Margaret liked, who was brisk, no-nonsense, but efficient and cheerful. She looked at all the latest scans. A bit of radiotherapy might help the pain in her shoulders, but not much. Really, it had now got to the stage where no amount of radiotherapy would help. Then she left the room.

Before that meeting with Dr Newby, Margaret had decided that whatever happened, she was giving up the chemo.

She had been on the heavy-duty cancer drugs for eight months, and chemo full time for a year. The side-effects were now unbearable. The quality of her life had so diminished that she did not want to take them any more.

At the end of the meeting, Margaret told Dr Newby she had decided to take no more chemo pills. Dr Newby nodded and said yes. She was going to say that herself.

So we left, got in the car and went home. Without talking. The only thing she did say was that she did not want the children or anyone to be told the exact prediction, about possibly having only three months to live. Say nothing about that, she said. If asked, just tell them the white blood cells were now stable. She did not want them getting more depressed and worried.

So that was it. After forty-three years of treatment for cancer, it was all over. No more treatment of any sort or any forms of cancer drugs. There was no point. They had run out of treatments.

I thought about the future, the future of medicine, the future of the world. Obviously there will be even more advances, perhaps proper cures, or at least decent cancer treatments which don't have awful side-effects. How fortunate for those in the years ahead who will benefit.

On the other hand, I also looked back into the past. Having the double mastectomy in the seventies did work, when I was convinced each time that she was a goner. Again, in 2007, I was sure it was the end. And yet once again she survived, and had had these extra nine years. So we had been lucky, living when we did, in these times, compared with those who had suffered in the distant past.

The next evening, over supper, I started crying. I have gone through life not crying or showing emotion.

'Oh help,' she said, a joke phrase in our family, mocking my mother, who always said it when someone got emotional or sentimental.

'I was just thinking,' I said. 'When I die, I will meet you again.'

'You are not going to turn soppy and religious, are you, in your old age?'

'Yeh I know, it is corny. It's what people always say. But it just came into my head. I couldn't stop it. While I live on, it will be a comfort to think we will meet again. Even though it is a stupid thing to say and of course we won't.'

'Oh help,' she said.

In bed that night, I leaned over and gave her a kiss, being careful not to touch her.

'I love you so much,' I said.

'And I love you. Now go to sleep . . .'

In fifty-five years of marriage I don't think either of us has said we loved each other, not since our pre-marriage courting days. We always mock people saying 'love you soooo much' or 'love you too' even when it is a ten-second mundane phone call.

# 23

# THE THREE HURDLES

In December 2015, Margaret got worse. She was still forcing herself up for an hour or two each day, but her hands and body were shaking, she staggered round the bedroom, the pains in her body were everywhere.

I rang the palliative care team leader and also our GP, Dr Stuart. They both came not long afterwards. They both assured Margaret that, these days, there was never any need to suffer pain. When it got unbearable, they would give her stuff, so not to worry. I was reassured. But Margaret was not.

She was given a prescription for morphine which I took round to Michael's, our local chemist. In the last year, I never seemed to be away from him. He is an expert, everyone agrees, the cleverest chemist in north London, if not the whole world, never knowingly stuck for an explanation, a diagnosis and of course a recommendation.

Margaret now had so much medication that she had a wicker basket, the size of a Harrods hamper, in which she kept all her pills and potions, covered in a pretty red and gingham piece of cloth. It looked so like a picnic hamper that I feared the younger granddaughters might open it and start scoffing.

The morphine came as a liquid, in a little bottle, like children's cough mixture. I wanted to have a small swig, but she would not let me. She took it for five days. The pain was a bit less, but she felt sick. It was changed to morphine pills. They did not seem to help much either, so steroids were added. Each time, the picnic hamper got bigger and bigger.

Six months earlier, I had booked my annual January trip to the West Indies, for the thirtieth year running, even though for the last eight years I had gone on my own. At the time I booked, she was still walking fairly well, but now it was clearly impossible, so I cancelled it. When I told her, she started crying. 'I am ruining your life enough as it is.'

I was now doing all the cooking, such as it was, shopping and cleaning, while she stayed mostly in bed. One night, I decided to cook some fillet steak for each of us, which I had bought at Lidl months ago after swimming. She said she felt sick at the very thought of it, but agreed to give me instructions on how to cook it, telling me which pan to use, how to chop the red onions, make sauté potatoes and boil the green beans. I ate it all, and it tasted quite nice, but nowhere as nice as all those years of having it made for me. And the mess afterwards, dear God, the kitchen was like a dump. It took forever clearing up and totally ruined the enjoyment of the meal. And the smell of cooking, which lingered long afterwards, was horrible.

For the last few years, Margaret had almost become a veggie, only agreeing to cook meat for me once a week. She said it was the sight of the raw meat that had put her off. I could now understand what she meant. I think cooking is overrated. All that fuss, and then you have to do it all again the next day.

I also got her to give me instructions for using the washing machine. And the first time I used it, I caused a flood. Don't know what I did wrong. But the water went all the way down the hall floor. What an idiot.

Margaret would still not discuss the future, or look back at the past. I was hoping to have some soppy conversations about the good times in our lives, the fun things we had done, you remember that hotel, wasn't that a brilliant holiday, and the children and grandchildren, remember the birth of Amelia. But she was not interested. Or she did not have the energy.

Then to my slight surprise she started talking about three upcoming events she wanted to make, to somehow stay alive, till all these three events were over. It showed she had been going over things in her head.

The first was the long-planned visit of Theo, her best friend from her Oxford days, with whom she had shared a flat, who had got married after Oxford and lived ever since in the USA. Her husband Van, a Rhodes scholar, had gone on to be an economist in the Carter administration and an academic.

We had never been to see them in Washington, as Margaret refused to go, even when she was well enough, though we had visited them many years ago when Van had been a professor at Swarthmore. Theo had visited us many times, in London and in Lakeland. And of course they had written to each other all the time.

Theo did come, in December, as planned. And they had long chats. Theo, after all these decades in the USA, is now thoroughly American, of a certain sort, and had brought lots

of books and literature about dying, which was thoughtful –
what to do, how it feels, what can be done.

Despite being incredibly fit and active, she and Van were
selling up their Washington house, where they had brought
up their three children, and had bought into what appeared
to be an apartment in sheltered housing. She brought videos,
photos, pamphlets to show us all the wonders and support
systems, which amused us. Being British, we privately scoffed.
Americans, eh. But we agreed it was all very sensible.

We ourselves had made no plans for the end of our lives.
Margaret personally had been donating money to Dignity in
Dying for years. She had said she would like to be put to sleep,
when the time came, not to suffer the pain and indignity of
dying, forcing others to witness her suffering. Now, she was
too ill to travel to Switzerland and be finished off. I don't think
in fact she would have done it, would endlessly have put it off,
till it was too late, which is what was now happening.

In my own fantasy ending of my life, I would never even
think of committing suicide. My plan is to stay in this house
and arrange carers to live in. I am going nowhere. And I hope
of course I will have enough money to pay for care and not
expect our children to be burdened. I often did mention this,
now and again, while having my evening drink and reading
the evening paper, then moved on quickly to pondering Spurs'
chances in the League.

The other event, after the visit of Theo, which Margaret wanted
to get through was Christmas. She had 'done' Christmas for
years, decades of it, for the whole family, and relations, extended
family and friends, massive Christmas dinners for which she did

all the cooking. For the last couple of years she had not been up to it, so the children had taken over the family baton, taking it in turns. This year we were all going to have it at Jake's.

She was not of course going to be there at his house, not the slightest chance of that, but she did not want do anything inconvenient, such as dying, and thus ruin the family gathering, deflecting us all from having a jolly, noisy, happy time.

For the first time in fifty-five years of marriage, I was allowed to go out and buy the Christmas tree for our house. I had never been allowed to do it, as I could not be trusted, and would come home with some rubbish tree just because it was cheap.

Now, she did not have the will or the energy to object when I said I would get it. I got a nice tree from a stall outside Morrison's, at a nice price, which was £15. The previous year she had paid £50 at a posh shop in Swain's Lane. But she pronounced it a nice tree, just as nice as any we had had in the past.

As usual, she listened to her Christmas carols. She never listened to music, had no interest in songs or music of any sort, and in the rest of the year she never put on a record or a tape. But each year at Christmastime she got out an old tape of King's College Cambridge choir singing carols. She always listened to them in the dark, on her own, with the Christmas tree lights on. If I or anyone else came into the room, she would turn it off, trying to pretend she had not been listening to the carols.

I once brought back from the West Indies a reggae version of some Christmas carols, which I and the children enjoyed. She listened once, and then refused to have it on again. She only wanted the traditional old-fashioned versions sung the old-fashioned way.

Somehow, she got through the Christmas period at home with no collapses. On New Year's Eve, she even managed to come downstairs in her dressing gown for our own New Year tradition, our annual ritual.

For over forty years, on New Year's Eve, we would sit up late – sometimes till five past ten – and do Our Predictions, which I would carefully list, in my best handwriting. Firstly, we take a look back at the year just gone, listing the highlights. Mainly family-related highlights, like a new baby, a leaking roof repaired.

We also had a short list of Current Topics. This was about the subjects currently worrying us, at that very moment, as that New Year arrived. I liked doing that one. A year later, when I read out last year's worries, we had totally forgotten most of them, the things that had been driving us mad.

Then we did the Predictions for the year ahead. If someone was pregnant, or sitting some exams, we would guess the outcome. Exact dates would have to be predicted for births – plus names. We never predicted sad things, never listed deaths or failures, just all the happy or relatively happy outcomes.

We did national and world things as well. If for example there was a General Election or Presidential Election coming up in the year ahead, we each had to guess the winners. With figures.

If there was a World Cup, we had to name the two finalists, same with the European Championship. And each year who would win the Premiership and the FA Cup.

I always liked reading out stuff from the distant past, asking her to guess where we were and what we were worrying about on New Year's Eve 1966, or in 1984.

I did ask her to guess where we were on 3 December 1983. I had looked it up and knew we were in the Böglerhof hotel in Alpbach, Austria, on a skiing holiday. We went to that same hotel three years running. Margaret loved it even though she did not ski, leaving that to me and Jake and Flora. Instead, she would go for a long walk in the snow.

She knew at once where we were that year, as she always knew dates and places, unlike me. But she said asking her to guess one year was enough. She did not want to go back over old stuff, least of all old predictions. Nor to bother her with boring football predictions. 'How long is this going on? I want to go to bed.'

But she played a bit of the game, to indulge me. I have now forgotten what she predicted on her last New Year's Eve – on 31 December 2015. I wasn't able to look it up till the next New Year's Eve. That was the rule. Neither of us would have predicted Leicester in 2016. I probably said Spurs to win the Prem. I do that every year. Could it be next year – the year after she has gone?

The third thing she was hanging on for was to get to 7 January 2016, and my eightieth birthday celebrations. I had planned two events, a dinner party for friends and neighbours in the street and a party at the Groucho Club for my work and media friends. This was what we had done in 1986, for our Silver Wedding.

For the actual birthday on 7 January, I had booked a room at the Groucho. I had invited all the family, including grandchildren and my sister and brother and his wife, who were coming down from Carlisle, along with my long-standing media friends and colleagues. I worried how they would all mix together. Then later, I had arranged a dinner for the neighbours, not at home as in 1986, but at a local bistro, Bistro Laz, beside the Heath.

Margaret was never going to go to either of them, even if she had been well. The very thought of either of them, especially the Groucho Club, appalled her. But she wanted to stay alive, not cause either of them to be cancelled, in order to please me. And also please herself. She looked forward to our three children, in turn, coming to see her after the Groucho Club and telling her, blow by blow, details of the full horrors of what she had missed. Different details, of course, as they would have their own take on what happened.

And it came to pass. The Groucho party was a great success. We had live music by the Quarrymen and I danced with my younger grandchildren all night long. One of the things about young grandchildren is that they are not embarrassed. Unlike teenagers.

And everyone mixed well, my family and my media chums, who included the editor of the *Sunday Times* and editor of the *New Statesman*, for whom I have been doing columns for many years, and also old friends dating back forty years, such as Jilly Cooper, Joan Bakewell and Melvyn Bragg. Melv was even persuaded to sing or at least shout 'Twist and Shout'.

Margaret was amused the next day to be taken through every detail, every awful thing I had done and said and had arranged, endlessly saying how pleased she was not to have been there.

She was pleased she had not ruined any of the three family events by something awful happening to her, such as dying, and it proved a distraction for her to hear all about the family Christmas lunch and my party, after they were successfully over.

Can you will yourself to live? I felt in this case, over those three weeks, she did. She had created three hurdles for herself, three family events to survive for, and had managed to stay alive for all three. With us in spirit if not in the flesh.

# 24

# Notes from a Hospice

## 8 January 2016

Today, the day after my eightieth party, the palliative care consultant came, Dr Philip Lodge, the first time we had seen him. Felt quite honoured, having the consultant coming to the house.

I had been ringing the palliative care nurse to say how worried I was that Margaret was falling, staggering, and shaking. I was scared she would fall and break something.

Dr Lodge was in his late forties, none of the autocratic manner of some consultants, or their remoteness, but seemed at ease, relaxed, natural. He managed to be concerned and caring without being creepy or false, a hard trick to pull off. Some of the palliative care nurses had driven me mad putting on their caring face and voice, the way Fergal Keane used to do on the radio.

From time to time, as he talked to Margaret, I noticed Dr Lodge managing to stare round our bedroom, looking at all the photos and stuff. I do like a nosy doctor. It shows they are involved, that patients are real people not numbers. I couldn't place his accent. Rather North London, which you don't find in many consultants.

He checked Margaret all over, including the old wounds on her chest, questioned her about the worst areas of pain, such as her back and shoulders, but fortunately did not ask her to go yet again through her medical history. He had read all the notes, so she didn't have to drag herself through her operations or treatment. I wish all doctors were like that.

He explained that going downstairs was more dangerous than going up, as the chance of falling was greater.

I told him how Margaret had suddenly lost the power in her right arm, so she could not lift things and, even worse, write postcards and letters, which she had done all her life. He nodded and said she would lose all the power in her legs soon. There was no change or lowering in his voice or demeanour, just a straightforward fact. Most doctors so far had shied away from revealing what the next stage would be, even when asked, which in this case Dr Lodge had not been. He just told us, which is how it should be.

Margaret was tiring, with all the questions about her pains, where exactly they were, how bad, and when. She tried to break in, cut him short, thanked him for coming, when she was sure he had so much to do.

'Sorry, Margaret, I have to ask you some more things. This is my bread and butter.'

It was quite a witty thing to say. On paper it might look facetious but we both smiled, understanding the nature of his self-deprecation, as if he was a shift worker in a factory.

He asked Margaret whether she wanted to remain in her

home or go into a hospital. Certainly not a hospital, we both said. She would rather die at home than in a Royal Free ward. 'I would really like an overdose now,' she said, 'something to knock me out for good. I've had enough pain.'

He smiled and said don't worry about the pain, we can control that.

He then got out a form which was marked Resuscitation Form. He filled in all Margaret's details and gave it to me. It said that in the event of a total collapse, such as a heart attack, Margaret Davies had not to be resuscitated. I had never heard of such a form. I carefully filed it away. Margaret had lost interest by now.

He gave us some numbers to ring. He would by chance be on duty tomorrow, and so would Shebo, our main palliative care nurse. I had to ring either of them if Margaret collapsed. It was clear he expected this to happen, possibly over the weekend.

## 9 January 2016

Margaret is in the Marie Curie Hospice in Hampstead. After a hellish twenty-four hours, she is in bed resting, peacefully, relatively pain-free at last, in a very quiet and very nice room with a large window and a view and absolutely excellent kind caring staff.

It has been a dramatic day. This morning there was a sudden increase in the pain – and the total loss of any strength or movement in her legs and in both arms. She has not eaten all day, because she couldn't move her arms, nor could she get out of bed to go the lavatory, as her legs are gone.

I rang the palliative care team, and rang Dr Lodge, as directed, and left messages. Quite soon afterwards Shebo rang me back. She said Dr Lodge had managed to get Margaret a room in the hospice. She told me to expect the ambulance in two hours.

I was taking the call upstairs in my room, on the portable extension, standing looking idly out of the window into our street as we talked. Such a familiar street scene, all the houses so familiar, one I had been staring at in idle moments for fifty-five years when I was supposed to be working.

I was thinking two hours, that's when she said the ambulance would come, no chance, pull the other, they won't get an ambulance here for ten hours. Then blow me, as Shebo was still telling me stuff, an ambulance drew up right opposite our house. 'Fucking hell!' I shouted in amazement. Then apologised to Shebo, who was still on the phone. She could not believe it either. It was quicker than ordering an Uber taxi.

I watched as the ambulance got parked, rather badly, on the corner of Laurier Road and our street, on a yellow line, tut tut. Two paramedics got out and rang our bell. I rushed down and took them upstairs and into Margaret's room.

They both stood there, looking glaked, which is a Scottish word my mother used, not sure how to spell it but it rhymes with 'naked', meaning dopey, confused. They had clearly no idea who Margaret was, her name or any details. I was rather bad tempered when they started going through a long list of dopey questions, such as had she had a heart attack.

It eventually emerged that they had been going to another emergency call which had been cancelled. By chance, they happened to be in the next street, Laurier Road, which is why they had arrived in two minutes. Hence they had had no time to find out about Margaret, who she was or her problem.

The main ambulance man then rang some number, got a few details and advice, and announced he would give Margaret a painkiller. This would make it more comfortable for her while riding in the ambulance.

He spent ages trying to inject the painkiller, totally failing to get it into any of her veins. She had had this trouble over the last few years, despite having endless bloody blood tests. Her veins, so we discovered, were too small.

They gave up in the end, having put her through all the extra pain and discomfort to supposedly relieve the pain.

They went back to the ambulance, got some equipment and carried her down the stairs. They laid her on a stretcher in the ambulance and I sat beside. The ambulance shook and shuddered going over every bump. Looking round I could see it was a pretty old ambulance, clearly knackered. As it bumped and jerked through the traffic, I could tell Margaret was in total agony. I thought she was going to pass out with the pain.

She then declared she was sure her arm was broken. The paramedics got alarmed when they heard this, exchanging glances. One asked if she had fallen recently. She said yes, two days ago. They looked at each other and started muttering about the Royal Free, which way was it.

Oh God. I knew that the plan was that she had to be taken to the Marie Curie Hospice, where a bed was ready for her. The last thing we wanted was for her to be taken instead to A&E at the Royal Free – on a Saturday evening. Oh God, that is the stuff of nightmares. But it is what the paramedics would have to do, if they thought she had had an accident and broken something.

I gave M a push and hissed in her ear. Dr Lodge had tested her only yesterday. He would have seen any broken arm. You are just imagining it. Otherwise you will have to go to A&E. She told the ambulance that it was just painful, not broken. Phew.

I explained to the ambulance men that Margaret was due at the hospice. Which one, they asked. I said Marie Curie in Hampstead. They had no idea where that was. I think their normal beat was out in Essex. So I directed them.

I know it well, and so does Margaret. She had treatment there nine years ago and my sister Marion was in there, towards the end of her life, so was Geraldine, mother of Jake's wife Rosa. I knew how comfortable and calming and caring it is and was relieved that we were on the way. I could not have coped any more at home, now she was immobile, her legs gone.

She is now in room 12, Heath Ward, on the first floor, all on her own, wonder of wonders, and even more amazing, it has brilliant views of the gardens and the street outside. Her room is in fact bigger than our bedroom at home. Well done Dr Lodge.

While Margaret was being settled in the bed, I was asked to have a meeting with the ward sister Louise, who wanted to talk to me. So we sat next door in the little lounge where visitors sit. She said officially that Margaret was in for respite care, till they get on top of the present pains. Then we will see.

She asked me family details, such as the names of our children. This is for privacy and security, she explained, so when they ring or visit, their names and relationships will be known. Over the years, quite a few well-known people have been in the Hampstead Hospice and they have had journalists trying to get in, find out details.

'Are the three children all your children?'

I was confused by the question. She explained that she just wondered if perhaps some were from a previous marriage. I said we have been married for fifty-five years – to each other.

I suddenly found myself starting to cry. I hadn't cried in the ambulance, even when Margaret was in agony. Yet this harmless question had started me off.

## 12 JANUARY 2016

When I was with M today in her hospice room a woman breezed in and said, 'Gin and tonic?' M said no thanks. 'Vodka, then?'

M has not had a drink for nine years. Once the chemo started, she lost the taste for drink. Apparently the woman is a volunteer who comes in once a week. All drinks are free for patients, but any guests have to pay. So unfair.

Later a well-spoken man arrived with a dog and stood by her bedside. He asked if Margaret would like some canine love. This turned out to be a chance to pat his dog. Amazing. I wonder if hospices all over the country have volunteers offering equally weird if wonderful services.

I walk each day to the hospice, which takes me about forty minutes. Sometimes I go too fast, trying to beat my record, and start wheezing, in which case I get the bus back. The walk is nice, as you end up in one of the best parts of Hampstead. The hospice is in Lyndhurst Gardens, surrounded by superior mansion blocks. It appears to be originally a pre-war mansion of some sort, with modern, concrete and glass additions and entrance hall. There is parking, unusual for anywhere in Hampstead, but I have got it into my head always to walk or bus. It will be my exercise for the day.

I am always surprised when entering her room. It is so light and airy and filled with flowers. Every visitor brings them. I am coordinating all her visitors, making a timetable each day, a copy of which I leave with her.

The staff are so kind and caring and calm, more like a hotel or a very high-class private clinic. It is so quiet, peaceful, feels almost empty, yet a patient can ring for help and someone will be there in minutes.

It has about thirty patients, as far as I can see, all presumably terminal, but you don't meet them. Almost all are confined to their beds. I just glimpse them through doors when walking down the corridor from the lift. There is one little ward of six, but everyone else has their own room. How on earth can they afford such high-quality staff and attention when we are not paying a penny?

M is even enjoying the food, which is a surprise. She has not been out to a restaurant for nine years, since the tumour in her back. 'But now a restaurant is coming to me – twice a day.'

She has a catheter and a plastic bag hangs over the side of the bed to receive the contents of her bowels. It gives a vague hum which I always think is a radio that has been left on. Regular painkillers are injected into her, which work much better than they did at home.

She can't sit up properly, as her arms have gone, so she lies flat on her back. She can't move her legs. They have to move her legs for her when she is washed and changed. She can't write anything, which she is desperate to do, wanting to write down the names and details of all the staff, doctors, nurses, cleaners and all the various volunteers. Her mind is so alert. In fact she seems to have been mentally stimulated by her new situation, talks to everyone.

There is a stream of volunteers and experts coming in offering various treatments, such as yoga and painting, as well as the regular physios. She gets very tired, but she seems stable. All the physio work, however exhausting, does seem to be helping. Is she really in for respite care – or is this it?

I would not say she was happy, as that word would be cruel, but all visitors remark afterwards on how bright and cheery she is.

I asked her today what it is like, being here. She thought for a while and said, 'pleasant'.

I did not expect her to say that. I expected her either to grunt or sigh, or dismiss it as a dopey question. The thought of her going into any institution, even a hospice, had been hanging over us for months. Who would have thought she would pronounce it pleasant.

All the children have been, and the four grandchildren, even the two little ones. They loved the room, inspecting all her hoists and contraptions. They didn't seem alarmed by the sight of Granny in bed.

They can't see how thin she has become, as she has the blankets over. She has lost a huge amount of weight – as well as height. At New Year, when we did our Predictions, we also always record each of our weights. She was down to 7 stone 6 lbs. She has lost a stone in a year. Her normal fighting weight, ten years ago, before the return of the cancer, was around 10 and a half stone. I am not revealing my weight. Too embarrassing. Okay then, when we got married I was 10 stone 11. I am now 12 stone.

## 15 JANUARY 2016

M today asked me to bring in a copy of *Significant Sisters*. I was surprised. She wants to give it to one of the cleaning staff who comes from the Philippines and wants to go to university and study feminism.

Margaret has gone through life never offering people her books, never mentioning she is a writer, changing the subject should she be asked. So what has come over her now, behaving like an ordinary normal author? The drugs? Being settled and comfortable?

I always tell everyone, whether they ask me or not, that I write books. I thrust copies on them all the time, usually remaindered copies, of which I have loads.

## 18 JANUARY 2016

She seemed in fine fettle today – or perhaps it was me. I had a lunch beforehand with our neighbour Derek John. We went nearby in Belsize Park, the restaurant next to the cinema, where M and I used to go for many years.

She was full of chat – about the staff and her visitors. I had to leave the room for half an hour, and go to the day lounge.

She was being given an injection before the physios arrived for her dreaded daily exercises. Margaret does not like being observed during her physio.

Yesterday, so she said, when the two physios were working on her, the usual young strapping gels, one of them collapsed, shouting in agony. She'd got cramp in her calf.

According to Margaret, she saved her. She maintains she caught the physio as she fell. Our hero, I mean heroine.

Don't totally believe her, sounds a bit like her Red Pike story, but it is a story she could easily have worked up, if she was fit and well, if she could write, if she were sending letters to her chums. I accepted it of course. Just as I believed she climbed Red Pike before breakfast.

### 19 JANUARY 2016

I went on the C11 bus today, as it was raining. It stops at the Royal Free, where lots of outpatients always get on. A tall, decrepit-looking man hobbling on two sticks got on, cheerful-looking, about my age, i.e. quite young really. A dyed-blonde, tattooed, overweight woman got up and offered him her seat.

'No thanks,' he said, in an Irish accent. 'I like to show off my disabilities.'

'Oh make the most it when you can, love,' she replied.

'Being an exhibitionist has nothing to do with your situation,' he said.

I made a mental note to repeat this conversation to M.

I rarely bring her physical things, apart from that day's *Independent* paper and any letters. I like to think I bring in chat.

I make a list of things that happened in the last twenty-four hours, or things I have thought. We have always relayed every bus stop story to each other, however banal. Who am I going to tell all my trivia chat to, when she goes?

## 20 JANUARY 2016

When I went into her room today, I noticed a walking stick on her bed, a proper walking stick, with a rubber ferrule at the end, the sort she has at home, the one she inherited from her father, which now hangs forlorn at the end of the hall shelf.

She has had a miracle recovery! That was my first thought. She wouldn't have a walking stick unless she was now trying to walk. Those strapping physios, perhaps the one who collapsed on her bed, and was saved by Margaret, have worked some magic.

She explained that in the night her brain started telling her to move her legs. Over and over again came the same message, yet she couldn't move either leg one inch. She felt herself becoming hysterical, unable to understand what was happening. She shouted for help and two night carers came, calmed her down.

One then pummelled her legs, till at last there was feeling. No movement, just feeling, the feel of blood flowing and a sense of touch. She said it felt wonderful, the circulation going again, as if she had got her legs back.

As they left, one of them got an old walking stick and gave it to M, telling her that when it happens again in the night to pummel her own leg. So that was why the walking stick was there. She now has some marginal use of her left hand, so she is able to give her legs a good pummel in the night, if and when she becomes hysterical.

We chatted for an hour and a half, me telling her what I was cooking for myself, gossip from the street, conversations I had overheard, when she suddenly said, 'There seems to be space between us.'

This caught me on the hop. I didn't quite know what she meant. Just as she was going to explain further, a doctor came into the room, a young blonde woman registrar.

I started to get up, thinking that if Margaret is being physically examined she will not like me to be present. But the doctor asked if I could wait, if I did not have to go? I said no, no, I would like to stay.

The doctor made it clear that Margaret would not be coming out. This was it. But she could not predict how long it would take. They have weekly meetings to discuss a patient's progress, but they can never get it exactly right. The paralysis is getting worse, and will creep up her body, but it is now unlikely that her brain will be affected.

So what will happen?

The doc muttered the usual stuff about an infection that might happen, or just gradually total weakness. M said she did not want antibiotics, just painkillers, as she did not want her life prolonged. The doc nodded.

On the way home across the Heath I met a man, Paul, a neighbour who lives in Grove Terrace. He asked where I had been and I told him Margaret was in the hospice.

'Oh I have missed her walking on the Heath. I always looked out for her orange coat. She is always so elegant.'

Elegant? I thought about that as I walked home. Should I tell her tomorrow? I know she has never enjoyed or fished for compliments, always deflecting them.

During our life together, the biggest compliment I ever give her is to say that she looks neat. Or sometimes I say clean. Neat and clean, you can't do better than that.

## 21 JANUARY 2016

I told M that story today, about being elegant. I think she was quite pleased.

I then asked what she meant by there being space between us. I had been thinking about it and wondered if she was becoming institutionalised. Or have we grown somehow apart since she came into the hospice?

She looked surprised, saying she had no memory of saying it. I promised her she did, because it caught me on the hop.

Then she decided what she must have meant was that there is a space around her. She is on her own most of each day, and all night, without my nonstop chattering. She meant there is space around her, not between us. She does still feel in contact with me.

She also said she has changed her views on hospices. She had always thought they were an indulgence, a luxury, all that money being spent to keep the dying alive when a lethal injection, which is what she had always wanted, would be so much better, saving time and pain and agonising for everyone. Now she feels the benefit. She is glad she is here. It is a comfort, not an indulgence.

## 22 January 2016

M had a bit of a scare last evening. Suddenly a Miss Havisham figure appeared in her bedroom doorway. It was a woman with wild grey hair piled up on top of her head, wearing some sort of flowing black robe or frock. M was half asleep at the time.

'What are you doing?' yelled the woman. 'Get out of that bed. That bed is mine! This room is mine!'

M was confused, thinking at first the woman was a ghost, or she had imagined her. Then she realised the woman was clearly a bit mad, so pressed the alarm bell. Two carers came to escort the woman away.

The woman, apparently, has had a brain tumour and has no idea who she is or what has happened to her. M laughed while telling the story, but at the time she had clearly been rather alarmed and a bit frightened.

Yesterday, when the posh drinks trolley woman had come round, asking 'Gin and tonic, darling?', Margaret, to my surprise, had asked if she could possibly have a small glass of white wine, with ice. It was duly produced – and Margaret loved it.

So today I took in a bottle of Pinot Grigio, some ice and a glass, and put them in her fridge. Oh yes, she has a fridge, all mod cons in the Hampstead Hospice, darling.

I learned today that some of the ever so affluent occupants of the large houses and mansion blocks in Lyndhurst Gardens, where the hospice is situated, have been complaining about having to look out from their windows at elderly half naked people in the hospice opposite being given bed baths. Bloody cheek. Why can't they avert their gaze, or close their curtains?

M told me that she had had two out-of-the-blue visits this morning from very eager, over-excited new people – an art therapist and a reflexologist. She agreed they could come back later, as she was waiting for the consultant. It's all go, in the Hampstead Hospice.

When Dr Lodge, the consultant, did come, he had students and two registrars in tow. They all stood around M's bed as Philip explained her situation. At the end, she asked him how long he thought she had. Not like M to be so direct. He said he didn't know.

When I arrived, Margaret told me all this. I asked if she felt the end was nigh.

'I don't think about it. I just take one day at a time.'

'You should really have been a football manager.'

'The days are still pleasant. I am not in pain. If asked during the day if I would like a lethal injection, I would probably say no. The evenings are different. It suddenly strikes you that you are stuck between these four walls, you haven't moved all day, you won't move again, you are going nowhere. The nights are awful. So if asked in the night, I would say yes, finish me off.

'Last night I imagined I was choking. I thought the tumour has got to my lungs, it was pressing on me, and I was losing my breathing. I knew I was imagining it. It took a huge effort to beat it, mind over matter, and get it out of my head.'


24 JANUARY 2016

Theo, Margaret's friend in Washington DC, has sent her a book to cheer her up – a book by the American humorist Art

Buchwald, who wrote a column in the *Herald Tribune* for many decades. It is about being in a hospice in the USA.

While there, he turns his room into an office and studio, giving interviews, making radio broadcasts. He then has a miracle recovery and after six months in the hospice he goes home.

Margaret did not find it at all amusing. Funny how humour dates. I didn't find it very funny either, though I did when I read his column many years ago. His smart remarks now seem laboured. But in the book, he praises the hospice system, describing how it is a British invention, but has become popular across the USA.

I had not been aware of it being a British creation. I had assumed some sort of system to care for the dying must always have been there, back to medieval times. But the system as we know it now was begun by Cicely Saunders (1918–2005). I looked her up and found she read PPE at Oxford and in 1940 became a nurse. In 1948 she fell in love with a patient, a Polish-Jewish refugee, working as a waiter, who had escaped from the Warsaw ghetto. He was dying of cancer. He bequeathed £500 to Cicely. This was the germ of the idea of starting a hospice. She later qualified as a medical doctor. She was made a Dame in 1979. I told Margaret all this the next day, but she was too tired to take it in.

I talked to Dr Lodge today and remarked how I noticed that there were empty beds in the little ward. I said that surprised me. 'Yet people must be dying to come into this hospice . . .'

He smiled wearily, no doubt having heard this joke before. He explained that the funding for the hospice was half provided by Marie Curie, which is a charity, and half by the

Royal Free. He for example works half his week at the Royal Free as a consultant, and half in the hospice. He walks between the two, which only takes ten minutes. He usually has his lunch on the way – munching a sandwich.

He said at the moment, they were okay for doctors in the hospice, and also for the cleaning and basic care staff. The problem was getting nurses. Nurses can't afford to live in London. This was why at present those beds were empty.

How awful to think of this wonderful building, with all its amazing staff, doing such good to so many people, yet for the lack of enough nurses, they have empty beds.

When I told Margaret, she got me to promise that when she died I would give a large donation to Marie Curie. She suggested £50,000. I coughed, said hmm, I'll think about it. That was what I gave a few years ago to a charity in Lakeland, the Cumbria Community Fund. Seems only fair we should give back something to both London and Loweswater. We have taken so much from both of them.

M has started trying to write a few words with her left hand, which still has a slight bit of movement. She does it ever so painfully and the result is appalling, like a spider crawling across the page, but she is persevering and has even written a few thank-you cards to her close friends.

'A new woman came today,' she said. 'I think she is from the Philippines, like most of them. Just arrived, at the bottom of the caring ladder. She was trying hard and asked me when she left the room if she could do anything else for me.

'I said, "Yes, there is one thing . . ."

'"What is that, Margaret?"

'"I would like you to smile,"' said Margaret.

The woman was confused. So with her left hand, Margaret pushed open her own lips, indicating what smiling was. At last the woman smiled.

'Oh you have a lovely smile,' said Margaret.

The woman left, smiling.

## 25 JANUARY 2016

M had more bad dreams in the early evening, convinced she could move her legs, but of course she cannot. She thought she was going mad, so wanted to ring for help, but could not find the switch. In doing so she knocked over her water jug. That helped as a distraction, taking her mind off the panic of failing to move her legs.

She then experienced a sudden flash of lightning in her head, right across her brain, light and noise and heat. After that, she felt fine. She went to sleep, her head cleared.

She told a nurse in the morning about this strange experience – but the nurse did not know what she was on about. Having only recently arrived from the Philippines.

More trouble in the night with the contraption for the bowels. There were explosions which she can't hear, or smell, till the care staff come in the morning and discover it. They then have to forcibly get out the rest of her shit. She can't feel a thing. Her body is dead from below the waist. She feels so sorry for the staff, having to do it, so cheerfully.

'Everyone has a poo chart, so they filled in mine when they had finished. Dear God, my own poo chart. I never thought it would come to this . . .'

She was almost amused, almost smiling.

She has a TV in her room, high up on the wall beside her bed, but has never put it on. She won't let others put it on for her either, even though I have suggested it might distract her in the evenings when she thinks she is going potty. But she is still listening to the radio, though she puts it off when staff come in.

She listened to *Saturday Review* on Sat, which she always listens to at home, but fell asleep before the end.

'When I woke up, I thought I will go downstairs now, see if Hunter has finished reading the *Guardian*. When I realised my mistake, I suddenly felt homesick. I haven't been homesick up to now.

'I am often at home in my mind, going round every room, checking things off, but it's the first time I thought I really was still at home ...'

## 26 JANUARY 2016

Shock news today. One of the registrars has told M that she could possibly be discharged.

At one level it is good news. It indicates she has been stable, that they have made her comfortable. But how on earth will we cope at home, providing twenty-four-hour care and attention? How can we inject her painkillers, work her bowels, give her an all-over body wash, give her physio and react at once in the middle of the night when there is a drama?

She has now been in the hospice almost three weeks. It was meant just to be respite care. So it only seems fair to make the bed vacant for someone truly at death's door.

She and I discussed where she will sleep, if she does have to come home. Downstairs is best — but not in the front of the main room as she does not want people looking in. So at the back, where she will get the garden view.

But I was too stunned to concentrate properly on the logistics. I had assumed this was the endgame, the final stage, she would never come out, that she would end her days here, and end them 'pleasantly'. She can't possibly feel pleasant at home. Even reorganising the whole house, getting round-the-clock care, medics visiting, she will be frantic, shaking, in a panic, a danger to herself, as she was when she was at home.

Before she entered the hospice, I wanted her to die peacefully at home, in her own bed. As she did. As most people do. But not now. I now know how wonderful the hospice is, so secure, so reassuring, perfect for the terminally ill. A house isn't. So what will happen now?

# 25

# THE BIG MEETING

## 29 JANUARY 2016

The meeting to decide Margaret's immediate future was today. Flora decided to come as well, and drove me over.

M was being washed when we arrived so we sat in the family room. A social worker came in, introduced herself, said she was coming to the meeting. She said we were lucky with M being semi-paralysed. That meant under Camden rules she would qualify for a full-time live-in carer. Oh wow, thanks a lot, great news, thanks for sharing.

The meeting was held at M's bedside. There was Dr Phil Lodge, the social worker, a sister in charge of discharge and another woman, not sure what she did, plus a medical student who just listened.

Phil did most of the talking – and so, surprisingly, did Flora. Yet she had said beforehand she would just sit and listen. She was very strong and outspoken, criticising them for suddenly springing on Margaret and on us the fact that Margaret might have to go home, when clearly she was in no state to go home.

It all seemed really to depend on Margaret herself expressing unhappiness, saying she feared going home, that she would
not survive at home. So we all waited to hear what she would
say about the proposal to send her home.

'In an ideal world,' she began, speaking slowly, with great
effort, forcing out each word, 'I would like to be at home.
If the same sort of help could be provided that I am getting
here. But how could it? There would be no bell to press in the
middle of the night for the night doctor to come.'

'What about a nursing home?' suggested Dr Phil.

Flora flew at him. 'She is NOT going into a nursing
home!'

'I understand,' said Phil, meekly.

I did say a few words about the sorts of emergencies already
happening, her bowels exploding in the night, having panic
attacks. How on earth could we cope with any of that at
home?

M looked very tired, the worst she had looked so far. It had
been an effort to talk, to formulate her words, and give her
opinion, which had always been so easy for her all her life,
whether asked for her opinion or not. Now she just wanted
it all over. She apologised for having no energy. Then closed
her eyes.

I asked when the decision would be made to chuck her out,
and who would make it and why?

Philip then started to speak, almost as slowly as Margaret.
He said she was in a bad situation, though there were some
who were worse. But, all things considered, it would be best
for her to stay here.

'Is that the decision then?' I asked. 'She can stay here?'

'That is it,' he replied.

Everyone smiled. It had been like a High Court case with the jury having finally reached a popular verdict.

Afterwards, in the lounge, the social worker said the decision was never in question, but they had to go through with the process. Hospice beds were in high demand. They were expensive, costing about £300 a day, as opposed to only £200 at home, even counting a full-time carer and a district nurse.

On the way home, I revealed to Flora something I had not told her, or Caitlin and Jake, as M had sworn me to secrecy. Almost exactly three months ago now, the oncologist had predicted that M had just three to nine months left.

Flora said she always knew we must have been told. And she had suspected it was three to six months, not nine. I then could not remember whether we had been told six or nine months. I said I would check when I got home. Good job I had been writing everything down.

## 1 February 2016

M said today how interesting it had been during the last three weeks having our three children coming to see her, each on their own, sitting by her bedside, making inconsequential chat, going on about what they had been doing. She saw different aspects of them. Jake seemed stronger. Flora was more dominant – especially at the discharge meeting – and Caitlin had an impulsive streak she had never been aware of.

## 2 FEBRUARY 2016

A bit ratty today.

I asked her when she wakes up in the morning does she immediately know where she is, realise what has happened to her?

'Yes, of course,' she said, curtly, as if she could not possibly be unaware of the state she was in. I said that after three weeks at home, on my own, I was still waking up and not knowing where I am. I never know what I do next, where I have put the kettle for my tea.

'You have always been like that.'

'So how do you feel when you wake?'

'Depressed of course, what do you think?'

'Does taking one day at a time help?'

'Not really. I feel trapped. That is the worst part. Being trapped. That is worse than knowing I am going to die. Because I can't move my legs, I can't move, not at all. So for three weeks, I have lain, twenty-four hours a day, on my back. All my life, I have never ever slept on my back.'


## 3 FEBRUARY 2016

M has always been so strong in every way – physically, mentally, intellectually, emotionally – all her friends and family were always struck by it, which is why they looked to her for her opinion and for her help. She never moaned or displayed any doubts, fears or weaknesses. It's tragic seeing her now, getting frailer every day, yet mentally still strong, clear and lucid, if very tired. There have been no tears, no signs of depression, at least on the surface. During the whole of the last year I have seen tears only once – that one night, in bed. She has been so strong.

## 4 FEBRUARY 2016

M was on oxygen when I arrived, so her breathing, which had been getting bad, was a bit better, but for the first time she did not seem mentally bright and alert.

She did not want to talk, answer any questions, got ratty when I kept on asking her things, about how she felt, what she was thinking.

'I don't think,' she replied, wearily. 'I've stopped thinking.'

She seemed blank, as if beginning to shut off. She had had Valerie Grove in the morning, one of our oldest friends, the author and *Times* journalist, who lives with her family in Highgate. She stayed forty-five minutes, though I'd said thirty minutes was now the limit. M said it had been fine, she had enjoyed having Valerie.

Some days, in the first few weeks, Margaret had been having four visitors, some at least an hour, without any appreciable tiredness. In fact she seemed to gain by them, as if stimulated by them.

But today she did not even have the strength to tell me any trivia about the staff, what they had said, or about a therapist who had visited. It was as if she could not be bothered any more.

She asked me to bring in one thing for her the next day – a pair of scissors. The staff are not allowed to cut toenails. A chiropodist could be called, but would cost £30. She knew I would not want to spend that. I ignored that remark.

She told me where her scissors were – in her yellow sponge bag, in her bedside drawer.

I dug it out when I got home. I never knew she had such a lethal-looking pair of medical-type scissors. But then I have never looked in her drawers, or her cupboards, or her desk or the shelves in her room or the sheaves of paper which have been lying on her desk for the last six weeks, covered with her immaculate handwriting. I know my place.

But I know that on her desk are the first sixty pages of a new novel. Over Christmastime she had told me about it, surprisingly. Surprising, because she never normally would admit to working on a novel.

## 5 FEBRUARY 2016

She looked exhausted today, totally blank, given up. She had the clipper things in her nostrils for the oxygen which was pumping away. No energy or desire to communicate. I chuntered on for a while, but got no reaction.

I then got out her nail scissors. I asked her where she had got them from. She said she had had them for years. Which is what she always said, if I happen to remark on a new blouse, a new top, new shoes, some new article of clothing. She would say she had had them for years. Then she would say typical, you never notice my clothes. I knew of course that she would never admit to having bought something new, unless I actually caught her, coming through the door with a Monsoon bag. And even then she would try to lie her way out of it, saying she had been in a charity shop.

I cut her toenails as carefully as possible. Her legs all the way up were dead, so she could not feel me cutting the nails. I presumed the blood would still flow, if I made a mistake and cut her skin.

I remember my mother asking me to cut her nails at the end of her life. Her nails were hard and crinkled and rock-like. Couldn't even cut off a sliver. They were like cast iron. We had to take her to the health clinic in the end. A proper chiropodist did it, using an industrial saw.

Margaret's skin seemed remarkably soft and smooth, her legs were not wrinkled or emaciated as I expected, despite not having moved them for so long.

It felt so highly personal and intimate, weird and strange and intrusive, yet she is my wife of fifty-five years. She would never have asked me do it if she had been fit and well. Feeling her skin felt funny. Looking at her naked legs, which of course she was not aware of, not being able to bend and look, or to feel my touch, I thought how I had never seen her naked for over forty years. Not since her first operation in 1975.

She said the doctor thought she had an infection. Which doctor? There were always lots of new young registrars. She didn't know, couldn't describe her. Yet a few days ago she knew the names of everyone. She said they had tested her urine. That was all she knew. Then she went back to sleep. I realised she was too tired to be cross-examined further. She didn't know, and didn't care, whether she had an infection or not.

I left her, wondering how long she would sleep. There did seem to have been a big decline in the last twenty-four hours. All she clearly wanted now was to be out of it, to fall asleep, forever.

As I was leaving, opening her bedroom door to leave quietly, she suddenly opened her eyes and woke up again.

'The Hoover bag,' she blurted out. 'It will need to be replaced. It must be full by now.'

'Fuck the Hoover bag,' I said.

But she was asleep again.


## 6 FEBRUARY 2016

Four weeks ago today she moved in. For three weeks she was in great form, lively, comfortable, not happy but content, relaxed, saying it was pleasant.

Today she was breathing badly, the oxygen connected, but she had no interest, no energy, eyes blank, lifeless.

I took in six novels which had arrived, newly published, sent from Becky Hardie [her publisher at Chatto]. She watched me blankly as I unpacked them, with no reaction. Just a week ago she would have responded immediately to each book – enthusiastically or otherwise. I read out the titles and authors. She said leave three – Julian Barnes, Anne Tyler, Rose Tremain. Take away the rest.

She would not answer any more questions, nor would she talk.

Was this finally the end? She clearly wanted to go. All these decades she had seemed a goner at times, then recovered. Could she possibly, miraculously recover life again?

I coughed and spluttered, then I said how much I loved her, how I will miss her.

'In my mind, you will not be gone,' I said. 'You will be with me, all the time. It will not feel sad or creepy, being in the house alone. I will always be talking to you.'

'You'll be fine,' she said, dismissing me and my soppy thoughts.

I said I will be back tomorrow. She said nothing.

'You'll be fine.'

Then she closed her eyes.


## 7 FEBRUARY 2016

Amazingly, she seemed much brighter today – alert, talking, listening, chatting. I stayed an hour, no bother. She even gave me some jobs to do – to send birthday cards and £20 each for Ella on Feb 18 and Noor on Feb 20, our great-nieces. Don't forget, she said. She was always brilliant on dates. I found it hard to remember who they were, far less their birthdays.

As I left, I met one of the young doctors. She said she did think M was going. She thought it would only be a matter of days. They would ring me, night or day. It clearly appeared imminent.


## 8 FEBRUARY 2016

I went to bed with both the mobile phone and the landline portable near me in the bedroom, which is something I never do.

At 7.30 in the morning, one of the phones did ring, but it took me a while to work out what the noise was, which phone it might be, and where it was. By the time I had located it, the call had ended. I immediately listened to a voicemail. A female foreign voice said that Margaret had died ten minutes ago.

I rushed out of the house, without washing or eating, and drove as fast as I could. Waiting at traffic lights crossing from

Pond Street I looked out at people in their cars, slumped, expressionless, going off as usual to their daily work, automatons, unaware of themselves, far less of me. They don't know that my wife of fifty-five years has just died. Should I open my window and tell them?

There was a new notice on Margaret's bedroom door when I arrived which had not been there the previous evening. It warned people not to enter this room without contacting a nurse. I went straight in.

Margaret was lying flat out in her bed, looking peaceful, tidy, neat, well wrapped. But undeniably dead.

Her catheter had been removed from her; all the medication and stuff taken away. She had not long been dead, for it was still hardly eight o'clock, but while I was driving over, the nurses must have tidied her up.

Her arms were clasped on her chest, a little cushion placed carefully below her neck, presumably to prop up her head, in case it fell, or if she dribbled. I felt her hands. They were still warm. I kissed both her hands. Then I kissed her on her cheek.

The room was dark and depressing, as they had pulled the curtains. I assumed they must do this, when someone has died. Some stupid mark of respect. I flung open the curtains, let the early morning light flood in, such as it was for early February, and then switched all the electric lights on.

I gazed out at the gardens and the houses opposite, wondering which local residents had complained about having to watch dying bodies. I wondered if Margaret had seen the light coming up on that brand-new day. If she had died at 7.20, as they had said, there must have been a hint of dawn. I like to think she might have been aware of it, going out on a new dawn, for the world and for those being left behind, if not for her. Which was a silly thought. She probably just drifted off hours earlier in the night.

I sat silently, looking at her, holding her hands. Slowly I could feel her hands getting colder. As I watched her, the colour draining from her face, becoming yellowish and parched, and yet looking at her, so peaceful, it was easy to imagine she was not dead. 'I am only sleeping,' as John Lennon sang.

The hospice was so quiet, as it was so early in the morning. The night shift was giving way to the day. I had seen no sign of any nurses or cleaners.

I was not sure what to do next. They had told me she had died, so I had vaguely expected someone would be there. I suppose in a hospice death is so common, there is no sense of drama. I had just walked in, nobody had seen me, nobody had spoken to me. Now I was sitting alone with my dead wife.

I got out my mobile and sent a text message to each of the children. I told them M had died at 7.30. I had just arrived at the hospice. I did not ask them to come. Caitlin, who always replies to all messages at once, as I do, said she would come at once.

I was still sitting on my own, beside her, observing further minute changes to her dead body, when a middle-aged man walked in. I assumed he was a doctor. I asked if he could do the death certificate as soon as possible. Sorry, he said, in very plummy tones, I am the chaplain.

Oh God, last thing I need. What sort? He said any sort, he looks after all faiths, but he is an Anglican cleric and works at a well-known church in central London.

He spoke nicely, sincerely to me, but as if I was a total idiot, asking me to lean on him. He asked if I would like a prayer. I said no, too late for prayers, but I would like a coffee. And he toddled off to get me one. Which was nice.

I felt sorry for him. He was only trying to do his job among unbelievers, but his timing was so awful, so wrong. He probably didn't know, nobody had been around on duty to tell him. He had just arrived, went to the first room, going on his rounds, and there was me, with my dead wife.

Caitlin came in just as he brought me my coffee. She wondered who he was. I introduced her to the chaplain, then managed to usher him out, explaining that now I had my daughter with me, I was fine, thanks, how kind.

Flora and Jake then arrived. We all sat by Margaret's bed, not knowing what to say. Flora was clearly very upset, but she was the only one who managed to kiss M, as I had done. The other two could not bear to do so.

All of them were obviously uneasy, sitting beside their dead mother, which so far had not really unsettled me. I suppose I had seen it coming for days, if not weeks, if not years. I just liked to be near her, even though she was dead, which they clearly found too distressing. So after fifteen minutes or so we all moved next door into the family room.

I asked Caitlin to go and find a doctor, any doctor. I said tell them we want the death certificate signed. I was desperate to get quickly on with the next stage.

We discussed what to do about a funeral. I wanted Margaret cremated as soon as possible, but no wake, I couldn't bear a wake.

We sat for some time in the family room, on our own, just

the four of us, talking, discussing what to do. It was good that we were being left in peace and quiet, but on the other hand, we seemed to have been forgotten. I wanted someone to tell us what the next procedure would be. In a hospice, they are all used to death. We are not.

It was two hours after I had first arrived that a doctor eventually appeared. I pleaded with her to provide us with a death certificate. I knew one was needed before you can contact an undertaker and get on to the next stage.

The doctor went to check her notes. She returned to say she could not sign the certificate. According to her notes, she had not physically seen Margaret in the last twenty-one days. Only a doctor who had seen the patient in that time could sign a death certificate. Oh God.

So, there was now another delay as we waited for any doctor to come on duty who had seen Margaret recently. I was now becoming distressed. Not simply because Margaret had died but because of all the palaver. But finally a doctor did appear who had treated her recently and was able to do the paperwork.

In the visitors' room I got a telephone directory, found the number for Levertons, our local undertaker in Kentish Town, and rang them. No one was on duty yet, so I left a voicemail, with details, asking them if they could arrange a funeral as quickly as possible.

Flora offered to go back into Margaret's room and clear her clothes and personal stuff, which was thoughtful. Over the last four weeks, a large amount of books and papers and stuff had gathered around her on her bedside table.

Levertons rang back and asked me to come to the funeral

parlour at four that afternoon. Jake said he would come with me. I said no thanks, it will just be boring paperwork; it will go on for ages, no need for you to come as well. I can do it, I can cope.

They went off in their cars, Flora carrying bin liners with Margaret's meagre possessions.

I went back into her bedroom for my last look, my last communion.

Two nurses were there, with plastic aprons firmly and fiercely fixed. I knew one of them, the sister who had checked me in four weeks ago, taken the family details. The one who had caused me to cry.

They were laying out Margaret's body, making her neat and tidy.

'Would you like her wedding ring?' asked the nurse.

I nodded. She then got out a can which she appeared to have in her pocket and sprayed Margaret's wedding ring finger with some solution, like a football referee spraying the pitch with white foam for a free kick. She eased the ring off Margaret's finger. The process was done as quickly and automatically as if she was swiping bananas on the Marks and Spencer till at Camden Town. She must do it all the time, every day probably, hence the handy can of finger softener. I wondered how many dead fingers she had done, how many dead fingers to a can.

# 26

# THE FUNERAL

Next day, having booked the funeral for the Friday, four days ahead, I then changed my mind. I decided we would have a wake. Margaret would not have wanted anything, but she is gone, we are the living, we can decide what suits us, what we want to do and how we choose to remember her.

One of the first people, outside the family, that I told about Margaret's death was our old friend Valerie Grove, whom we have known for well on forty years. These days she writes a lot of obituaries for *The Times*, so she said she would contact them. She has kept all Margaret's letters for years and I suspect had been making notes for several weeks about a Margaret obituary.

I put a short obituary announcement in the *Times* Deaths column and got rung by the Press Association. They asked me a few questions, saying they would send out a brief statement, which would save me being bothered again. Before they rang off, I said don't forget to send a copy to the *Cumberland News*. It would save me telling all our Loweswater friends and neighbours.

Over the next two days, I was surprised and amazed by the coverage. Every newspaper, including the tabloids, did a piece about Margaret. The *Times* obit – by Valerie – ran to two pages. The *Daily Mail* did a whole page. Even the *New York Times* did a page.

Then the letters of condolence came in, hundreds of them, and hundreds of e-mails. I was unable to answer them all for weeks, what with trying to organise the funeral. The *Sunday Times*, where I have written my Money column for almost twenty years, asked for an appreciation of Margaret. I said I would try to do 800 words but in the end it got to 3,000.

This brought in even more letters, from friends of Margaret and mine we had not seen or spoken to for fifty years. Mike Thornhill, who had been best man at our wedding in 1960, and with whom we had lost touch in recent years, contacted me and arranged to meet.

A Danish friend called Karin, who used to be one of our neighbours, till she and her family moved to California, wrote and told me about the death of her husband, a few years ago.

'One of the things that really bothered me, when Bill died,' she wrote, 'was the friends and neighbors who would grab me and cry and look deep into my eyes, saying what a wonderful man Bill was, making me cry even more. I knew how wonderful he was, but I was really angry with him for dying before me. No doubt you will get plenty of that too. Oh and don't worry about answering all those letters. I don't think people would expect it. I still haven't opened a lot of the letters I got.'

Almost all the letters I got were handwritten, kind and thoughtful, and posted in nice envelopes. Not with black borders, as in the olden days, but on quality paper. The art of handwriting is not dead, or perhaps people only turn to handwriting these days when someone is dead.

I wanted to answer every one, which is what Margaret always did, making me scream, in her perfect handwriting. I would say she could have written a new book, instead of all these letters to fans. She would send readers a reply on one of our house postcards, which were not cheap, thus giving away our home address, which I said would lead to further correspondence. She also put a first-class stamp on her replies, which made me scream at the expense, when there was no urgency.

In the end, when the volume got too much, and I wanted to reply to everyone before the month was out and everyone had forgotten, I created a round robin which I then sent out.

*Thank you so much for your kind sentiments about Margaret.*

*The response and the coverage have been remarkable – whole page obits all over the shop, from D Mail to NY Times, plus BBC radio.*

*My theory at first was not many dead – must have been a quiet day in the Obits office. Then I thought perhaps it was some sort of reaction to all the Big Male Beasts who died in last few weeks, D Bowie and T Wogan. They cleared the decks for days, and were criticised for overdoing it.*

*Then along comes this quiet literary lady, whom the general public does not know, so they think, let's give her a nice show.*

*I put these theories to Caitlin, our oldest and tallest, and she said I was being patronising. The reaction on Twitter – whatever that is – to her death had been enormous, with people eager to tell us about their favourite Margaret Forster book. This was picked up by the newspapers and in fact they lifted some of the remarks on Twitter, so Caitlin says.*

*Any road, the extensive, wide spreading of the sad news has resulted in hundreds of cards and letters and messages. Handwriting is not dead, pretty headed note paper is alive; people still do want to share their feelings.*

*But, it means I am having to do a round robin reply, otherwise I will be writing cards till Easter. Sorry about that. (Round robins? Surely owls are rounder?)*

*Thanks ever so. Much appreciated*

Hunter

We booked the funeral for first thing on the Friday morning, 12 February, a rather awkward time for people not living in London, and even for those who do, but it was the only time Levertons – they tend not to add an apostrophe – could book it for us. I was desperate not to have to wait till the following week.

I had been quite surprised by the inside of the Leverton and Sons funeral parlour in Kentish Town, the first time I had ever been in it, though I had passed it for decades. Rather functional and modest, compared with their plush limos, their registration numbers beginning with LEV, which have been easing their way up Highgate West Hill for as long as we have lived here, driving me mad when I get stuck behind them.

I never knew Levertons were so venerable, dating back to 1789. They have six offices in the London area and have helped the departures of some very famous folks over the centuries, including Princess Diana (and are in line to help bury the Queen).

You can't really escape hiring an undertaker, wherever you live. Someone has to look after the body, get it buried or cremated, arrange lots of things which the ordinary person doesn't realise have to be done.

I was determined to have the cheapest, simplest package, so I sat in Levertons looking at the price lists. There was a huge variety of coffins, ranging from £1,825 for something called American Metal down to £395 for a plain veneered coffin.

I could have had a horse-drawn hearse with a team of four plumed horses that would impress the neighbours. A snip at £1,800, if you happen to be an East End gangster.

In the end, I opted for what they describe as their Direct Cremation Option at £1,900, payable in advance. Good job

I had my Visa card on me. This covers all basic costs and dis-bursements – i.e. fees to doctors and the crematorium. It does not include limos for the mourners or a cleric to officiate.

I have always hated it at funerals when the cleric in charge has clearly never met the deceased and is working from notes shoved in their hands at the last minute. They do give the service a suitable, solemn setting, but as neither of us had been churchgoers since we were teenagers, it did not seem necessary.

I know Margaret would have preferred the humblest funeral, as we managed to get married with only two others present, but I had decided, despite my first reactions, that I wanted all the family and relations to be invited, plus neigh-bourhood friends, and also Margaret's publishing friends, including Carmen Callil who, while at Chatto, had published many of her books, and her present publisher, Becky.

We created and home-printed the programme for the ser-vice ourselves, my daughter-in-law Rosa laying it out. I even included a few jokes, well what I considered were amusing remarks, and some stories about Margaret.

Altogether forty people turned up on Friday 12 February 2016 at Golders Green crematorium in north London for Margaret's funeral. It was cold and wintery, pretty miserable for everyone having to get there so early – and then stand around waiting for the previous funeral to finish. My brother Johnny and his wife had come down from Carlisle the day before.

While I waited, I stood and read the plaques to people who have been cremated at Golders Green – Sigmund Freud, Marc Bolan, Kathleen Ferrier, Joyce Grenfell, Ivor Novello, Tommy Handley, Keith Moon, Anna Pavlova, George Bernard Shaw. You wouldn't see such names in Loweswater churchyard.

I had decided to lead the service myself – with the help of my children. Two of them spoke, Jake and Flora. Caitlin, who has the nicest voice, and is used to public speaking, decided she could not face it. But her daughter Ruby, aged sixteen, gave an excellent speech. I went round afterwards saying that all that money on her education had not been wasted. I like to think that Margaret would have been proud of them all.

Afterwards, all the forty mourners went back to our house for Tea and Buns. That was the wording in the programme. We did of course have loads of food and drinks, wine and whisky, in the Scottish fashion, which my children paid for and arranged beautifully.

Only one thing went wrong in our homemade service. I had given the undertaker three songs I wanted played and he said, no problem, he would get them on a CD.

Margaret was totally non-musical, so this was my own self-indulgence. When she went on *Desert Island Discs*, it was explained she had to pick eight records. 'On a desert island, I wouldn't want any records – just silence, and a book.' So when she went on the programme, I picked some nice Beatles songs for her, including 'And I Love Her'.

For the funeral service, the music I chose was 'The Holly and the Ivy', as Christmas carols were the only sort of music she liked and it was still the depths of winter, and 'And I Love Her' by the Beatles. At the end of the service, as we trooped out, I wanted 'Georgy Girl' to be played. A pretty naff tune, which Margaret would have hated, but quick and jaunty and it makes people smile.

Somehow, what got played was a cover version of 'Georgy

Girl', not the original by the Seekers. It was slow and painful and awful. Not at all the sprightly version I wanted. I don't think most people realised, but I moaned to everyone afterwards, and explained the mistake.

Two days later, Andrew Leverton himself rang – the eighth generation in the family firm – and apologised. To make amends, he said they would give a £300 donation to Marie Curie Cancer.

The funeral tea, at our house, turned into quite a jolly party, with the forty people crammed into our living room, eating and drinking and gossiping, staying most of the morning, getting noisier and noisier.

When they had all gone, it was like suddenly turning off a noisy concert on the radio, or an over-acted BBC drama. The house seemed instantly so quiet, deader and more echoing than it had ever been.

I had been alone in the house since 9 January, when Margaret went into the hospice, so I should I have become accustomed to the silence, got used to pottering around on my own. For over fifty years it had rattled with the noise of children and then grandchildren. Now I was left on my own, in an empty three-storey house. All those years we had manoeuvred and bribed to get the whole house to ourselves. And now I had it all to myself. The last thing I wanted.

I went up to Margaret's office on the half landing at the back of the house. I looked through her glass door at her desk, where the sheets of her novel lay unfinished, her Waterman pen and ink at the ready, waiting for her return.

I knocked on the glass panel, as I always did, without thinking. It was a little ritual we had somehow got into, knocking before entering the other person's work place. Having knocked, and realised she would not answer, never again, I then could not face opening the door, and certainly not going inside. Not yet. But I knew I would have to, sometime. Already in my mind I was forming a huge list of things to do, yet none of which I wanted to do. Not now. Not ever, really.

So, is that it? That was the title of a very good autobiography written by Bob Geldof. Some roadie had used the phrase, when they were finally packing up after the first Live Aid concert in 1985. 'Is that it?' And he thought he would apply it to his life story.

What am I going to do now? At the age of eighty, I didn't have much leftover life to kill. That was the title of another good book – by Caitlin Thomas after the death of her husband Dylan.

I came downstairs and looked out at our empty wintery garden and the backyard and the gleaming York stones, not long laid, which in the end Margaret had approved of and enjoyed.

Shall I stay in the house? Should I convert the top floor, get a lodger?

What about our Lake District house? Can I really live up there in isolation in Loweswater on my own for five or six months of the year?

Can I live alone, just by myself, anywhere? I have never lived alone since we got married in 1960, nor ever felt alone since 1956 when I first went out with Margaret.

Decisions, decisions. As I walked slowly down the stairs, I could hear Margaret's voice from her hospice bed, almost the last words she said to me.

'You'll be fine ...'

# BIBLIOGRAPHY

By public demand – okay, because I wanted to know the total myself – here, in chronological order, is a list of all of Hunter Davies' books, of all sorts. To qualify, they must have their own ISBN number and have Hunter's name on the title page. They cover fiction, non-fiction, children's books, guides, collections and edited books, but not counting reprints or revised editions.

\* *Subsequently appeared in new, revised editions*
± *Copyright given to charity*

1    *Here We Go Round the Mulberry Bush* (fiction) Heinemann, 1965
2    *The Other Half: Ten Candid Looks into the Lives of Britain's New Rich and New Poor* (non-fiction, social history) Heinemann, 1966
3    *The New London Spy: A Discreet Guide to the City's Pleasures* (ed., non-fiction, travel) Anthony Blond, 1966
4    \**The Beatles: The authorized biography* (non-fiction, biography) Heinemann, 1968
5    *The Rise and Fall of Jake Sullivan* (fiction) Weidenfeld & Nicolson, 1970
6    *I Knew Daisy Smuten* (ed., fiction) Weidenfeld & Nicolson, 1970
7    ±*A Very Loving Couple* (fiction) Weidenfeld & Nicolson, 1971

8  *Body Charge* (fiction) Weidenfeld & Nicolson, 1971

9  *\*The Glory Game: A Year in the Life of Tottenham Hotspur* (non-fiction, sport) Weidenfeld & Nicolson, 1972

10  *\*±A Walk Along the Wall: A Journey along Hadrian's Wall* (non-fiction, travel) Weidenfeld & Nicolson, 1974

11  *\*George Stephenson: A Biographical Study of the Father of the Railways* (non-fiction, biography) Weidenfeld & Nicolson, 1975

12  *±The Creighton Report: A Year in the Life of a Comprehensive School* (non-fiction, social history) Hamish Hamilton, 1976

13  *The Sunday Times Book of Jubilee Year* (ed., non-fiction) Michael Joseph, 1977

14  *\*A Walk Around the Lakes* (non-fiction, travel) Weidenfeld & Nicolson, 1979

15  *\*William Wordsworth: A Biography* (non-fiction, biography) Weidenfeld & Nicolson, 1980

16  *\*Book of British Lists* (non-fiction, reference) Hamlyn, 1980

17  *±Beaver Book of Lists* (non-fiction, reference, children's) Hamlyn, 1981

18  *The Grades: The First Family of British Entertainment* (non-fiction, biography) Weidenfeld & Nicolson, 1981

19  *\*Father's Day: Scenes from Domestic Life* (non-fiction, humour) Weidenfeld & Nicolson, 1981

20  *\*A Walk Along the Tracks: Britain's Disused Railways* (non-fiction, travel) Weidenfeld & Nicolson, 1982

21  *Great Britain, A Celebration* (non-fiction, culture) Hamish Hamilton, 1982

22  *England! 1982 World Cup Squad* (non-fiction, sport) Futura, 1982

23  *Flossie Teacake's Fur Coat* (fiction, children's) Bodley Head, 1982

24  *Flossie Teacake – Again!* (fiction, children's) Bodley Head, 1983

25  *A Walk Round London's Parks* (non-fiction, travel) Hamish Hamilton, 1983

26  *The Joy of Stamps* (non-fiction) Robson Books, 1983

27  *London at Its Best* (non-fiction, travel) Macmillan, 1984

28  *The Good Guide to the Lakes: The First Guide to English Lake-land with Real Opinions (non-fiction, travel) Forster Davies, 1984

29  Flossie Teacake Strikes Back! (fiction, children's) Bodley Head, 1984

30  Come On, Ossie! (fiction, children's) Bodley Head, 1985

31  Ossie Goes Supersonic! (fiction, children's) Bodley Head, 1986

32  The Grand Tour (non-fiction, travel history) Hamish Hamilton, 1986

33  Ossie the Millionaire (fiction, children's) Bodley Head, 1987

34  ±Back in the USSR (non-fiction, travel) Hamish Hamilton, 1987

35  The Good Quiz Book to the Lakes (non-fiction, reference) Forster Davies, 1987

36  The London Quiz Book (non-fiction, reference) Forster Davies, 1988

37  Lakeland Towns and Villages (ed., non-fiction, travel) Forster Davies, 1988

38  *Beatrix Potter's Lakeland (non-fiction, biography) Warne, 1988

39  Saturday Night (fiction, young adult) Penguin, 1988

40  STARS OF THE SIXTH: Fit the for the Sixth (fiction, young adult) Penguin, 1989

41  STARS OF THE SIXTH: Rapping with Raffy (fiction, young adult) Penguin, 1989

42  STARS OF THE SIXTH: She's Leaving Home (fiction, young adult) Penguin, 1989

43  STARS OF THE SIXTH: Party Party (fiction, young adult) Penguin, 1989

44  STARS OF THE SIXTH: Ice Queen (fiction, young adult) Penguin, 1989

45  STARS OF THE SIXTH: When Will I Be Famous? (fiction, young adult) Penguin, 1990

46  STARS OF THE SIXTH: Who Dunnit? (fiction, young adult) Penguin, 1990

47  *STARS OF THE SIXTH: A Case of Sam and Ella* (fiction, young adult) Penguin, 1990

48  *STARS OF THE SIXTH: The French Connection* (fiction, young adult) Penguin, 1990

49  *STARS OF THE SIXTH: Playing Away* (fiction, young adult) Penguin, 1990

50  *STARS OF THE SIXTH: Let's Stick Together* (fiction, young adult) Penguin, 1990

51  *STARS OF THE SIXTH: Summer Daze* (fiction, young adult) Penguin, 1990

52  *My Life in Football* (non-fiction, memoir) Mainstream, 1990

53  *Snotty Bumstead* (fiction, children's) Bodley Head, 1991

54  *In Search of Columbus* (non-fiction, biography) Sinclair-Stevenson, 1991

55  *Striker* (fiction) Bloomsbury, 1992

56  *Snotty Bumstead and the Rent-a-Mum* (fiction, children's) Bodley Head, 1993

57  *Hunting People: Thirty Years of Interviewing the Famous* (non-fiction, biography) Mainstream, 1994

58  *The Teller of Tales: In Search of Robert Louis Stevenson* (non-fiction, biography) Hamish Hamilton, 1994

59  *\*Wainwright: The Biography* (non-fiction, biography) Michael Joseph, 1995

60  *Living on the Lottery* (non-fiction, hobbies) Little, Brown, 1996

61  ±*Flossie Teacake Wins the Lottery!* (fiction, children's) Bodley Head, 1996

62  *Born 1900: A Document of Our Times* (non-fiction, social history) Little, Brown, 1998

63  *London to Loweswater: A Journey through England at the End of the Twentieth Century* (non-fiction, travel) Mainstream, 1999

64  *Dwight Yorke: The Official Biography* (non-fiction, biography) Deutsch, 1999

65  *Flossie Teacake's Holiday* (fiction, children's) Bodley Head, 2000

66  *Hurry, Hurry While Stocks Last: A Sideways Look at the Economic, Social and Shopping History of Cumbria as Seen Through Local Advertisements 1850–1940* (non-fiction, social history) Bookcase, 2000

67  *A Walk Around the West Indies* (non-fiction, travel) Weidenfeld & Nicolson, 2000

68  *Joe Kinnear: Still Crazy* (non-fiction, biography) Deutsch, 2000

69  *The Quarrymen* (non-fiction, biography) Omnibus, 2001

70  *The Eddie Stobart Story* (non-fiction, biography) HarperCollins, 2001

71  *Boots, Balls and Haircuts: An Illustrated History of Football from Then to Now* (non-fiction, sport) Cassells, 2002

72  *Best of Lakeland* (non-fiction, travel) Dalesman, 2002

73  *The Best of Wainwright: A Personal Collection* (non-fiction, travel) Frances Lincoln, 2003

74  *Relative Strangers: A History of Adoption and a Tale of Triplets* (non-fiction, social history) Time Warner, 2003

75  *\*Gazza: My Story* (ghosted, non-fiction, autobiography) Headline 2004

76  *Strong Lad Wanted for Strong Lass: Growing up in Carlisle* (non-fiction, autobiography) Bookcase, 2004

77  *Hunter Davies' Lists: An Intriguing Collection of Facts and Figures* (non-fiction, reference) Cassell, 2004

78  *The Fan* (non-fiction, sport) Pomona, 2004

79  *Mean with Money* (non-fiction, collection) Pomona, 2005

80  *Being Gazza: My Journey to Hell and Back* (ghosted, non-fiction, autobiography) Headline, 2006

81  *The Beatles, Football and Me* (non-fiction, autobiography) Headline, 2006

82  *Wayne Rooney: My Story So Far* (non-fiction, autobiography, sport) HarperSport, 2006

83  *I Love Football: A Match Made in Heaven* (non-fiction, sport) Headline, 2006

84  *The Bumper Book of Football* (non-fiction, sport) Quercus, 2007
85  *Prezza: Pulling No Punches* (ghosted, non-fiction, John Prescott autobiography) Headline, 2008
86  *Confessions of a Collector: Or How to Be a Part-time Treasure Hunter* (non-fiction, hobbies) Quercus, 2009
87  *Cold Meat and How to Disguise It: A Hundred Years of Belt Tightening* (non-fiction, social history) Frances Lincoln, 2009
88  *Postcards from the Edge of Football: A Social History of a British Game* (non-fiction, sport) Mainstream, 2010
89  *Behind the Scenes at the Museum of Baked Beans: My Search for Britain's Maddest Museums* (non-fiction) Virgin, 2010
90  *Sellafield Stories: Life in Britain's First Nuclear Plant* (ed., non-fiction, history) Constable, 2012
91  *The John Lennon Letters* (ed., non-fiction, biography) Weidenfeld & Nicolson, 2012
92  *The Biscuit Girls: Love, Life and Hardship in a Northern Factory* (non-fiction, social history) Ebury, 2014
93  *The Beatles Lyrics: The Unseen Story Behind Their Music* (ed., non-fiction, music) Weidenfeld & Nicolson, 2014
94  *The Co-op's Got Bananas!* (non-fiction, memoir, vol. 1, 1936–60) Simon & Schuster, 2016
95  *Lakeland: A Personal Journey* (non-fiction, travel) Head of Zeus, 2016
96  *The Beatles Book* (non-fiction, encyclopaedia) Ebury, 2016
97  *A Life in the Day* (non-fiction, memoir, vol. 2, 1960–2017) Simon & Schuster, 2017
98  *Diary of an Unknown Schoolgirl: Margaret Forster's Diary, 1954* (ed., vol. 1 of my wife's diaries) Chatto & Windus, 2017

# INDEX

# Index

# Index

# Index

# Index